THE
ECCLESIASTICAL
TEXT

Borrowed from
Earl Zetterholm

I CAN DO
ALL THINGS
THROUGH
HIM
WHO
STRENGTHENS ME.
PHILIPPIANS 4:13

THE
ECCLESIASTICAL
TEXT

Text Criticism, Biblical Authority
and the Popular Mind

THEODORE P. LETIS, PH.D.
Institute Director

The Institute for Renaissance and Reformation Biblical Studies
Philadelphia • Edinburgh

LCC #97-74091
ISBN 0-9658607-0-1

The Institute for
Renaissance and Reformation Biblical Studies
6417 N. Fairhill
Philadelphia, PA 19126

Visit our Web Site: www.thetext.com

Contents

The fall of the tele-evangelists a few years ago in the United States was the clearest and most public indication that Christianity, "American style," was in an intolerable state. The question naturally suggested itself at the time, and still reverberates throughout the ecclesiastical world: just how could such a sophisticated culture as this find a place for such religious enterprising media figures? The harsh reality is that Americans are not as sophisticated as they would like to believe.

We are presently confronted in the United States with a generation that is decidedly less literate, both in the narrow and in the wider sense, than in that nation's recent past. Allan Bloom's troubling work: *The Closing of the American Mind*, subtitled: *How Higher Education Has Failed Democracy and Impoverished the Soul's of Today's Students"* tells this story in painful detail.

While the souls of today's students, however, may be intellectually impoverished, their influence as consumers has not been lost. As long as big-business can still appeal to their uninhibited sexuality with rock and roll and a clear complexion, why should anyone expect generation X to think on top of that? It is, after all, economics that has contributed in large measure to the closing of the American mind and the loss of Johnny's ability to read.

During the Reagan administration's first term a plan was launched to turn the tide on this threat to America's future (even the corporate world would eventually suffer if lack of education and reading skills resulted in an insufficient consumer class to buy the nation's goods). One result was a report prepared by the National Commission on Excellence in Education, titled: *A Nation At Risk: The Imperative for Education Reform*. One of the conclusions reached in this study was that

> [t]oo few experienced teachers and scholars are involved in writing textbooks. During the past decade or so a large number of

texts have been "written down" by publishers to ever-lower reading levels in response to perceived market demands.

That is to say, in order to assure that a textbook will be purchased and used by teachers, a sixth grade text may be written down to a fourth grade reading level in order to assure that all the students can read it. This also, obviously, lessens the work load of the teacher.

It is a rather simple exercise to translate this same development into the modern American Bible publishing industry context. The challenges presented to Bible publishers to make lucid, ancient Near-Eastern sacred texts—originally written in Hebrew, Aramaic and Greek—to a population on a downward slide from literacy, are simply monumental.

Things were not so difficult in the past when children and adults grew up hearing and learning the phraseology of the old Anglican Bible, with its literary and literal rendering of Biblical imagery, Hebrew and Greek idiom, and technical theological and religious vocabulary. Today, however, one can no longer assume such knowledge, either in religious communities, or in the culture at large, and ironically, the modern publishers of the English Bible are certainly to blame to a large extent.

Today these sacred texts must have none of the smell of the ancient Near-East upon them; they must be made to speak in an American colloquialism that offers neither a window to the transcendent, nor an entry way to the religious consciousness that animated the communities that composed, preserved and transmitted these materials as a sacred trust. Hence, today we have Bibles that have been custom fitted to the immediacy of the modern situation, primarily for marketing purposes, but always under the guise of "needing to communicate." One publisher alone, the Zondervan Publishing House, has excelled in this endeavor, aiming for every consumer group imaginable. This, however, is diversification gone mad:

The Quest Study Bible
The New Student Bible
Women's Devotional Bible

The Adventure Bible
The Teen Study Bible
Men's Devotional Bible
Couples' Devotional Bible
The NIV Life Application Bible
The NIV Study Bible
Youthwalk Devotional Bible [?!]

This is a scandal beyond belief.

The *New York Times* for September 5th, 1996 had a headline in their business section which read: "The Bible, a Perennial, Runs into Sales Resistance." The article went on to say how "the $200 million market for bibles is as flat as a leather Bible cover." This is because, as Oxford University Press explained, "we've reached saturation point." In short, there is a glut in the market because "several hundred versions of the bible, catering to every niche of reader" has resulted in "too many Bibles for too few faithful." Perhaps there is a pattern here: with the trivialization of the sacred, could it be that we have a corresponding disinterest in religion and hence the loss of a market for these masters of communication? If so, this, too, is another wonderful irony. Thomas Nelson, publisher of the *New King James Bible*, was recorded losing $1.4 million in the first quarter of 1996 with "Bible revenue" down 6 percent!

This development is the result of the Bible slipping out of the hands of the ecclesiastical communities that produced it, and into the hands of 20th century "Bible Societies" who have developed their own communications theories about how the Bible should be made relevant to the consumer standing at the threshold of a new millennium. A recent exposé in *World* magazine (March 29, 1997), announced on its cover: "The Stealth Bible: The Popular *New International Version* Bible is quietly going 'gender-neutral,'" while the title of the article read: "the Feminist Seduction of the Evangelical Church: Femme Fatale." Here we learn the inside machinations of an unholy triangle of intrigue between a profit-making, multi-national corporation owned by media tycoon Rupert Murdock, who is the owner of the Zondervan Publishing House, and the not-for-profit "International Bible Society," and the rotating hired-hands who constitute the committee responsible for producing the NIV.

In this article, and its follow-up (April 19), we discover that part of the need to "communicate" (read="market"), involves actually altering what in the past religious communities regarded as inspired and sacrosanct Biblical content, in order to reflect the cultural concerns of ideological feminism. Even the rather non-confrontational, Evangelical author, J.I. Packer, was heard to decry: "Adjustments made by what I call the feminist edition are not made in the interests of legitimate translation procedure. These changes have been made to pander to a cultural prejudice that I hope will be short-lived."

Not likely. How one defines "legitimate translation procedure" is up for grabs these days. Pandora's box has been pried open and the Bible, no longer in the possession of the Church and her specific theological criteria for a religious understanding of the translation task, is now a commodity of the "Bible society" and the Bible landlords of the corporate world. In this, one has an inkling of what must have enraged Luther when he saw Father Tetzel at work. Things had simply gone too far.

The essays and reviews that are to follow are, each in their own way, attempts to address this crisis. Not unlike the wonderful collection recently published, with the ever so appropriate title: *Reclaiming the Bible for the Church* (Eerdmans 1995), these essays aim in the same direction. This present collection, however, will be more concerned with how we arrived at where we are rather than offer a programmatic solution (though the book reviews will be where I tip my hand). This, I believe, is the historian's duty.

The essays were written while I was doing research for the Ph.D. degree at the University of Edinburgh and were, more often than not, written by invitation and subsequently published in journals both academic and popular. Some were formal lectures delivered before various academic society meetings. They range from historical studies proper, to text critical studies, to themes treating Renaissance/Reformation and post-Reformation approaches to the text critical task and translation philosophy. There are also four reviews of rather pivotal works also addressing these themes. While I am working from a post-critical point of reference, it will be evident soon enough that I do not readily fit into anyone's category comfortably. Nevertheless, it is certainly true to say that my *tendenz* is *pro ecclesia*.

Chapter one saw its beginnings as the second chapter of my master's thesis written at Emory University, *Edward Freer Hills's Contribution to the Revival of the Ecclesiastical Text*, unpublished M.T.S. Thesis, 1987. It was subsequently revised and submitted for publication to the *Christian Scholar's Review,* but was rejected with the hopeful explanation that the peer assessors were "almost persuaded." I next submitted it to the *Journal of the Presbyterian Historical Society* (now known as *American Presbyterians*) and it was accepted, appearing in the Autumn of 1991. It was delivered as a guess lecture before the Evangelical Theological Society (of which I have never been a member) on 9 December 1987 and before the students and faculty of the *Theologische Universiteit van de Gereformeerde Kerken in Nederland, Kampen* on 8 June 1989. At least two Ph.D. dissertations have addressed it to date and Appendix A contains a series of peer assessments of its merit from a cross-section of historians and theologians. The thesis of the essay is that Warfield was primarily responsible for finally cutting Princeton Seminary off from her 17th century orthodox roots by means of the introduction of the German practice of text criticism at that institution.

Chapter two was an early version of a chapter of my Ph.D. dissertation which was delivered as a lecture before the Rutherford House Dogmatics Conference in Edinburgh, Scotland, 30 July, 1989. The editor of the *Scottish Bulletin of Evangelical Theology* was present and asked me to allow the journal to published my essay, which then appeared in the May 1990 issue. It explains just what was the 17th century orthodox view of textual variants and the paradigm of Biblical authority with which they worked. It was this paradigm, I argue, that Warfield overturned.

Chapter three was an essay I was asked to write by several who were beginning to grapple with the issues I was raising, addressing the shift in language in the 19th/20th century from "infallible" to "inerrancy" and how the terminological alteration coincided with the changed paradigm introduced by Warfield.

It was presented as a lecture at the Lutheran study centre at Cambridge University, the Westfield House, as "Orthodox Lutheran Dogmatics and the Language of Biblical Authority in Light of Anglo-American Modernist Developments," 22 June, 1993. It was subsequently submitted to *Logia* magazine, which rejected it because it denounced the use of the word "inerrancy;" it was also rejected by the journal *Pro Ecclesia* because it denounced the Church of England's decision to begin ordaining women. It was readily accepted by the British publication, *Calvinism Today* (subsequently renamed *Christianity and Society*) and appeared in the July 1995 issue.

Chapter four is part of the introduction to my doctoral dissertation with added material (the bulk of the essay). It treats what I see to be the significance of Brevard Childs's canonical approach to Biblical studies and interpretation for confessional and catholic traditions looking for a post-critical articulation for old and time honored paradigms. Portions of this essay were also delivered at the Westfield House during the same conference mentioned above and was called: "Brevard Childs and the Catholic Moment: An Occasion for Re-Appropriating Classic Lutheran Orthodoxy in the Post-Modern Milieu." It was accepted for publication by the Evangelical forum within the Church of England, the *Churchman*, the third number in 1991.

Chapter five originally appeared as a term paper at Concordia Seminary, Fort Wayne. It then appeared in the first issue of *The Bulletin for the Institute for Reformation Biblical Studies* (now renamed *The Institute for Renaissance and Reformation Biblical Studies*) as "The Gnostic Influences on the Text of the Fourth Gospel: John 1:18 in the Egyptian Manuscripts" (1989). It has been substantially revised since being given as a lecture at the annual meeting of the Tyndale House Fellowship, Tyndale House, Cambridge (Summer, 1996). While controversial it attempts in light of current research, to revive theories first brought forth addressing the variants at this place in John's prologue by John William Burgon and Herman C. Hoskier. It is also an occasion to offer an explicit example of how Childs's canonical approach might look in a specific application to an important textual variation in the N.T. MS tradition.

Chapter six was an essay I was asked to write for a special Reformation edition of the American publication *The Standard Bearer* and appeared in the October 1993 issue. It draws an uncomplicated contrast between the dominant translation philosophy of the American Bible Society with that of the Renaissance Reformation era.

Chapter seven is a reply to both Daniel Wallace and the late Kurt Aland, as they in turn offered assessments of the revival of the Ecclesiastical (i.e. Byzantine, Traditional, Majority, Koine) text. In so doing it offers a post-critical explanation for why this development is not only legitimate but reasonable and perfectly justifiable on Professor Aland's own terms. It appeared as both an essay in the *Bulletin* (1990), and as a contribution to a *festschrift* (1996).

Chapter eight is the most extensive essay in this collection and treats a parallel movement which has arisen with the scholarly revival of the Ecclesiastical text. As a young undergraduate I had it explained to me that in setting forth one's case one must make equally certain not just to make clear what one *is* saying, but also to make clear what one is *not* saying. While this is no doubt painfully obvious to most I recall the vivid effect this bit of advise about rhetoric had on me. This essay documents what the revival of the Ecclesiastical texts does not involve. It first appeared in the British journal *Calvinism Today* (July 1992), and later was published as a monograph in Great Britain that same year. It has the distinction of being the first monograph publication of the *Institute* and contained twelve woodcuts and a cover boarder by Albrecht Dürer.

The appendices and reviews should be self-evident. The reviews all appeared in the early numbers of the *Bulletin*, while the review of D'Amico also appeared in the American Academy of Religion's *Critical Review of Books in Religion, 1991* (howbeit, in a rather poor state, the new technology of scanning having betrayed the copy editor when it came to Latin terms and my surname!).

Theodore P. Letis
Atlanta, Georgia

CHAPTER ONE

B. B. Warfield, Common-Sense Philosophy and Biblical Criticism

Traditionally within evangelical circles, higher criticism has been viewed as the forbidding realm of destructive subjectivism. On the other hand, since the late nineteenth century, the lower, or textual criticism, has been viewed as the safe domain where all are thought to be constrained by "objective" data which ultimately demonstrate the reliability of the Biblical text.[1] An historical study of the discipline of lower criticism, however, proves this to be a rather recent development.

Perceptive historians have long noted that it was specifically the *lower* criticism that originally haunted conservatives because of the threat it posed to their view of *verbal* inspiration. Thus it was that the lower criticism precipitated the nineteenth century, autographic inerrancy theory, adopted by "several Protestant orthodox theologians . . . after they had to face the results of textual criticism."[2]

---

[1]Accurate was L. Harold DeWolf's assessment: "The intimate and inseparable relation between textual and historical studies of the Bible seems not to be adequately appreciated by some conservative scholars. For example, Edward J. Carnell praises unstintedly the devotion, skill, and results of textual criticism . . . on the other hand, when the same writer considers the work of historical or 'higher' criticism, he has nothing to say for it." *Theology in the Liberal Perspective* (Philadelphia: Westminster, 1959), pp. 51–52.

[2]William F. Orr, "The Authority of the Bible as Reflected in the Proposed Confession of 1967," *Pittsburgh Perspective* VII (March 1966): 29. For other sources highlighting the innovative nature of the autographic inerrancy theory, cf. Thomas M. Lindsay, "The Doctrine of Scripture: The Reformers and the Princeton School," *The Expositor* I (1895):291–93; Henry P. Smith, *Inspiration and Inerrancy: A History and Defense* (Cincinnati: Robert Clarke and Co., 1893), pp. 142–159; B.B. Warfield, *The Westminster Assembly and Its Work* (Oxford: Oxford University Press, 1931), p. 237, n. 46; Mark A. Noll, ed. *The Princeton Theol-*

It is sometimes forgotten that *textual* criticism, as Kümmel reminds us, provided one of the most "decisive stimuli" to the scientific, critical study of the Bible in the beginning.[3] Moreover, it was the Deist, Anthony Collins, who in the eighteenth century used John Mill's early collection of 30,000 N.T. textual variants as an argument for replacing *revealed* with *natural* religion.[4] And on the American scene, Joseph Stevens Buckminster, persuaded the officials at Harvard College in 1809 to publish an American edition of Griesbach's critical Greek New Testament, because he saw its value in promoting text criticism, in his opinion, "a most powerful weapon to be used against the supporters of verbal inspiration."[5]

Benjamine Breckinridge Warfield (1851–1921), Professor at Princeton Seminary from 1887–1921, was the most astute and critically aware N.T. scholar at Princeton during his tenure. While he also retained the old scholastic view of *verbal* inspiration, he did so, keenly aware of this "weapon" in New England.

A good deal of Warfield's early academic career, therefore, was spent mastering the discipline of N.T. text criticism so as to

---

ogy 1812–1921: Scripture, Science, and Theological Method from Archibald Alexander to Benjamine Breckinridge Warfield (Grand Rapids: Baker Book House, 1983), p. 272; Jack B. Rogers, *Scripture in the Westminster Confession: A Problem of Historical Interpretation for American Presbyterianism* (Kampen: J.H. Kok, 1966); Jack B. Rogers and Donald McKim, *The Authority and Interpretation of the Bible: An Historical Approach* (San Francisco: Harper and Row, 1979); Lefferts A. Loetscher, *The Broadening Church: A Study of Theological Issues in the Presbyterian Church Since 1869* (Philadelphia: University of Pennsylvania Press, 1957), pp. 30–31; John C. Vander Stelt, *Philosophy and Scripture: A Study in Old Princeton and Westminster Theology* (Marlton, New Jersey: Mack Publishing Company, 1978), pp. 294–302. On the innovative nature of the word "inerrant," see Arthur C. Piepkorn, "What does 'Inerrancy' Mean?" *Concordia Theological Monthly* 36 (September 1965): 577–593.

[3]Werner G. Kümmel, *The New Testament: The History of the Investigation of its Problems* trans. by S. McLean Gilmore and Howard C. Kee (Nashville: Abingdon, 1972), pp. 40–50.

[4][Anthony Collins], *Discourse of Free-Thinking, Occasion'd by the Rise and Growth of a Sect Called Free Thinkers* (London, 1713), pp. 87–89.

[5]Jerry W. Brown, *The Rise of Biblical Criticism in America, 1800–1820: The New England Scholars* (Middletown, Conn.: Wesleyan University Press, 1969), p. 23. Brown adds, "The publication of a critical text of the New Testament was an important event in the development of American biblical studies" p. 24.

tame and neutralize this threat. How he went about his task helps to explain three developments at Princeton in his life time and his lasting influence on the current evangelical view of Scripture: 1) why he gave a distinctive emphasis to the autographic inerrancy theory; 2) how text criticism came to be viewed by evangelicals in the twentieth century as a safe, neutral realm that can only support the evangelical cause and never harm it; 3) how Warfield contributed to a climate that was more tolerable toward genuine biblical criticism at Princeton at a time when such criticism was perceived to be threatening in the extreme.[6]

Warfield and Scholasticism

Warfield's first step in this process was to distance himself from the Protestant scholastic approach to text critical matters, while retaining the scholastic view of *verbal* inspiration. This was not an easy move. In the old scholastic system these two aspects went hand and hand—two parts of a whole.[7] Neverthe-

---

[6]Only eight years after Warfield's death, Princeton was prepared to fully embrace even the higher criticism. On the circumstances which led to Princeton's reorganization in 1929, which allowed the higher criticism entry, see John W. Hart, "Princeton Theological Seminary: The Reorganization of 1929," *Journal of Presbyterian History* 58 (Summer 1980): 124–140. Unfortunately, however, there is no attention given to the shift in attitude toward biblical criticism in preceding years, leading to the controversy. Loetscher, *The Broadening Church,* treats the influence of biblical criticism but does not treat Warfield's contribution by way of text criticism. Mark A. Noll, *Between Faith and Criticism: Evangelicals, Scholarship, and the Bible in America* (San Francisco: Harper and Row, 1986), pp. 117, notes that today text critical problems "have long been set to rest among academically qualified conservatives," but he has no discussion of the crisis this discipline posed during the nineteenth century, nor is there any mention made of Warfield's introduction of this discipline to Princeton, the very dawning of biblical criticism proper at this institution. Other recent works treating the reorganization of Princeton are, R.T. Clutter, *The Reorientation of Princeton Theological Seminary 1900–1929,* unpublished Th.D. thesis, Dallas Theological Seminary, 1982; B.J. Longfield, *The Presbyterian Controversy 1922–1936: Christianity, Culture, and Ecclesiastical Conflict,* unpublished Ph.D. thesis, Duke University, 1988.

[7]By scholastic approach, with regard to the issue of text criticism and variants, I mean that approach used from the time of Theodore Beza (1519–1608) to Francis Turretin (1623–1687) whose dogmatics was the primary text at Princeton from 1812

less, in contrast to Charles Hodge's view, which we shall treat below, Warfield began by deprecating the established text (what was called the *textus receptus*—the "received text") which had hitherto been the locus of the verbal view of inspiration. For Warfield, the scholastics had stumbled when their reverence for the Word of God, perversely but not unnaturally exercised, erected the standard or received text into the norm of a true text.[8]

Warfield was the first from Princeton to break so decisively with the old text standard. He did so with the confidence that a far better text was then emerging.

Nevertheless, to abandon this standard meant he would be abandoning the text thought to be verbally inspired by the Divines who produced the Westminster Confession of Faith. In order to save, therefore, his verbal view of inspiration—the last vestige of Francis Turretin's influence—he was forced to now relegate inspiration to the inscrutable autographs of the biblical records.

These, he now also argued, when once reconstructed, would be inerrant in a way which far surpassed the text thought to be inspired by the Westminster Divines. Contrary to most critical evaluations of Warfield, the primary influence on him at this point was not Reformed scholasticism, but rather, the Enlightenment.[9]

---

to 1872. This involved fencing in the Masoretic O.T. text and the *textus receptus* N.T. text by creedal statements regarding their respective, providential preservation and sanction, over all rivals, as the locus of verbal inspiration. While there was a rational component to the posture—when data was brought forth in its defense—it was fundamentally a theological *a priori* and exceedingly important to the dogmaticians; as important as Warfield's shift to centering final authority in the autographic text from 1881 on ward. On this, see, Theodore P. Letis, "The Protestant Dogmaticians and the Late Princeton School on the Status of the Sacred *Apographa*," *The Scottish Bulletin of Evangelical Theology* 8 (1990): 16–42.

[8]B.B. Warfield, *An Introduction to the Textual Criticism of the New Testament* (London: Hodder and Stoughton, 1893), p. 216.

[9]Donald McKim sums up the position we are countering: "Some scholars have argued that the Princeton doctrine with its emphasis on the 'inerrancy' of the Scripture, particularly in the original (now lost) autographs, owes its origin to the scholastic theology of the seventeenth-century Reformed orthodoxy and especially to the writings of the Swiss theologian Francis Turretin (1623–87)." Donald K. McKim, *What Christians Believe About the Bible* (Nashville: Thomas Nelson, 1985),

The true test for determining if one is an heir of the Reformed scholastics is found in the role the Westminster Confession plays in locating final Scriptural authority. Archibald Alexander (1772–1851), Charles Hodge (1797–1878), and the Southern Presbyterian, Robert Dabney (1820–1890) were genuine heirs of Turretin. They focused authority in present, extant copies of the biblical texts (*apographa*), with all the accompanying textual phenomena, as the "providentially preserved" and sanctioned edition (Westminster Confession of Faith, 1:8).

Warfield, on the other hand, was the first professor at Princeton to allow his Common-Sense Philosophy the role of reconstructing the text according to the canons of German criticism.[10] Moreover, this German approach to reconstructing the text shared an organic connection with the more radical *higher* criticism. It demanded that Scripture be approached "as any other literature," and it legitimized the use of the radical technique of *conjectural emendation*—the very foundation of the higher critical method. In this development, Warfield must be credited with introducing genuine biblical criticism at Princeton, which would receive acceptance at Princeton after the reorganization of this institution in 1929.

Archibald Alexander, Charles Hodge and Caspar Wistar Hodge

Prior to Warfield's arrival at Princeton, no Princetonian had attained expert status in the young discipline of New Testament text criticism. Germany was the domain of these studies. It is interesting to note that in the absence of this, the founding professor at Princeton Seminary, Archibald Alexander, felt no com-

---

p. 64. Rather, the real impetus for Warfield's position was both the need to answer the challenge of text criticism to *verbal* inspiration, as well as his personal agenda of wanting to legitimize German text criticism by a new interpretation of the Westminster Confession, by means of which he would actually abandon scholasticism altogether. These are both post-Enlightenment, nineteenth century influences.

[10]For an excellent treatment of the influence of the Scottish Common-Sense Philosophy within American academia at this time, see, Mark A. Noll, "Common Sense Traditions and American Evangelical Thought," *American Quarterly* 37 (Summer 1985):216–238.

punction about admitting the autographs were not inerrant, noting,

> that it is even possible that some of the autographs, if we had them, might not be altogether free from such errors as arise from the slip of the pen, as the apostles and ["had"] amanuensis [-es] who were not inspired.[11]

Alexander could afford to admit this error, because for him, as it was for the scholastics to whom he was indebted, the primary locus of authority was the in-hand texts at his disposal. For him there was no radical discontinuity between the lost autographs and the text he had before him. Therefore, if the extant text manifested errors the likelihood was strong that they were there originally.

Furthermore, though Alexander was aware of at least 60,000 textual variants in his day, he was confident that they did not affected doctrine in any way. Like the scholastics, Alexander saw the uniformity of the extant text—in spite of some diversity—as explicit evidence of the enduring validity of the Westminster Confession's promise of providential preservation.

He acknowledged that though God *could* have miraculously maintained inerrant perfection (if He had chosen to provide it in the first place) in the *transmitted* text—always the locus of his attention, not the autographs—he chose not to. Like the scholastics, he attached "more weight to the *number* of attesting manuscripts" (emphasis mine), rather than in the need to reconstruct an inerrant archetype. He preferred a "MS. written with care" over "one carelessly written, other things being equal." Like Turretin, he was disinclined to consider translations over Greek copies. In short Alexander is a fair representative of the seventeenth century Reformed dogmatic tradition.

Unlike Alexander, who never encountered German methods first hand, Charles Hodge studied in Germany for two years between 1826 and 1828.[12] He established significant relationships

---

[11]Lefferts A. Loetscher, *Facing the Enlightenment and Pietism* (Westport, Conn.: Greenwood Press, 1983), p. 228.

[12]Alexander A. Hodge, *The Life of Charles Hodge* (New York: Arno Press, 1969 [originally published in 1881]), pp. 100–101.

with the more conservative Germans, Tholuck and Neander, and heard other noteworthy theologians such as Schleiermacher. After his return home, he continued to read the journals, *Zeitschrift, Evangelische Kirchen-Zeitung*, and several others. Tholuck kept him supplied with the best German works on language, literature and exegesis of the Old and New Testaments. While Hodge was still in Germany, Alexander had warned him,

> I hope while you are separated from your earthly friends, you will take care to keep the communication with heaven open! Remember that you breathe a poisoned atmosphere. If you lose the lively and deep impression of divine truth—if you fall into skepticism or even into coldness, you will lose more than you gain from all the German professors and libraries.[13]

It never seems to have entered Alexander's mind that the influence could work in the other direction, Hodge bringing fresh air to the Germans.[14]

While Hodge did manage to keep his faith, he also became fully aware of the current state of text criticism, as his lecture notes on biblical criticism, given at Princeton, make clear. Two unpublished collections of notes, his "Biblical Criticism: Introductory Lecture," given before he left for Germany, (November 1822) and "Laws of Criticism of the New Testament," presented after he returned (August 1834), reveal how text criticism was treated at Princeton under Charles Hodge.[15]

In the former lecture he notes the various dangers to which the texts of Scripture have been exposed, including intentional scribal alterations. Since "the integrity of the Text is the great

---

[13]*Ibid.*, p. 160.

[14]Tholuck expressed the following sentiments to Hodge in a letter sent while Tholuck was in Rome and Hodge was in Halle: "I cannot express what I feel at the idea of my not seeing you again. You have been sent to me through God's mercy as a messenger of glad tidings, as a comforter in cheerless hours, as an elder brother to show me the simple ways to heaven." *Ibid.*, p. 189.

[15]Unpublished lectures found in the Speer Library, Princeton Theological Seminary.

foundation on which rests all Christian doctrines and all Christian hopes, it is of all points the last to be taken for granted." Those who are "stewards of the mysteries of God" should be able to prove to both friends and enemies that the Bible has come down to us "essentially the same" as "God at first delivered to His Church."

In his lectures on "Laws of Criticism," he acknowledges that the canons he lists are taken from Griesbach's *Prolegomena*. Nowhere in the lecture, however, does he ever apply these accepted canons to individual passages.

Like Alexander before him, and his son, Caspar Wistar Hodge, after him, he regards as a "fixed law" the illegitimacy of practicing *conjectural emendation* on the texts of Holy Scripture, because, "it would be exceedingly injurious as every critic would think himself authorized to make alterations and thus certainty and authority of S.S. [sacred Scripture] would be destroyed."

Hodge provides a brief history of the published editions of the Greek New Testament, noting that the confidence that one can have in any given edition will be based on "the qualifications of their several editors." This is of great import to him because "these editions differ in some instances very materially from each other," and we must determine which is correct.

He remarks favorably on the editions and editors in the Complutensian/Erasmian tradition while respecting the critics of that tradition. The following became his definitive opinion, however, regarding the state of New Testament textual studies at Princeton Seminary in 1834:

Altho' it must be confessed that subsequent editions have greatly enlarged the stock of materials whence the true reading of the sacred text is to be obtained and may in some instances have pointed out and corrected mistakes in the Elzevir editions yet it may well be doubted from the principles on which they have proceeded [subsequent editors] whether they have formed any edition which taken as a whole is worthy of as much confidence as is justly due to the edition of 1624 [Elzevir].—It was the beauty of this edition and the character the Elzevirs had obtained for correctness that brought it into general use, so that it was soon looked upon as the standard and gained an ascendancy it has never lost.[16]

For Hodge, as with Archibald Alexander and the earlier dogmaticians, the *textus receptus* was still regarded as the reigning standard at Princeton in the first half of the nineteenth century. Nevertheless, Hodge never really offered a substantive critique of Griesbach, the then current "critical" edition, although he did at one point reveal a concern about his principles:

> Of his talents, learning and authority and honesty, there is a general agreement. Of opinion of the correctness of his critical principles there is considerable diversity.—Whatever doubt attaches to the correctness of these principles must attach to the text founded upon them.[17]

Furthermore, Hodge was worried because in his first edition Griesbach "published an explicit declaration of his faith in the divinity of our Saviour. This declaration he afterwards withdrew." Moreover, Griesbach's exegetical writings were "very much in accordance with the prevailing sentiments of the continental critics."

At the end of his lecture, while listing for further reading on the subject, Michaelis's *Introduction to the New Testament, the Prolegomena* of Mill, Wetstein and Griesbach, he also listed Laurence's *Strictures on Griesbach's System* and Nolan's *On the Integrity of the Greek Vulgate*, the most comprehensive defense of the *textus receptus* published in Hodge's day.

Because the standard text of the day was suitable for Hodge, he felt no need to plea for an inerrant autograph. In fact, in a letter from his son, A.A. Hodge, to B.B. Warfield, the younger Hodge acknowledged his understanding of his father's view regarding errors and the Bible:

---

[16]Hodge, *Laws of Criticism*. Note that Hodge's commentary on the book of Romans was published the following year in 1835.

[17]*Ibid.*

But the question remains was this book [the bible] with its (1) human (2) oriental & (3) Hebrew characteristics *intended to stand the test of microscopic criticism as to its accuracy in matters of indifferent detail?* It appears my father [Charles Hodge] was speaking of the possibility of infinitesimal inaccuracies of no importance relating to the end designed, in *Systematic Theology* Vol. I, p. 170. I say so too—very heartily. But the question remains what degree of minute accuracy do the facts prove that God designed to effect? That is for you critics and exegetes to determine.[18]

This quote stands in striking contrast with Warfield's agenda: unlike Alexander, Charles Hodge, and apparently A.A. Hodge as well, Warfield felt he could abide *no* errors and so posited the inerrant autograph theory.

Caspar Wistar Hodge, Charles Hodge's other son, can be seen as a transitional figure between the old scholastic approach of earlier Princeton, and what would become the new Warfieldianism of later Princeton.

While he published little, his lecture notes on New Testament criticism are extant. Here he, too, makes no plea for the inerrant autograph theory. Rather, he poses the question, "What has God done? Not what ought he to have done?"[19]

Furthermore, he sensed the problem confronting the Princeton view of Scripture, asking, "What are we to say of verbal inspiration when the Church cannot agree as to the words of the text?" His confidence in the Common-Sense approach assured him, however, that a thorough investigation could only "do away with difficulties," but for a few obstinate points.[20] By his day the accumulation of textual variants had reached the sum of 120,000, but he judged that no more than 1600 to 2000, mostly minor points, yet remained in doubt.[21]

---

[18]Letter from A.A. Hodge to B.B. Warfield, in Warfield's papers, November 14, 1880, Speer Library, Princeton Theological Seminary.

[19]C.W. Hodge, *Lectures on New Testament Criticism* 1878, MS. in the library of Westminster Theological Seminary, p. 1.

[20]*Ibid.*

[21]*Ibid.*, p. 3.

He mentioned that doctrinal considerations—both orthodox and heretical—had led to deliberate alteration of the transmitted text. This admission, which he had accepted from Griesbach, had implications he may not have ever fully grasped.[22] He freely rejected the controversial *comma Johanneum* (IJn. 5:7), and Acts 8:37, on the ground that they had both been interpolated by orthodox scribes. Griesbach convinced him that when variants were involved, all readings favoring *orthodoxy* were to be immediately regarded as suspect.[23] He was perfectly willing to give up these passages as accretions, however, because such a loss failed to affect "the integrity of the book or . . . doctrine."[24]

C.W. Hodge, unlike his father, was less willing to acknowledge, if indeed he was aware of it at all, the connection in Griesbach's method with the higher critical framework. He naively believed Griesbach to be working "entirely free from prejudice in his labors."[25]

As a matter of fact, Johann Salomo Semler (1725–1791), Griesbach's mentor and one of the decisive architects of the higher-critical method, had provided Griesbach with his text critical principles.[26] Semler believed the canon and text to be ac-

---

[22]*Ibid.*, p. 4. This is a distinctive trait of the German method. It presupposes real development of the text from a simpler, to a more theologically rich and complex form, the result of doctrinally motivated redactors. Certainly C.W. Hodge's father, who studied in Germany, would have been aware of such implications. A few years later, Westcott and Hort, who would have an important influence on Warfield, attempted to escape such implications by denying that doctrine played any role whatsoever in creating textual variants. In this way they gave their own particular application of the German method a less ominous and threatening dimension. Westcott and Hort, *The New Testament in the Original Greek*, Introduction, p. 282. No one now accepts such a dogmatic and optimistic stance.

[23]Griesbach had as one of his canons of criticism: "When there are many variant readings in one place, that reading which more than the others manifestly favors the dogmas of the orthodox is deservedly regarded as suspicious." Johann Jakob Griesbach, *Novum Testamentum Graece* (Halle, 1796), p. 62.

[24]C.W. Hodge, *op. cit.* p. 5.

[25]*Ibid.*, pp. 25–26.

[26]Metzger says of Semler, "Often regarded as the father of German Rationalism, [he] made noteworthy contributions to the science of textual criticism . . . . Semler was the first to apply the term 'recension' to groups of New Testament wit-

cidents of history; he saw neither as inspired nor authoritative, since both reflected the local concerns of their various authors and redactors.

C.W. Hodge did not employ Griesbach's method uncritically, though. While holding that Griesbach was "entirely free from prejudice," he nevertheless had doubts about his recensional theory. Furthermore, while he saw the oldest evidence as the best, he granted that late manuscripts could reflect an early form of the text. Ultimately, he thought the highest value belonged to evidence from remote, independent sources.

When he evaluated examples he proved himself both independent and inconsistent. He criticized F.H.A. Scrivener for choosing, based on subjective or theological reasons, readings in the later manuscripts. Yet after acknowledging that the best authorities, manuscripts as well as critics, rejected the latter part of John 3:13, i.e. "no man hath ascended up to heaven but he who came down from heaven *even the son of Man who is in heaven*," he sided with Scrivener and the late MSS., simply on the grounds that "the verse is genuine and important." He could be as subjective as anyone.

Along with the Germans, he also rejected the Markan authorship of the long ending to this gospel, though he retained the passage as nevertheless canonical, and therefore, inspired. He also rejected Matt. 6:13; John 5:3, 4; and John 7:53–8:11, which he regarded as non-canonical, though probably an actual historical event. In John 1:18 he retained the received reading *only begotten son*. As already mentioned, he rejected Acts 8:37, even though it had been retained by another Princetonian, J.A. Alexander, in his commentary on this book.[27]

---

nesses (*Hermeneutische Vorbereitung*, iii (I) [Halle, 1765]). Properly a recension is the result of deliberate critical work by an editor." Metzger, *The Text of the New Testament* 2nd ed., p. 115 and n.2.

[27]J.A. Alexander, *A Commentary on the Acts of the Apostles* (1857), pp. 349–350. The scholastic element can be detected in Alexander's final assessment of this verse: "It is therefore one of those cases, in which the external testimony may be looked upon as very nearly balanced, and in which it is the safest course to let the scale of the received text and traditional belief preponderate." Warfield would scorn such sentiments.

On the problem of how to treat textual variants C.W. Hodge saw two schools on the horizon. The first consisted of the Germans, Tregelles, and Westcott and Hort; these are they who rely on "ancient MSS." The second was represented by Scrivener, who seemed to rely on "modern MSS." This diversity offered no challenge to C.W. Hodge's optimistic view of the Common-Sense approach, however, because, "as this is a question of evidence," the two schools would "agree after a time."

In summary, C.W. Hodge had a fairly tolerable understanding of the state of the discipline, but seemed to lack an awareness of the higher critical framework of the German method. Or, if he did recognize it, he chose to ignore this. Furthermore, when the consensus went against what he considered a doctrinally vital point, he opted for the traditional reading. He would accept text criticism only as far as his Common-Sense criteria would let him. Yet, his belief—more a projection than a true reading of the state of affairs—that German text criticism had attained an unbiased, scientific method, allowed him to conclude, "criticism satisfactorily answers the question as to what the words of the N.T. are." Eventually, even most Germans would give up such a notion.

B.B. Warfield

Warfield became a protégé of Charles Hodge and in 1887 he took his chair at Princeton Seminary. Like Hodge, he knew one had to study in Germany to respond intelligently to their biblical criticism. Like Hodge, he knew that New England was now the fount of German criticism in America and that it was the *lower* criticism that offered the greatest threat to verbal inspiration. Buckminster at Harvard had brazenly declared, "any rational person aware of the history of the New Testament text could not hold a rigid theory of verbal inspiration."[28] Charles Hodge had attained to such knowledge to a degree; but he seems to have retained his belief in verbal inspiration by keeping text criticism at arm's length.

---

[28]Brown, *The Rise of Biblical Criticism*, p. 24.

By Warfield's day, however, text critical studies had moved from Germany to the more moderate climate of Britain.[29] C.W. Hodge had sensed this and made a start toward accepting the practice of text criticism. It was Warfield, however, who now felt fully confident about plunging ahead. If English churchmen (Westcott and Hort) could do text criticism without damage to the faith, so could Princetonians. In time, Warfield would be the first American to produce a primer on the German practice of N.T. text criticism.[30]

On the advice of C.W. Hodge[31] and with a letter of introduction written by Philip Schaff, Warfield entered the University of Leipzig in 1876 for a year's study. He returned to the United States, fully abreast of the state of German criticism. After spending a year as an assistant pastor he became an instructor of New Testament Language and Literature at Western Theological Seminary (today it is called Pittsburgh Seminary) in 1878.

The title of his inaugural address, *Inspiration and Criticism,* reflected what I believe Warfield saw as his particular calling— the integration of biblical criticism with the scholastic view of *verbal inspiration.*[32]

---

[29]Though the non-conformist, Plymouth Brother, S.P. Tregelles, had begun to turn attention to text critical matters in England, earlier in the century. In fact, Warfield may have been indebted to Tregelles for using the argument of divine providence to sanction the use of text criticism. Tregelles had argued, "As God in his providence has preserved Holy Scripture to us, so can He Vouchsafe the needed wisdom to judge of its text simply on grounds of evidence," *An Account of the Printed Text of the Greek New Testament* (London, 1854), p. 186. Cf. also pp. 37–38; 176.

[30]B.B. Warfield's, *Introduction to the Textual Criticism of the New Testament* was first published in England in 1886 and saw seven editions there from 1886–1907, with two American editions published in 1887 and 1907. While Philip Schaff did write a *Companion* three years earlier than Warfield which contained a great deal of text critical information, it had several contributors—including Warfield—and was too broadly based to be regarded strictly as a primer in the discipline.

[31]Letter from C.W. Hodge to Warfield, June 6, 1876, Warfield Papers, Speer Library, Princeton Seminary.

[32]"Inspiration and Criticism," in *Discourses Occasioned by the Inauguration of Benjamine B. Warfield to the Chair of New Testament Exegesis and Literature in Western Theological Seminary* (Pittsburgh: n.p., 1880), pp. 1–46; reprinted in Warfield's *Revelation and Inspiration* (New York: Oxford University *Press, 1972), now titled,* *The Inspiration and Authority of the Bible* (Phillipsburgh, N.J., 1948).

In the lecture he refers to a "certain looseness of belief" within the Church and in the face of this he assured the audience of his own steadfastness. He saw the problem as focused in the German attack on verbal inspiration.

He quickly disavowed any dictation theory of inspiration, affirming that the actual mode was inscrutable. He avoided altogether, however, any mention of the threat textual variants posed to verbal inspiration, calming his listeners in a confident tone, affirming that "a careful revision of the text" would place the Bible beyond doubt.

Here we see that criticism now becomes the ally of faith. With C.W. Hodge, he was certain that because the *lower* criticism deals with "facts," it was immune to the "speculations" of the *higher* criticism. He felt that "modern negative criticism neither on internal nor on external grounds has been able to throw any doubt on the authenticity of a single book of our New Testament." In fact, "modern criticism has gone step by step with traditional faith."

What Warfield failed to address was the fact that large blocks of material traditionally found in those books were now, in his opinion, to be dispensed with as corruptions of the text, "facts" produced as a result of modern criticism. Warfield was now prepared to go beyond what anyone at Princeton had ever been willing to do—doubt the inspiration of one of the resurrection accounts.

On December 2, 1882, Warfield had published in the popular *Sunday School Times* an article treating the long ending to Mark's Gospel. Here he declares that this resurrection account is "no part of the word of God." "We are not then," he added, "to ascribe to these verses the authority due to God's word."[33]

Professor N.M. Wheeler, of Lawrence University, challenged him on this point. Insisting that Warfield's view of the matter implied that "we must ask the critics every morning what is the latest conclusion in order to know what is that Scripture inspired of God," Wheeler sensed the near relationship between

---

[33]B.B. Warfield, "The Genuineness of Mark 16:9–20," *Sunday School Times* 24 (December 2, 1982): 755–756.

what Warfield was doing and what was being proposed on the higher critical plain.[34]

Certainly the textual data for this passage consisted of hard "facts," but these "facts" permitted two opposing reconstructions or interpretations. Warfield, along with C.W. Hodge before him (to a lesser extent),[35] adopted what was the German conclusion. This position supported the higher critical interpretation regarding the doctrinal development of the Gospels: this section was added late to provided the oldest Gospel account with a supernatural conclusion, in harmony with the later Gospel treatments of the resurrection.

The English theologian, F.C. Conybeare, a contemporary of Warfield's, summed up the higher critical understanding of the implications of such variants as this:

> These facts speak for themselves. Our Greek texts, not only the gospels, but of the epistles as well, have been revised and interpolated by orthodox copyists. We can trace their perversions of the text in a few cases, with the aid of patristic citations and ancient versions. But there must remain many passages which have been so corrupted, but where we cannot to-day expose the fraud.[36]

Nevertheless, Warfield was certain that by accepting the consensus of opinion regarding text criticism, currently coming out of Germany, it could only ultimately assist the faith, even if some major adjustments would be called for. The English critics, Westcott and Hort, gave him this confidence.

The English Connection: the Influence of Westcott and Hort

As soon as the critical Greek text of Westcott and Hort appeared (1881), Warfield gave it a review that would forever endear it to conservatives in the United States:

---

[34]N.M. Wheeler, "Uncanonical Inspiration," *Sunday School Times* 25 (January 6, 1883): 4.

[35]Recall that while C.W. Hodge doubted the Markan authorship of the verses, he, nevertheless, regarded them as canonical.

[36]F.C. Conybeare, *History of New Testament Criticism* (London: Watts and Co.,

We cannot doubt but that the leading principles of method which they have laid down will meet with speedy universal acceptance. They furnish us for the first time with a really scientific method.[37]

Philip Schaff, himself an accomplished textual scholar, was so impressed with Warfield's elucidation of Westcott and Hort's method of genealogy in this review, he invited Warfield to explain this in Schaff's own, *Companion to the Greek Testament and English Version*.[38] This was tantamount to elevating Warfield to the first rank in this discipline in America, since Westcott and Hort were considered to represent the very cutting edge of textual studies.

Westcott and Hort were, in turn, merely adopting the method of Griesbach, whose name they venerated "above that of every other textual critic of the New Testament."[39] While they felt they must make a few adjustments to his theories, they made clear it is his approach they adopt, holding that "no valid objection can, we believe, be brought to bear against the greater part of Griesbach's historical view."[40]

In this review of Westcott and Hort, Warfield revealed his command of both the history of text criticism and the methods of Westcott and Hort. With encouragement from readers of the review, he decided to produce his own handbook on textual criticism, after the "scientific" methods of Griesbach and Westcott and Hort. In the preface to this work, Warfield clearly revealed his debt to Westcott and Hort, making "no claim to orig-

---

1910), p. 77. Mark's long ending was one of the classic paradigms that allowed critics to extrapolate further in the quest for origins.

[37]Warfield's review of Westcott and Hort, in *Presbyterian Review* 3 (1882) p. 355. Southern Baptists would adopt Westcott and Hort via Professor A.T. Robertson, who dedicated his handbook, *An Introduction to the Textual Criticism of the New Testament* (London: Hodder and Stoughton, 1925), "to the memory of B.B. Warfield."

[38]Schaff, *Companion*, pp. 208–224.

[39]Westcott and Hort, *Introduction*, *The New Testament in the Original Greek*, p. 185.

[40]*Ibid.*

inality" because "obligations to previous works can scarcely be acknowledged."

Believing that Westcott and Hort had established a scientific method in tune with his own Common-Sense criteria, Warfield reproduced their theories and method in his own handbook. He accepted their claim to have reconstructed a "neutral" text, based on principles established by the German critics themselves and so beyond the pale of *their* criticism. The two English scholars claimed to have discovered "seemingly the pure stock from which all others in existence appear to have diverged."[41] Furthermore, they arrived at such a determination without calling on the help of theology. This made their arguments all the more compelling.

In Enlightenment fashion, therefore, Warfield said that in text critical matters, the faithful follow the same method as the Germans, treating Scripture like any other piece of literature, without reference to either inspiration, or the uniqueness of the Bible. This he had learned from Westcott and Hort, who argued,

> The principles of criticism explained . . . hold good for all ancient texts preserved in a plurality of documents. In dealing with the text of the New Testament no new principle whatever is needed or legitimate.[42]

Note carefully Warfield's echoing of this sentiment in his own handbook:

> It matters not whether the writing before us be a letter from a friend, or an inscription from Carchemish, or a copy of a morning newspaper, or Shakespeare, or Homer, or the Bible, these and only these are the kinds of evidence applicable [i.e., nontheological, canons of text criticism][43]

Another aspect of the German method that Warfield adopted via Westcott and Hort was the practice of *conjectural emenda-*

---

[41]Warfield's review of Westcott and Hort, pp. 342–343.
[42]Westcott and Hort, *Introduction*, p. 73. Cf. also pp. 276–277.
[43]Warfield, *An Introduction to Textual Criticism*, p. 10.

tion.[44] We have already established that no N.T. scholar at Princeton had, until Warfield, accepted this method of guessing, aside from manuscript evidence, at what the true reading was (based on the assumption that all extant copies are, at this point, corrupted). One reason the Princetonians were sensitive to this issue is because it is precisely here that an organic link is formed with the *higher* criticism. A.A. Hodge revealed his fear of this method in classic style in his *Evangelical Theology:*

> There is an arrogant phase of the 'higher criticism' that is far more ambitious and attempts to correct, or even to reconstruct, the existing text by wide inductions from the history of the times, from the other writings, and from the known or supposed character, knowledge, style, situation, or subject of the writer . . . . but it is very plain that this process of 'higher criticism' is liable to be coloured, and even wholly controlled, by the subjective conditions of the critic—by his sympathies, by his historical and philosophical and religious theories, and by his *a priori* judgments as to what the sacred writer ought to say.[45]

Warfield had used nearly every one of these arguments to reject the long ending of Mark.

Little wonder, therefore, that once Warfield's views on Westcott and Hort became public, by way of his review of their text in 1882, he received a most interesting letter from Charles Augustus Briggs of Union Seminary in New York. Briggs would later be defrocked for advocating some of the same methods as endorsed by Warfield.[46]

---

[44]On this see Warfield's review of Westcott and Hort, pp. 347–348, where he remarks, "It may be said here, again, that thus a wide door is opened for the entrance of deceitful dealing with the Word of Life. The danger is apparent and imminent. But we cannot arbitrarily close the door lest we incur the same charge" p. 347. Cf. also his treatment of this in his handbook, pp. 207–210,

[45]A.A. Hodge, *Evangelical Theology: a Course of Popular Lectures* 1890), pp. 66–67.

[46]For a brief introduction to Briggs's trial, see, Max G. Rogers, "Charles Augustus Briggs: Heresy at Union," in George H. Shriver, ed., *American Religious Heretics: Formal and Informal Trials in American Protestantism* (Nashville: Abingdon Press, 1966), pp. 89–147. For a more detailed treatment see, Channing R. Jeschke, *The Briggs Case: The Focus of a Study in Nineteenth Century Presbyterian*

In his letter Briggs protested to Warfield that he, (Briggs), Robertson Smith, and others, were merely "working in the O.T. as Tischendorf, Westcott and Hort [were] in the N.T." and that he could "see no difference of spirit or methods between your article [review of Westcott and Hort] and that of Professor Smith."[47] Why is it that Warfield could be seen as engaging with higher critics in his task of lower criticism, without receiving the same condemnation as Briggs and Robertson Smith?[48]

B.B. Warfield, the Westminster Confession of Faith and Inerrancy

In 1880, two years before Warfield would write his review of Westcott and Hort, A.A. Hodge invited him to co-author an essay for the new *Presbyterian Review* on the doctrine of inspiration. Hodge complained that for months Charles Briggs had pestered him to put in print such an essay because Hodge was regarded as a representative of the *old orthodoxy*. Briggs wanted to initiate an exchange on the subject in the new journal.

Hodge began his request to Warfield by acknowledging his own inability to address the critical theories of Briggs:

> I can after a fashion restate the old orthodoxy *common*-place as to inspiration and fence it somewhat on the *a-priori* or meta-

---

History, unpublished Ph.D. thesis, University of Chicago, 1966. For a recent monograph treating Briggs, see, Mark S. Massa, *Charles Augustus Briggs and the Crisis of Historical Criticism* (Minneapolis: Fortress Press, 1990).

[47]Letter from Charles A. Briggs to B.B. Warfield, March 10, 1882, in the papers of Warfield, Speer Library, Princeton Theological Seminary. William Robertson Smith (1846–1894) was a Scottish Old Testament scholar whose articles "Angels" and "Bible," prepared for the *Encyclopedia Britannica*, raised a storm of protest and led to a charge of heresy. He was suspended from his position as Professor of Hebrew and Old Testament Exegesis in the University of Aberdeen the same year A.A. Hodge and Warfield published their essay on inspiration.

[48]For a treatment comparing and contrasting Warfield and Briggs, see, Trevor W.J. Morrow, *Infallibility as a Theological Concept: a Study in the Use of the Concept "Infallible" in the Writings of B.B. Warfield and C.A. Briggs,* unpublished Ph.D. thesis, The University of Edinburgh, 1984. Unfortunately, as in most treatments of Warfield, their is little attention paid to the significance of his work in text criticism.

physical side, but I can do nothing on the side of stating or answering the positions of the hostile criticism, as to origin or genesis or dates of the books of either testament or as to the alleged
contradictions of detail.[49]

He invited Warfield to write the essay with him, with Hodge
writing the first half dealing with the doctrinal aspects,

to be followed by a discussion statement illustration [sic "illustrating"] proof of the truth as to 1st [sic] the effect of the preva-
lent new criticism.[50]

Hodge begged Warfield to address "the state of actual facts
(as to the *New* Testament) in regard to the asserted inaccuracies—or contradictions."

Hodge had considerable confidence in Warfield who had
spent a year at Leipzig just three years earlier, mastering the
"facts." He was just the champion to go up against Briggs who
had also studied in Germany. It would indeed be this essay that
would reveal to the critics of the old orthodoxy that in Warfield
they had a worthy opponent.

Warfield must have felt a grave responsibility being asked to
come to the rescue of Princeton. His challenge was to address
Briggs, and other critics, and yet to also protect his own reputa-
tion as an emerging authority on N.T. text criticism—the one
discipline that seemed most directly to undermine the Princeton view of verbal inspiration.

Warfield had to admit, along with all post-Enlightenment
critics, that in text critical matters, the Bible was to be treated
like any other kind of literature. He had also to maintain, however, that it was the verbally inspired Word of God. This was a
demanding task for one governed not by the *both/and* of the
German dialectical method, but by the *either/or* of Scottish
Common-Sense Philosophy. It was not, however, beyond Warfield's abilities. Warfield's answer was to,

---

[49]Letter from A.A. Hodge to B.B. Warfield, October 20, 1880, in the papers of
B.B. Warfield, Speer Library, Princeton Seminary.
    [50]*Ibid.*

not assert that the common text, but only that the original autographic text was inspired. No "error" can be asserted, therefore, which cannot be proved to have been aboriginal in the text.[51]

Furthermore, Warfield provided an ingenious new interpretation of the Westminster Confession of Faith that would allow him to claim creedal validation for the new criticism. The confession which had once taught the providential *preservation* of the extant Church texts, was now used to affirm the providential *restoration* of an inerrant original text, by means of modern text criticism. Because, he argued,

> we believe in God's *continuous* care over the purity of His Word, we are able to look upon the labors of the great critics of the nineteenth century—a Tregelles, a Westcott, a Hort— . . . as instruments of providence in preserving [read: *restoring*] the Scriptures pure for the use of God's people.[52]

This, then, is how Warfield accomplished his weighty task: if the correct interpretation of the WCF was, in Warfield's opinion, that it taught the locus of providence was now *restoration*, via Enlightenment criticism, rather than the *preservation* of the traditional texts, then we need not concern ourselves with the criticisms lodged at the human element in the text of Scripture presently (and historically) used in the Church. This stance allowed Warfield to actually join with the critics of the Princeton position as God's providential agents in the task of restoring the *inerrant* original, now the *new* locus of both inspiration and providence.

Ironically, Warfield was able to engage in *lower* criticism, with *higher* critics, with complete impunity, and thus retain his integrity in that field. He could do so because he retained the

---

[51]A.A. Hodge and B.B. Warfield, "Inspiration," *Presbyterian Review* 2 (1881), p. 238.

[52]B.B. Warfield, *Critical Reviews* (New York: Oxford University Press, 1932), p. 36. Cf. also very similar remarks in his *Westminster Assembly and its Work* (New York: Oxford University Press, 1931), p. 239.

traditional language of the Confession. Furthermore, he was also able to retained the old scholastic doctrine of verbal inspiration, though this required a change *interpretation* of the Confession, shifting the old Princeton doctrine of Scripture back into the mists of time, now resting it on a yet to be reconstructed *inerrant* original autograph.

Briggs, on the other hand, while also employing the new criticism at Union, such as he saw Warfield now advocating, nevertheless, chose not to shift the historical understanding of the Westminster Confession, in the way Warfield did. As a result, he suffered severe recriminations. Briggs had history on his side, however, when he simply argued that, "The Westminster divines did not teach the inerrancy of the original autographs."[53]

Recent Defenders of Warfield

When Warfield was challenged for his innovative formulation, based on his demythologization of the Westminster Confession of Faith, his response was to merely assume what he could not historically prove. Recently, however, contemporary Warfieldians have returned to the now century old argument and have attempted to offer historical evidence for Warfield's position.

Randall H. Balmer has culled (with the help of John D. Woodbridge and Mark Noll), a mass of quotations from nineteenth-century, American, theological journals, which he believes distinguishes, just as did Warfield, between original autographs and copies.[54] Furthermore, he believes this evidence helps to prove that Warfield's view was that of early Princeton.

The missing element in Balmer's treatment, however, is the role that text criticism played, or did not play, in these discussions throughout the developing nineteenth century. Certainly all the Princetonians admitted there was some degree of error in the copies, declared to be providentially preserved by the WCF.

---

[53]Charles A. Briggs, *Whither?* Edinburgh: T. and T. Clark, 1889), p. 69.

[54]Randall H. Balmer, "The Princetonians and Scripture: A Reconsideration," *The Westminster Theological Journal* 44 (Fall, 1982):352–365.

Furthermore, like the Westminster Divines, they all believed that only the original autographs were *given* by inspiration.

But unlike Warfield, we have shown that important early Princetonians admitted error in the autographs. Moreover, we never discover them making an appeal to original autographs as the sole repository of inspiration, because this was not the position of the Reformed scholastics, from whom they derived their theology. Futhermore, like the Protestant dogmaticians before them, because of their naive, underdeveloped knowledge of, or adoption of text criticism, they never believed there to be a radical discontinuity between the original text and copies. Warfield, however, certainly did.

There was no primer on text criticism published in America until Schaff's *Companion* (1883) and Warfield's handbook (1886). Text critical data, or an agreed upon means for employing it, did not really become widespread, outside of the liberal Northeast institutions, until the publication of the *Revised Version* (1881). Ira V. Brown recognized that,

> the way was prepared for acceptance of higher criticism by the appearance of the Revised Version of the Bible in 1881 (N.T.) and 1885 (O.T.). . . . This was a high point in lower or textual criticism. . . . The mere publication of a new translation, founded upon revised Hebrew and Greek texts, helped to modify the traditional concept of infallibility.[55]

It has been the burden of this essay to demonstrate just what was the particular modification of the Princeton view, at the hands of Warfield.[56]

---

[55]Ira V. Brown, "The Higher Criticism Comes to America, 1800–1900," *Journal of the Presbyterian Historical Society* 38 (December, 1960): 197. N.M. Wheeler, who had challenged Warfield on his views treating the long ending of Mark, made the following observation in this regard: "This question [the "inauthenticity" of Mark's ending], too, will gain increasing emphasis and pertinence as plain Bible-studying people become more familiar with the other similar phenomena in the New Testament, a familiarity which it is one of the functions of the Revised Version to transfer from the limited circle of scholars to the widening circle of intelligent Bible readers." *Op. cit.* p. 4.

[56]Contrary to the opinion of Robert Hoefel, who asserted, "Warfield . . . worked within the Princeton system . . . . [and] saw no need to re-evaluate or

The many quotations offered by Balmer are not coming from authors who as yet have felt the need to make the kind of adjustment which Warfield made. For the most part, they would not have sensed any great discontinuity between the original and traditional copies. In fact, one example used by Balmer illustrates this quite explicitly. One Reformed author quoted argued,

> We all know that in copying by hand mistakes are liable to creep in, as they do sometimes even in printed books . . . . the translation contained in our common Bible is a far better one, and much more conformable to the meaning of the original, than any that have been intended to supplant it.[57]

Such evidence flies directly in the face of the point Balmer is attempting to establish. By the author's analogy we get a notion of what kind of errors he had in mind when speaking of present copies: such errors as occur at the printing press—purely technical blunders. The above author is not arguing, as Warfield did, that large blocks of material have been purposefully interpolated into the common text, in order to support a resurrection account, or some other important theological tenet.

Rather, this author argues in just the opposite direction. Sounding very much like Charles Hodge, he affirms that the common, extant text, "is more conformable . . . to the original, than any that have been intended to supplant it." This certainly was not the opinion of Warfield.

The discipline of New Testament text criticism had simply not arrived in America for conservatives at the time most of these quotations were published. Therefore, it is unlikely that any of them were arguing for the adjustment that Warfield felt compelled to make.

Moreover, if Warfield's position was consistent with earlier Princetonian tradition, why did he have to defend his position

---

modify this model." "B.B. Warfield and James Orr: Contrasting Approaches to Scripture," *Christian Scholar's Review* 16 (September 1986):45.

[57]"On the Correctness of the Common Bible," *Utica Christian Repository* 3 (1824): 294, as quoted in "the Princetonians," p. 363.

to contemporaries against the charge of innovation?[58] Warfield was actually begging the question when he assumed that the Presbyterian Church had always held his view.

It would appear that even A.A. Hodge himself had trouble with Warfield's method of bifurcating. After reading an early draft of Warfield's portion of their co-authored essay treating *inspiration*, Hodge asked Warfield,

> If you think it proper—I wish you would *express* one point differently. Instead of putting *authenticity* and *genuineness* as essential prerequisites to inspiration—I would say that any criticism which denies the truth of any testimony of Christ . . . is inconsistent with inspiration.[59]

Warfield evidently caused Hodge to adjust his opinion.

Eventually, Warfield persuaded nearly everyone within the old Princeton tradition, during the heat of the dispute, that his apologetic technique was correct. It placed Scripture forever beyond the reach of antagonistic critics since only the yet to be reconstructed autographic text could be criticised; while also allowing Reformed critics to freely enter into the contemporary "quest for the historical text." But his advance proved to be short-lived.

Conclusion

If Briggs could see his own method reflected in that of Warfield's, so would others. Only eight years after Warfield's death, the higher criticism entered Princeton and the seminary was reorganized to accommodate this. The facile certainty that Westcott and Hort's system seemed to offer Warfield evaporated. Later text critics abandoned the hope of reconstructing a "neutral" text and today despair of ever discovering an *urtext*, the

---

[58]Cf. his "Inerrancy of the Original Autographs," *The Independent* (March 23, 1893), reprinted in Mark A. Noll, *The Princeton Theology 1812–1921* (Grand Rapids: Baker, 1983), p. 272.

[59]Letter from A.A. Hodge to B.B. Warfield, cir. Jan. 3–4, 1881, in Warfield's papers.

final resting ground of Warfield's doctrine of inspiration and inerrancy. Warfield had given earnest expression to his hope that,

> The autographic text of the New Testament is distinctly within the reach of criticism . . . we cannot despair of restoring to ourselves and the Church of God, His book, word for word, as He gave it by inspiration to men.[60]

Fifty years later, the Harvard text critic, Kirsopp Lake, offered a more modest assessment:

> In spite of the claims of Westcott and Hort . . . we do not know the original form of the Gospels, and it is quite likely that we never shall.[61]

Warfield's Common-Sense adoption of German methods would be more fully developed by others at Princeton who would no longer find his appendage of the inerrant autographs theory either convincing, or any longer relevant for N.T. studies. This latter aspect of his legacy would be preserved, however, at the break-away institution, Westminster Seminary. And since it was the Westcott and Hort method that Warfield canonized as the *scientific* means, based on his reinterpretation of the Westminster Confession, of restoring the inerrant autographs, Westminster has been frozen in time, still advocating their method, while the discipline has moved on.[62]

On this point of text criticism, Warfield was not a scholastic. It was Warfield who was most responsible for abandoning the scholastic, creedal approach of the earlier Princetonians and who first introduces genuine Biblical criticism to Princeton. He de-

---

[60]"The Rights of Criticism and of the Church," *The Presbyterian* (April 13, 1892):15.

[61]Kirsopp and Sylvia Lake, *Family 13 (The Ferrar Group* (Philadelphia: The University of Pennsylvania Press, 1941), p. vii. By default, *eclecticism* became the standard approach and dominates to this hour, cf. Eldon Jay Epp, "The Eclectic Method in New Testament Textual Criticism: Solution or Symptom?," *Harvard Theological Review* 69 (July–October, 1976): 211–257.

[62]See, John Skilton, "The New Testament Text Today," in John Skilton, ed. *The New Testament Student and His Field* (Phillipsburgh: Presbyterian and Reformed Publishing Co., 1982), pp. 19–20.

termined that if text criticism—German, Enlightenment text criticism—could be separated from the higher criticism, with common-sense at the helm, it could lead the Church safely into the seas of modernity, through the destructive winds of assault.[63]

Furthermore, by modifying the historical understanding of the Westminster Confession in order to accommodate this adjustment, Warfield felt he was constructing an apologetic that offered the same kind of certainty to modern Presbyterians, that the Westminster Confession had offered to the scholastics in their day. Moreover, it allowed him to 1) fully engage the discipline of text criticism and join in the quest for the historical text; 2) to retain the old scholastic view of verbal inspiration by now relegating this paradigm to the original autographs alone, which text criticism, not the Church, would now present to the world; 3) to give Scripture just the kind of scientific criteria it would need in the modern era, namely, the characteristic of inerrancy, something even the scholastics could not claim because they had bound themselves to the common, extant text.

The measure of Warfield's success in attempting to hitch the Princeton view of Biblical authority to the star of nineteenth century textual criticism, has been little assessed. To date, the inerrant autographs have yet to emerge. Perhaps George Marsden's analysis of the role of science within American evangelical academia may help to cast further light on the significance of Warfield's project:

---

[63]Most Reformed scholars today have recognized the impossibility and dishonesty of erecting such a wall of separation between higher and lower criticism. Harry Boer observes: "In view of the history of higher and lower criticism in the past one hundred years there is a profound irony in the relationship in which these two disciplines are regarded in the Church. Whereas higher criticism has a bad name in large parts of the Church, lower criticism has an eminently favorable name. Both kinds of criticism are governed by methods that . . . have an identical basic rational, scientific approach to their specific task. . . . The two forms of criticism are so interrelated and basic in the study of the bible that it is impossible to use the one properly without acknowledging the legitimacy and necessity of the other." Harry R. Boer, *The Bible and Higher Criticism* (Grand Rapids: Eerdmans, 1981), pp. 20; 18.

Rather than challenging modern science's first principles, the [American evangelical academics] came to be among the chief defenders of these principles. They were entirely confident that objective scientific inquiry could only confirm Christian truth. . . . The Christian community, having thoroughly trusted science and the scientific method, had welcomed them, even parading them as their staunchest friends. . . . This superficial accommodation left them with no defenses when the celebrated ally proved to be a heavily armed foe. . . . Biblical criticism turned the fire power of such scientific historical explanation point-blank on the origins of . . . the Bible itself. With awesome swiftness the edifice built by the method of addition that had worked so well for Christians in accommodating Christianity to the first scientific revolution had been demolished by the second.[64]

---

[64]George Marsden, "The Collapse of American Evangelical Academia," in Alvin Plantinga and Nicolas Wolterstorff, eds., *Faith and Rationality: Reason and Belief in God* (Notre Dame: University of Notre Dame Press, 1983), p. 223. Since the appearance of this essay a chapter from at least one Ph.D. has been written in response: "Critical Methodology in Defense of the Faith: B.B. Warfield's Overlooked Efforts in the field of New Testament," chapter three of Kim Riddlebarger's *The Lion of Princeton: B.B. Warfield on Apologetics, Theological Methodology and Polemics,* Ph.D. dissertation, Fuller Seminary. Here the author kindly states that ". . . Letis, has broken important new ground. . . . Letis contends that Warfield's importation of critical methodology to Princeton ultimately backfired, and led to an increasing historical skepticism that was antithetical to the work of the earlier Princetonians" (p.47). Moreover, Donald G. Bloesch has recently acknowledged the essay in his contribution to the "Christian Foundations" series: *Holy Scripture: Revelation, Inspiration and Interpretation:* "Theodore Letis makes a good case that Benjamine Warfield is mainly responsible for locating the final source of authority in the original autographic text rather than the *textus receptus,* the 'received text.' According to Letis, Warfield is to be seen as a daring innovator—"anbandoning the scholastic, creedal appraoch of the earlier Princetonians'" (p. 397, n. 18).

CHAPTER TWO

The Protestant Dogmaticians and the Late Princeton School on the Status of the Sacred Apographa

> *"... it is undisputed that from the 16th to the 18th century orthodoxy's doctrine of verbal inspiration assumed ... [the] Textus Receptus. It was the only Greek text they knew, and they regarded it as the 'original' text."*
>
> —Kurt Aland, "The Text of the Church?"
> *Trinity Journal* 8 (Fall 1987):131.

I. DEFINITIONS

A. Protestant Dogmaticians:

By Protestant dogmaticians I mean those much maligned heirs of Luther and Calvin from the post-Reformation era of the seventeenth century.[1] They have been discounted since the Enlightenment for two reasons: 1) they resorted to system building beyond what is considered the dynamic genius of the sixteenth century Reformers. This, in turn, prompted the formulation of creeds and confessions, considered by most today to reflect a propensity for over-definition. 2) They resorted to the Aristotelian method of the medieval schoolmen in their post-Tridentine battles with Rome.[2]

What we sometimes fail to realize is their era demanded such response. Theirs, after all, was a different age requiring a differ-

---

[1]The best treatment of the Lutheran dogmaticians on Scripture is Preus (1957). For Reformed scholasticism in general the most recent treatment is Muller (1987) and on Scripture Muller (1993).

[2]For a survey of recent literature on this as well as a fresh assessment of Protestant scholasticism see Muller (1986).

ent response to the freshly articulated Romanism of Trent, rather than that of the medieval schoolmen with whom Erasmus, Luther and Calvin had to contend. It was the special burden of the seventeenth-century Protestants to make certain the Reformation experiment of the sixteenth century continued to thrive within the new context of a now militant counter-Reformation age.

Most of the Protestant theology written at this time, along with the confessions and creeds, was prefigured by the systematic challenges presented to them by counter-Reformation theologians fighting for the very life's breath of the Latin Church.[3] If we fail to sympathize with what Frederic Farrar characterized in his Bampton Lectures in 1885 as, "a period in which liberty was exchanged for bondage; universal principles for beggarly elements; truth for dogmatism; independence for tradition; religion for system . . ." (Farrar 1886:358), perhaps it is because we need to reacquaint ourselves with *their* age and its peculiar demands.

B. The Sacred *Apographa*

By sacred *apographa* I mean the final referent of Biblical authority in the opinion of the Protestant dogmaticians—both Lutheran and Reformed. These are the faithful copies of the originally inspired *autographa.* The latter word is derived from the Greek noun αὐτόγραφα, original manuscripts written with one's own hand; The former word is derived from the Greek noun ἀπόγραφα meaning transcripts, copies from an original manuscript. By sacred apographa I mean those copies the Protestant dogmaticians regarded as faithful and authoritative

---

[3]Regarding the Lutherans, Preus maintains, "It is worth remembering that scholastic method was to some extent thrust upon the Lutheran dogmaticians of the seventeenth century. Tholuck has pointed out that a scholastic method was first used by the Wittenberg theologians in an effort to fight the Jesuits with their own weapons" (Preus:xvi). Muller remarks regarding the Reformed, "Note also that many of the late sixteenth and early seventeenth-century systems devote considerable energy to developing a theology technically capable of refuting Bellarmine" (Muller 1986:194, n.6).

copies of the original as opposed to corrupted or inauthentic copies.[4]

It is not my intention to address to what extent the dogmaticians fairly reflect the position of the Reformers since that is quite another issue, though an important one.

I will begin with the Lutheran dogmaticians. I will then treat the Calvinists, establishing that on the point of the sacred *apographa* we have one more rare category that finds near complete agreement in both families of the Reformation.

II. THE LUTHERAN DOGMATICIANS

If the first generation of Lutheran reformers could be called "ink theologians," to use Eck's words (Preus:207), because they believed all Christian doctrine should be derived from Scripture alone, the Lutheran dogmaticians must be seen as those who appended a Protestant *"traditio"* onto *sola Scriptura*.[5]

---

[4]For an excellent definition of these terms see R. Muller (1985) under *"autographa." Apographa* does not pertain to translations. Translations were regarded as inspired to the extent they reflected faithfully the content of the sacred *apographa*. Because, however, only Scripture in the original languages can be the norm for theology, the Lutheran Quenstedt argues, "Versions of the Bible are the Word of God in content and words, but the apographa are the Word of God in content, words and very idiom." (Preus:138). The Reformed Turretin says, "Although they are of great value for the instruction of believers, no other version can or should be regarded as on par with the original, much less as superior. (1) Because no other version has any weight which the Hebrew or Greek source does not possess more fully, since in the sources [*apographa*] not only the content (*res et sententiae*), but also the very words, were directly spoken (*dictata*) by the Holy Spirit, which cannot be said of any version. . . . Although a given translation made by human beings subject to error is not to be regarded as divine and infallible verbally, it can be properly so regarded in substance if it faithfully renders the divine truth of the sources [*apographa*]." (Turretin:152;154)

[5]Ladd has observed, "Protestantism thus came very near to adopting substantially the same false principles of hermeneutics, and of the nature of scriptural authority, as the Roman Catholics themselves. To a large extent in theory, and to a yet larger extent in practice, the Protestant theologians set up the tradition of dogma in the place of the fictitious tradition of unwritten apostolic doctrine, as a supreme authority through its influence upon the interpretation of the Bible" (Ladd 1883 vol. 2:180–181). The key words here are *very near*. Regarding the

The most valuable study of the Lutheran dogmaticians on Scripture is still probably Robert Preus's, *The Inspiration of Scripture: A Study of the Theology of the Seventeenth Century Lutheran Dogmaticians.*[6] The first to respond to the Council of Trent, however, and so begin Protestant scholastic tendencies, was Martin Chemnitz (1522–1586) who is not treated by Preus. This is because for Preus, the dogmaticians do not emerge in their fullest expression until the seventeenth century. Therefore, we will return to Preus's study after a look at Chemnitz.

A. Chemnitz (1522–1586)

Chemnitz's statement on Scripture is critical, appearing in his exhaustive four volume *Examen Concilii Tridentini*, which appeared during the years 1565–1573.[7] As a tribute to the importance of this work it is said in Lutheran circles, "if the second Martin (Chemnitz) had not come, the first Martin (Luther) would scarcely have endured" (Kramer 1971:24).[8]

Lutheran dogmaticians Preus is careful to note, "Only Scripture in the original languages is the *norma normans* of theology" (Preus:138). The important parallel between Rome and the Protestants, however, is found in their both making *ecclesiastical* determinations as to the exact locus of Biblical authority. Specific ecclesiastical recensions of the Biblical texts were sanctioned. The Reformed did this by way of their confessions, e.g. the Westminster Confession (1646), The Savoy Declaration (1658), The Helvetic Consensus Formula (1675), as did Rome in The Decrees of Trent (1564). The Lutherans, however, made such determinations in the persons of their dogmaticians and their published statements on the texts of Scripture. On this see the accompanying chart. As with the canon of Scripture, however, Protestants maintained that they were recognizing God's providence working in and through the Church, while Roman Catholics maintained it was the Church's authority itself which gave the texts their authority and sanction.

[6]This was a Ph.D. dissertation, *The Inspiration of Scripture as Taught by the Seventeenth Century Lutheran Dogmaticians*, 1952, written under the direction of Professor Thomas Torrance at New College, the University of Edinburgh. It was then published in Edinburgh in 1955. A second edition appeared in 1957 and this was reprinted by the Concordia Heritage Series, St. Louis, 1981 and is still in print so far as I know.

[7]I will be referring to the English translation, (Kramer 1971).

[8]A good monograph treating Chemnitz view of Scripture as compared with Luther's is Klug (1971). Klug sums up their relationship on Scripture as follows: "Chemnitz stands between Luther and the theologians who followed after him as a true bridge over which Luther's theology, especially of the Word, was carefully

In Chemnitz's treatment of the Decrees of Trent, he recorded the Council's statement on a given tenet and then responded accordingly. On Scripture, Trent set forth its case in the First and Second Decrees of the Fourth Session, on April 5, 1546. In the Second Decree, the *Vulgata Latina* was asserted to be the only authoritative edition of Scripture. The newly restored Greek text of Erasmus was officially put on the index of forbidden books even though the first edition had been dedicated to Pope Leo X and was commended by him.

Chemnitz spent most of his effort refuting the claims of Trent regarding the Roman Catholic Church's prerogative to be the sole interpreter of Scripture. This also included the claim that the Church had a fuller body of authoritative teaching beyond Scripture alone, as found in the on-going oral tradition. Hence, for Chemnitz, the issue at stake is still the Reformation tenet of *sola Scriptura*.

In section seven, however, he begins to address the issue of translations and their relationship to the original language texts:

> But what if that common edition [the *Vulgata Latina*] has not rendered what is in the sources, whether it be Hebrew or Greek, correctly, suitably, and adequately. . . . Will one be allowed to prefer the fountainheads to the brooks (Chemnitz:201)?

The answer that Chemnitz derives from the decree of Trent is "no," to which he replies:

> Truly, this must not be tolerated in the church, that in place of the things which the Holy Spirit wrote in Hebrew and Greek sources something should be foisted onto us as authentic which has been badly rendered . . . and that in such a way that one may not reject them even after he has examined the sources (Chemnitz: 202).[9]

---

carried, and not as an evolutionary rung in the ladder that led to a structuring of a theology of the Word quite different from that of the Reformer. . . . There is no real advance or development, other than a sharpening of thought and formulation" (247).

[9]There has been much controversy over the years as to just what the Council of Trent meant by, "precisely the ancient and widely current [*vulgata*] edition

Chemnitz then refers to the findings of the Renaissance humanists, Erasmus and Valla, on the many problems with the Vulgate. He lists examples of distortions in the Vulgate that seem to support various distinctives in the belief and practice of the Roman Church.

Up to this point it looked as though the Protestants had everything their way. This was short lived. A very important shift was precipitated by a new debate concerning the pointing of the Hebrew text. I will not go into detail on this controversy, but allow me to sum up what was at stake.[10]

---

that had been approved by long use within the Church for so many centuries . . . should be held as *authentic*." (emphasis mine) There can be little doubt that the Protestant dogmaticians understood the post-Tridentine theologian's interpretation of *authentica* as referring to the Vulgate as superior to extant Greek and Hebrew texts when these sources differed. In September of 1943, however, Pope Pius XII released an encyclical, *Divino afflante Spiritu*, defining "authentic" as applying "only to the Latin Church and to its public uses of the Scripture; that it diminished in no way the authority and value of the original texts, Hebrew and Greek; that the decree in effect affirmed that the Vulgate was free from any error whatever in matters of faith and morals and so could be quoted with complete authority in disputations, lectures, and preaching—that, in short, the term had been used primarily in a juridical rather than a critical sense; and that there had been no intention to prohibit the making of vernacular versions from the original texts rather than from the Vulgate." (*New Catholic Encyclopedia* s.v. "Bible,":454) Nevertheless, the first Roman Catholic English translation, the Rhemes New Testament, 1582 (Old Testament translated at Rhemes but published at Douay, 1609), reads on the title page, *The New Testament of Jesus Christ, translated faithfully into English, out of the authentical Latin . . . diligently conferred with the Greeke and other editions in divers languages."* This would have left the impression that priority was given to the *Vulgata Latina* over the Greek. Furthermore, even the young Bellarmine did not possess the clarity on just what *authentica* meant, as finally provided by the later encyclical (Brodrick:47). This all seems to indicate development on the interpretation of Trent's decree as found in the later papal encyclical not unlike fundamentalist *reinterpretation* of the Westminster Confession claiming it had reference to the original autographs rather than extant copies. Both this modern Protestant adjustment and Pius XII's 1943 Encyclical appealed to Providence for an explanation for this development.

[10]On this debate see Ladd (189–191); Bruce (1970:154–62); Freiday (1979: 9–11;89–95); Bowman (1948); Gundry (1967); Muller (1980); Letis (1987A: 35–70).

B. The Hebrew Vowel Points.

Both Luther and Calvin had admitted the pointing in the accepted Hebrew text of their day could be wrong at times and so felt nothing crucial was at stake (Muller 1980:53–54). When once it was suggested, however, that the system of pointing was the result of the Masoretes and not Moses or Ezra; and because of Jewish hostilities towards the Christian interpretation of the Old Testament the pointing had been adversely influenced by the Jews, *sola Scriptura* began to look tenuous. John Bowman has provided a good assessment of the debate:

> It would be quite erroneous . . . to form the opinion that the Protestants and Roman Catholics held opposing views on the points, merely to be consistent in their opposition to one another. The skein is more tangled than that. In claiming the late origin of the vowel-points, the Roman Catholics saw a way of championing the Vulgate translation as more reliable than the present Massoretic Hebrew text, which latter was regarded by Protestants as the very Word of God. Further, if the introduction of the Massoretic points was late, no one could have learned the Scriptures without the oral tradition of the Jewish church. The Protestants were professed antitraditionalists; they refused to accept the tradition of the Church of Rome, yet accepted the results of the tradition of the Jewish church. In this way the Catholics sought to show Protestant inconsistency (Bowman:47).

In fact, John Morinus, a former French Protestant turned Roman Catholic priest argued, "God gave the Old Testament without vowels because he desired men to follow the church's interpretation, not their own, for the Hebrew tongue without vowels as it was given is a 'very nose of wax'" (Bowman:51–52).

It was the Jesuit Bellarmine who used this argument with the most force. He argued that an earlier, authentic and uncorrupted form of the Hebrew text was employed by Jerome and for that reason only the *Vulgata Latina* can now be trusted (Muller 1980:56).[11] As Richard Muller has recognized, this lifted

---

[11]Bellarmine's biographer assessed Bellarmine as "only an amateur Hebraist." (Brodrick 1961:46)

the issue of the *correct edition* of the original language texts "to doctrinal status" (Muller 1980:63). For Protestants this was the ecclesiastical recension of the medieval Greek Church; for the Roman Catholics it was a theoretical textual base underlying the medieval Latin recension.

C. Gerhard (1582–1637)

In response to this claim of Bellarmine and others, Gerhard argued for the providential preservation of the *apographa*:

> Divine Providence did not permit those books to be corrupted and perverted; otherwise, the foundation of the church would totter and fall. . . . Were one to grant that something in Holy Scripture was changed, most of its genuine authority would disappear. On the other hand, however, Christ declares, Matt. 5:18 "Until heaven and earth pass away, not a iota, not a dot, will pass from the law until all is accomplished." Also Luke 16:17: It is easier for heaven and earth to pass away than for one dot of the Law to become void." . . . Just as Paul testifies that "the Jews are entrusted with the oracles of God," namely, those described in the books of the Old Testament, Rom. 3.2; so too, we can say in regard to the primitive Christian Church that it is entrusted with the oracles of God described in the books of the New Testament. You see, it has received the autographs from the very evangelists and apostles and has faithfully preserved them in the patriarchal churches so that they could correct the copies [*apographa*] and other versions according to the tenor of the autographs (Gerhard:505; 502).[12]

---

[12]I believe J.S.K. Reid misses Gerhard's meaning when he argues, "Gerhard, on the other hand, is rather stricter, holding that only the original Hebrew and Greek manuscripts are authentic." Rather, Gerhard quotes with approval Sixtus of Sena who said, "We say that this Greek codex which we are now reading in the church is the very same one which the Greek Church used at the time of Jerome and all the way back to the days of the apostles; it is true, genuine, faithful and contaminated by no fault of falsehood, as a continual reading of all Greek fathers shows very clearly." (Gerhard:553) It appears Reid has confused the Lutheran dogmatician's arguments in favor of the exclusive authority of the original *language* texts against versions, with an argument for the exclusive authority of the original *autographic* texts, a decidedly later position.

D. Quenstedt (1617–1688)

Quenstedt took up the theme of preservation of autographic quality in the *apographa* and gave it further specificity:

> Our argument runs as follows: every holy Scripture which existed at the time of Paul was θεοπνευστος (2 Tim. 3:16) and authentic. Not the autographic (for they had perished long before), but the apographic writings existed at the time of Paul. Therefore the apographic Scripture also is θεοπνευστος and authentic. . . . For although inspiration and divine authority inhered originally in the autographa, these attributes belong to the apographa by virtue of their derivation [radicaliter], since they were faithfully transcribed from them so that not only the sense but also the words were precisely the same (Preus:48).[13]

Elsewhere, Quenstedt was even more detailed:

> Not only the Canonical books of the sacred volume themselves, but even the letters, points, and words of the original text survive without any corruption, that is, the Hebrew text of the O[ld] T[estament] . . . and also the Greek text of the N[ew] T[estament] . . . have been preserved by the divine providence complete and uncorrupted (Piepkorn 1965:589).

E. Baier (1647–1695) and Musaeus (1613–1681)

Preus records of these two,

> Baier, following Musaeus, maintains that the apographa can rightly be called inspired since they possess the same *forma,* or content, as the autographic Scriptures. All the apographa have been either mediately or immediately copied from the auto-

---

[13]Reid also misses Quenstedt's meaning, asserting, "Quenstedt holds . . . inspiration applies to original manuscripts or autographa, not properly to the apographa" (Reid 1957:88). Yet a few lines later he admits that for Quenstedt, "a good copy is inspired like the original writing"(?) (89). G.W. Bromiley agrees with Preus and myself: "Quenstedt, however, took the even more difficult position that the apographs are fully inspired because the words as well as the content of the autographs are substantially retained in them" (Bromiley 1978:320).

grapha. Hence to day, in spite of the many codices extant with their many material variations, the meaning or the inspired sense of the autographa is with us (Preus:48).

F. Hollaz (1648–1713)

Hollaz, "seems to go further. He asserts that the very words as well as the content of the autographic texts are today in the apographa. A good copy of an inspired writing is inspired like the original writing" (Preus:48)

G. The Status of the *Autographa*

Preus notes that the decisive issue for Lutherans in this debate with Rome never centered around the nature of the theoretical autographic text;[14] this would grant precious ground to the Roman theologians:

> Most Catholic teachers would have granted that the ancient Greek and Hebrew autographa were authentic. They argued that the MSS which we have today, however, cannot be regarded as authentic because, after many years of copying, they have become corrupt and impure. This thought naturally led back to a discussion regarding the integrity of the contemporary text . . . Bellarmine contended that the Vulgate could not err because it enjoyed the approbation of the Church. (Preus:139).

One of the major criticisms directed at Erasmus by Roman Catholic dogmaticians was that he was returning to the corrupted Bible of the schismatic Greek Church. Rome's theologians believed, based on the unerring authority of the Papal Church, that the *Vulgata Latina* alone preserved the original content of the autographic texts. In response to this clear-cut position of Rome Quenstedt offered the definitive Protestant response, aptly capturing both the Lutheran and Reformed sentiment in the seventeenth century:

---

[14]"Dannhauer says that it is as needless and foolish to suppose that we must have the autographa today as to think that we need the cup from which Christ drank before the Eucharist can be rightly celebrated" (Preus:49).

We believe, as is our duty, that the providential care of God has always watched over the original and primitive texts of the canonical Scriptures in such a way that we can be certain that the sacred codices *which we now have in our hands* are those which existed at the time of Jerome and Augustine, nay at the time of Christ Himself and his apostles [emphasis mine] (Preus:48).[15]

To this, Preus adds after surveying eighteen of the most important Lutheran dogmaticians of the seventeenth century, "This was the Lutheran position in a nutshell."[16]

However, because the Lutheran dogmaticians also shared the seventeenth century with a developing, independent, philological tradition—the seeds of which were in Erasmus—the argument "the text of the Bible has gone through essentially the

---

[15]There were minority positions. Preus mentions that Huelsemann relegated inspiration "properly spoken of only in reference to the original manuscripts" (Preus:48). Also, in the Reformed camp Curcellaeus, Cappelus, and Usher argued that while we could not always be certain of the integrity of the apographic text, no fundamental tenet of the Christian faith was disturbed by textual variants. Curcellaeus seems to be the author of this perspective (although most attribute it to Bentley in his response to Anthony Collins) that would eventually undermine the position of the Protestant dogmaticians. Bentley again takes up the position in England, Bengel does so in eighteenth century Germany and Tregelles employs it again in England in the mid nineteenth century. By the time of Westcott and Hort it has become a moot point.

[16]Preus is understandably a bit apologetic about the dogmatician's arguments for the absolute authority of the apographic texts: "He [Quenstedt] would hardly have considered the apographa of his time in the same category as those which Paul and Timothy used. However, his statement indicates that he is not alive to the significance of the fact of variant readings" (Preus:49). I believe, however, that this position of the dogmaticians was in fact fashioned as a specific response to textual variants—those textual differences between the *Vulgata Latina*, which Roman Catholic theologians claimed came from superior editions of the original Hebrew and Greek texts, and the apographic texts employed by the Protestants and given to them by the Greek Church. Someone as early as Gerhard (d. 1637) spends time treating these and other textual variants raised by Bellermine (Gerhard:556–564). Furthermore, from Erasmus, Grotius and the London Polyglot, Quenstedt knew of an entire plethora of textual variants. I believe the arguments in favor of the absolute quality of the *apographa* were arguments in favor of ecclesiastical *traditio* (the Greek Church) preserving the correct recension of the Greek text (Erasmus also believed this but perhaps not with the same specificity as the dogmaticians) in deliberate response to textual variants.

same changes which belong to all other ancient writings," (Ladd:188) began to take its toll. G. T. Ladd argued that with the arrival of John Gottlob Carpzov, "The necessity . . . for transferring the quality of verbal infallibility from any extant manuscript or manuscripts to an ideal non-existent text, became more and more apparent." This new view, however, by no means prevailed within Lutheranism until late in the nineteenth century.

III. The Reformed Dogmaticians

A. John Owen (1616–1683)

The publishing of Brian Walton's *London Polyglot* (1657) provided the occasion for one of the most systematic defenses of the *apographa* by a Reformed dogmatician. John Owen, the leading Puritan theologian at the time of the publishing of the Polyglot was distressed at Walton's naked display of every variant to the N.T. text—sometimes with a significant degree of redundancy—known at that time. Owen bemoaned Walton's list of textual variants that took up as many pages in Walton's Polyglot as did his entire N.T. text. To Owen, this constituted both a crisis and a scandal: a crisis because this left the impression the very wording of the N.T. was greatly in doubt, a scandal because Walton had so indiscriminately published this for the world to see. Owen responded to Walton in his essay, "*Of the Integrity and Purity of the Hebrew and Greek Text of the Scriptures, 1659.*" In this work, Owen argued the polyglot gave material support to the Roman Catholic position by leaving the impression,

> the original [language] copies of the Old and New Testament are so corrupted ("ex oro tuo, serve nequam") that they are not a certain standard and measure of all doctrines, or the touchstone of all translations . . . . Of all the inventions of Satan to draw off the minds of men from the Word of God, this *decrying the authority of the originals* [the *apographa*] seems to me the most pernicious (Owen 1850–53:285).

Owen clearly understood the implications for Protestant authority in this threat from the polyglot:

> Besides the injury done hereby to the providence of God towards His Church, and care of His Word, it will not be found so easy a matter, upon a supposition of such corruption in the originals as is pleaded for, to evince unquestionably that the whole saving doctrine itself, at first given out from God, continues entire and incorrupt [sic] (Owen:302).[17]

Richard Kroll has correctly seen the significance of the *London Polyglot* as the "critical method [that] served at once scholarly, epistemological, and political purposes, forming an early Arminian and Latitudinarian assault on Catholic and Puritan claims to absolute certainty" (Kroll 1986:21). This was a continuation of the Erasmian project begun with the publishing of his critical edition of the *Greek* New Testament, which was "an avowed part of his desire to recall the Church to its pristine origins and to permit the individual to make probable judgements for himself" (Kroll 1986:11). Brian Walton, the editor of the *Polyglot* had clearly declared in the preface that "Now care is taken that every private man may have [the original texts], and use them as his own" (Kroll 1986:21).

That Walton clearly saw his project as a furthering of Erasmus's is stated quite explicitly in his reply to John Owen, in Walton's *The Considerator Considered* (1659):

> This is no new thing, that endeavours to promote the public good should be thus [poorly] rewarded; for in former ages we find, that those who laboured most about the sacred oracles of

---

[17]Here Owen is addressing the more moderate position of Cappellus, Usher, et al. which is while the traditional apographic text is not a near perfect replication of the *autographa*, no doctrine is at stake. Ladd notes correctly, however, the rationale of the dogmaticians who argued contrariwise, "the Bible is throughout the infallible Word of God, and that, if its text do [sic] not lie before us in autographic integrity, it cannot be the medium for this infallible Word. . . . It was urged . . . that, if a single concession were once made to the critics, they would not stop in their discoveries and demands until they had captured the entire field" (Ladd:188).

God, to restore them to their primitive and original lustre, and to wipe off that dust which by injuries of time and ignorance or negligence of transcribers was contracted, and so to transmit them pure and incorrupt to posterity . . . have yet been aspersed and slandered, their labours calumniated, and their aims perverted. . . . Erasmus's extraordinary pains in publishing the Greek Testament by comparing ancient Copies and Translations, was sufficiently railed at by some friars and ignorant zealots, as if he took upon him *to correct the Word of God*; as appears in his preface to his Annotations of 1535. . . (Walton 1821:3–4).

In response to the claims of the editors employed in the *Polyglot*, that certain translations had greater authority at times than did the common Greek and Hebrew texts, Owen defended the *apographa*:

Let it be remembered that the vulgar copy we use was the public possession of many generations that upon the invention of printing it was in actual authority throughout the world with them that used and understood that language, as far as any thing appears to the contrary; let that, then, pass for the standard, which is confessedly its right and due, and we shall, God assisting, quickly see how little reason there is to pretend such varieties of readings as we are now surprised withal (Owen:366).[18]

Against the claim there is a superior original language text underlying certain translations, Owen argues for,

the purity of the *present original copies* of the Scripture, or rather copies [*apographa*] in the original languages, which the Church of God doth *now* and hath for many ages enjoyed as her chiefest treasure (Owen:353). [emphasis mine]

---

[18]Note the parallel in language between Owen's appeal above to the common tradition of the Greek Church and that of the Council of Trent's appeal to the common Latin tradition in the Western Church. Trent argued that it was "precisely the ancient and widely current [*vulgata*] edition that had been approved by long use within the Church for so many centuries . . . should be held as authentic."

B. Francis Turretin (1623–1687).

Moving to the Continent, a contemporary of Owen's, Francis Turretin, was making the same point in his *Institutio theologiae elencticae* (1688). From his post as Professor of Theology at the University of Geneva, where he was appointed in 1653, Turretin argued in his chapter "The Purity of the Original Text,"

> This question is forced upon us by the Roman Catholics, who raise doubts concerning the purity of the sources in order more readily to establish the authority of their Vulgate and lead us to the tribunal of the church (Turretin 1981:113).

Like Owen, Turretin refers to the "original texts" as a *terminus technicus*:

> By "original texts" we do not mean the very autographs from the hands of Moses, the prophets, and the apostles, which are known to be non-existent. We mean copies (*apographa*), which have come in their name [*autographa*] because they record for us that Word of God in the same words into which the sacred writers committed it under the *immediate inspiration* of the Holy Spirit. . . . Faithful and accurate copies, not less than autographs, are norms for all other copies . . . and for translations [emphasis mine] (Turretin:113; 128).[19]

C. Reformed Confessions

While the Lutherans never codified this position on the sacred *apographa* in a confessional statement, the Reformed did. Thirteen years before Owen published his response to Walton, the Westminster Confession was drafted (1646) affirming,

---

[19]Some have argued that the words "immediately inspired" meant that only the autographs were inspired and authoritative. Whereas, while Turretin uses the same language as the WCF, for him the *apographa* also share this quality. Thus Turretin stands in direct opposition to this modern reinterpretation of the meaning of these words as they are used by the authors of the WCF. Furthermore, John Owen, like Turretin, also affirmed explicitly the inspiration and authority of the *apographa* and so recognized no distinction in the language in the WCF between immediate inspiration and the providentially preserved copies when adopting this exact language in his own Savoy Declaration (1658).

The Old Testament in Hebrew . . . and New Testament in Greek . . . being immediately inspired by God, and by his singular care and providence kept pure in all ages, are therefore authentical. Chapter one, Section eight (Leith 1973:196).

Note that by using the word *authentical*, the Westminster Divines were sanctioning the Greek Church's recension of the New Testament and the common Jewish, Masoretic text in response to Trent which referred to the *Vulgata Latina* as *authentica*.

Later, in 1675, Turretin of Geneva, Lucas Gernler of Basel and John Henry Heidegger of Zurich, composed the *Formula Consensus Helvetica,* which stated:

God, the supreme Judge, not only took care to have His Word, which is the "power of God unto Salvation to everyone that believeth" (Rom. 1:16), committed to writing by Moses, the prophets, and the apostles, but has also watched and cherished it with paternal care ever since it was written up to the present time, so that it could not be corrupted by craft of Satan or fraud of man. Therefore the church justly ascribes it to His singular grace and goodness that she has, and will have to the end of the world, a "sure word of prophecy" and "holy Scriptures" (2Tim. 3:15), from which, though heaven and earth perish, "one jot or one tittle shall in no wise pass" (Matt. 5:18). Chapter one (Leith:309–10)

Since the late nineteenth century there has been considerable debate about the authorial intent of the Westminster Confession on this point.[20] We know for certain, however, that the *Formula*, just quoted, was directed against developments at the University of Saumur regarding the authority of the Hebrew vowel points. Moreover, considering all the previous testimony surveyed thus far it must be evident that the Westminster Confession is but reflecting what was in the theological air at that historical moment, within both confessional Lutheranism as well as confessional Calvinism. Ladd well summed up the Protestant dogmaticians and their confessions on the status of the sacred *apographa*:

---

[20] On this see Rogers (1966).

No relief was allowed to the dreadful pressure of the post-Reformation dogma by way of attaching the quality of infallibility only to the original text; for, to maintain the dogma in its efficiency, it was further claimed that the biblical text had been supernaturally preserved in infallible form (Ladd:182).

John Robinson did a commendable job in treating these subjects within Reformed orthodoxy in his Ph.D. dissertation, *The Doctrine of Scripture in Seventeenth Century Reformed Theology* (1971), and here we will just survey his conclusions.

He clearly states that while Calvin held to the infallibility of Scripture, because this was always assumed to adhere to extant editions, "Calvin must have felt the tension between his doctrine [of Scripture] and the problems he confronted in the text, but he did his best to hold to the one and deal honestly with the other" (Robinson 1971:37). Unfortunately, Robinson's desire to prove that sixteenth and seventh-century Reformed orthodox theologians held to the modern doctrine of inerrancy, tends to dominate how he uses his data.[21] Nevertheless, the evidence is clearly set forth by him (though he seems at times to miss its full significance):

> The strength of the Reformed position . . . lay in demonstrating the successful transmission of the original texts to their own day. Some Reformed theologians were so convinced of the Bible's textual purity and authenticity that they apparently did not even refer to the received texts as apographs. Many referred to them as "original texts" which conveyed the impression that they were speaking of the autographs (Robinson:98).

Here Robinson has misunderstood the nomenclature of the

---

[21]For example when he argues that "the main point concerning textual infallibility was that no errors of any kind were admitted to have been present when the original text was recorded" (41), he does not ever address in this context the issue that was paramount to the dogmaticians, namely, that such a quality was found in extant editions (what the dogmaticians called the *apographa)* and was never relegated to lost autographs such as modern fundamentalists argue. Robinson does treat this issue elsewhere but never seems to fully grasp its significance for the dogmaticians.

dogmaticians because of the modern fundamentalist emphasis on "original autographs." When the dogmaticians refer to the "original texts" they nearly always have as their referent the extant *apographa* or original *language* texts, as opposed to original *autographic* texts. The confusion was never in their minds only in a modern reading them through the lens of twentieth century categories and debates.

Nevertheless, in spite of this confusion, Robinson does eventually get it right by acknowledging:

> Reformed theologians were not arguing for the obvious authenticity of the no longer extant autographs. Instead, they were claiming authenticity for the received texts which they viewed as equivalent to the original manuscripts, and which they referred to as the "authentic sources," the "first editions," the "Greek and Hebrew originals," the "original texts," etc. The authenticity of Greek and Hebrew "sources" was held to be absolute both in form and content. . . . In summary, the Reformed theologians held that only the received Hebrew text of the Old Testament and the Greek text of the New Testament were authentic, authoritative editions of the Scripture (98; 101–102).

Like most moderns, however, Robinson passes a bad judgement on the Reformed dogmaticians here because this was

> a weak point in the counter-attack upon the Vulgate developed from the Reformed conviction of the full authenticity and integrity of the Greek and Hebrew texts. This provided a vulnerable point for textual criticisms which were to affect not only the status of the versions but the authority of Scripture as well (102).[22]

According to Robinson, the defense of the *apographa* was carried on the same basis as that for the canon—"the key arguments were dogmatic . . . . the demonstration was com-

---

[22]This in turn prompted the modern fundamentalist adjustment which now claims that only the original autographs are authoritative, once they have been reconstructed.

pleted by an appeal, explicitly or implicitly, to the providence of God" (103). This dogmatic claim was then validated by Scriptural exegesis. Ecclesiology was also always close by: "The faithfulness of the Christian Church, the religious views of the Jews, the carefulness of the Masoretes, and the multitude of the manuscripts were also added to the proofs of non-corruption" (104).

Not unlike the Roman Catholics when Louis Cappel published his *Critica sacra* (1650), challenging the integrity of the Hebrew Text, the Reformed dogmatic response was the *Formula Consensus*, discussed above, which Robinson judges, "represented the general Reformed position" (116).

Why the Westminster Confession was subject to a new and different interpretation brings us to the Princeton Seminary of the late nineteenth century.

IV. The Princeton School

The Lutheran, Authur Carl Piepkorn, in an essay written in 1965 treating the history of the recent use of the word "inerrancy" in reference to Scripture, said of the position held by the Lutheran dogmaticians outlined above, "This is a position which modern textual criticism renders untenable. As this has become more and more apparent, the claim of inerrancy has increasingly been posited only of the originals [*autographa*]" (Piepkorn 1965:589). B.B. Warfield provided the fundamental paradigm for this shift in Reformed circles and by the mid-twentieth century his influence began to make its impact on Lutherans as well.

A. Early Princeton

1. Archibald Alexander (1772–1851)

When the dogmaticians encountered a difficulty in the text occasionally they would ascribe this to an error in transcription. Because, however, for them the sacred *apographa* were authoritative, more commonly such problems, tended to be brushed aside. Verbal peculiarities and the well-known discrepancies continued to be ascribed to the accommodation of the Holy Spirit (Vawter 1972:81).[23]

This reflected the feeling that all the phenomena found in the sacred *apographa* had to be taken seriously. Archibald Alexander, the first instructor at Princeton Seminary (1812), and heir of the dogmatic tradition of Francis Turretin, goes so far as to admit that minor errors in the text may have arisen not from scribal transmission but at the original time of composition, since the amanuenses of the apostles did not compose by inspiration. (Loetscher 1983:228)[24]

2. Charles Hodge (1797–1878)

Regarding Charles Hodge, I agree completely with the judgement of Ernest Sandeen in an earlier treatment of the Princeton theology when he highlighted a controversial passage in Hodge's *Systematic Theology* (1872–73). Here, Hodge admits to small, unimportant errors in Scripture.[25] Again, this reflects an attempt to take seriously all the phenomena of the *apographa* as a final and authoritative expression of the Word of God.

---

[23]On this score Ladd cites the following example: "The difference of readings, for instance, between 2 Sam. xxii. and Ps. xviii. was explained by assuming a double purpose of the Holy Spirit: differences in the spelling of proper names showed the freedom of the same Spirit" (Ladd:188). Preus also points out that Pfeiffer responded by saying contradictions "simply do not exist. If Scripture seems to contradict itself we must confess our ignorance and say, 'Thus it has pleased the Lord to say much which seems wrong and impossible'" (Preus:85).

[24]Preus notes that, "Some theologians at the time of the orthodox period had maintained a distinction between errors of the inspired writers themselves and occasional slips of the pen on the part of their secretaries, opposing the possibility of the former while granting the possibility of the latter, but to the dogmaticians neither possibility could be conceded" (Preus:78).

[25]The passage reads as follows: "The errors in matters of fact which skeptics search out bear no proportion to the whole. No sane man would deny that the Parthenon was built of marble, even if here and there a speck of sandstone should be detected in its structure. Not less unreasonable is it to deny the inspiration of such a book as the Bible, because one sacred writer says that on a given occasion twenty-four thousand, and another says that twenty-three thousand,

B. Late Princeton and B.B. Warfield (1851–1921)[26]

On October 20, 1880, A.A. Hodge wrote B.B. Warfield, then professor at Western Theological Seminary (today it is Pittsburgh Theological Seminary). Hodge pleaded with Warfield to co-author an essay with him in the young *Presbyterian Review* on the Princeton doctrine of inspiration in light of modern scholarship. Hodge confessed,

> I can after a fashion restate the old orthodoxy *common*-place as to inspiration and fence it somewhat on the *a-priori* or metaphysical side, but I can do nothing on the side of stating or answering the positions of the hostile criticism, as to the alleged contradictions of detail (Hodge 1880A).

Hodge directed Warfield specifically to address "the state of actual facts (as to the *New* Testament) in regard to the asserted inaccuracies—or contradictions" (Hodge).

In November of that same year Hodge posed the problem as he saw it with an explicit reference to his father's controversial statement in the first volume of the *Systematic Theology*. This is

---

men were slain. Surely a Christian may be allowed to tread such objections under his feet. . . . The universe teems with evidences of design, so manifold, so diverse, so wonderful, as to overwhelm the mind with the conviction that it has had an intelligent author. Yet here and there isolated cases of monstrosity appear. It is irrational, because we cannot account for such cases, to deny that the universe is the product of intelligence." By his metaphor it is obvious that Hodge allows for the presence of unexplainable phenomena in the apographic text which at one point he calls "errors" (although he does seem to hold out the possibility that these may be resolved in the future). Since no other ideal universe (*autographa*) which is without such *montrosities*, is referred to in his argument, unlike Warfield he thus concedes this element as part of the phenomena of Scripture itself since it is part of the sacred *apographa*. E.D. Morris came to the same conclusion in his major study of the Confession: "Still it may be necessary, after all such explanatory processes, to admit that there may remain in the Scriptures as we now possess them what has been well described, (Hodge, Syst. Theol.) as here or there a speck of sand-stone showing itself in the marble of the Parthenon—an occasional variation, difference or even discrepancy of statement which, so far as we can see, may have been in the original text as written by holy men moved by the Holy Ghost." *Theology of the Westminster Symbols* (Columbus: n.p., 1900):88.

[26]A bit of this material has already been covered in the opening essay.

a particularly important letter because it provides us with A.A. Hodge's exegesis of his father's statement:

> But the question remains was this book [the Bible] with its (1) human (2) oriental & (3) Hebrew characteristics *intended to stand the test of microscopic criticism as to its accuracy in matters of indifferent detail?* It appears that my father [Charles Hodge] was speaking of the possibility of infinitesimal inaccuracies of no importance relating to the end designed, in *Systematic Theology* Vol. I, p. 170. I say so too—very heartily. But the question remains what degree of minute accuracy do the facts prove that God designed to effect? That is for you critics and exegetes to determine (Hodge 1880B).[27]

This invitation and challenge to Warfield placed an immense burden of responsibility on his shoulders. When Sandeen judges that "Princeton Theology, especially in its latter days, continually fell victim to this besetting sin of pride, unable to make any distinction between Paul and Princeton," (Sandeen 1962:313) I am tempted to alter his words. They seemed not to be able to make out the difference between the Westminster Divines and the Protestant scholastic tradition they represented, and B.B. Warfield.

In order to answer this call to come to the rescue of Princeton, Warfield found it necessary to demythologise the Westminster Confession of Faith. Furthermore, when he accomplished

---

[27]A.A. Hodge's instincts as reflected in this assessment seemed to be quite good. Were it not for Warfield's influence he may have carried on the Old Princeton tradition with but slight modification as opposed to Warfield's radical new agenda. Sandeen noted that A.A. Hodge made no reference to original autographs in his first (1860) edition of his *Outlines of Theology*, but added these words to his 1879 edition. (Sandeen:316) Whether this was a result of Warfield's influence, or that of Francis Patton, who argued in a similar vain (1869:112–115), I have not yet been able to determine. Patton differed from Warfield, however, in acknowleding that the *apographa* were inspired to the extent that they reflected autographic content. Furthermore, he did not feel the common text needed to be replaced with an earlier recension, as did Warfield. For Patton, the common text represented "an infallible autograph" that "has been perpetuated by the industry of transcribers, and has been changed only in some unimportant details through the mistakes of copyists" (115).

his mission he looked back over his shoulder to discover he single-handedly converted to his perspective most of the General Assembly of the Presbyterian Church in the U.S.A. in 1893. (Rogers: 396).

In the process, however, he destroyed forever the dogmatician's view of the sacred *apographa*. For Warfield, the Westminster Confession no longer taught providential *preservation* of the text but rather its providential *restoration* in the latter part of the nineteenth century.[28]

In his treatise on inspiration, co-authored by A.A. Hodge, he felt himself completely in keeping with the authentic teaching of the Confession when he argued,

> We do not assert that the common text, [*apographa*] but only that original autographic text was inspired. No "error" can be asserted, therefore, which cannot be proved to have been aboriginal in the text (Warfield/Hodge 1881:238).

With this strategy, Warfield won the battle but he may have lost the war that seemed so critical to the Protestant dogmaticians. As perhaps the leading American authority on the state of New Testament text critical matters in the late nineteenth century, he thought it necessary to then go on a crusade against the uninspired *apographa*.

On December 2, 1882, he demonstrated how serious he was about his agenda. In the lay publication, *Sunday School Times,* he asserted to the reading Christian public that Mark's long ending was "no part of God's word." Therefore, "we are not then to ascribe to these verses the authority due to God's Word." (Warfield 1882:755–56) No Princetonian prior to this had ever doubted the canonical authority of these verses. This is

---

[28]He did so by arguing, "In the sense of the Westminster Confession, therefore, the multiplication of the copies of the Scriptures, the several early efforts towards the revision of the text, the raising up of scholars in our own day to collect and collate MSS., and to reform the text on scientific principles—of our Tischendorfs, and Tregelleses, and Westcotts and Horts—are all parts of God's singular care and providence in preserving [=restoring] His inspired Word pure" (Warfield 1931:239).

all the more provocative in light of Bruce Metzger's recent judgement on these verses in his monograph treating the canon. Here, Metzger accords the long ending canonical status, even though it is not Markan (Metzger 1987:269–270).[29]

However, all was not gloom and doom. Warfield held out hope, promising,

> The inerrant autographs were a fact once; they may possibly be a fact again, when textual criticism has said its last word on the Bible text. In proportion as they are approached in the processes of textual criticism, do we have an ever better and better Bible than the one we have now (Warfield 1892:557).[30]

Warfield's new proposal did not go unanswered.

C. Some Responses to Warfield

1. Preserved Smith (1847–1927)

The American Church Historian, Preserved Smith, protested Warfield's reinterpretation of the Westminster Confession in the following terms:

> Warfield in an article in the *Presbyterian Review* stated the doctrine [inerrancy] is not concerned with the accuracy of our present Bible, but interests itself in affirming a perfection of the original autographs which has in some cases at least been lost in transmission. . . . None the less does the new theory depart widely from the confessional doctrine. That the Word of God as we now have it in Scripture is infallible . . . this is the affirmation of the Confession. Its interest is in the present Bible for

---

[29]"Already in the second century, for example, the so-called long ending of Mark was known to Justin Martyr and to Tatian, who incorporated it into his *Diatesseron*. There seems to be good reason, therefore, to conclude that, though external and internal evidence is conclusive against the authenticity of the last twelve verses as coming from the same pen as the rest of the gospel, the passage ought to be accepted as part of the canonical text of Mark."

[30]Note by contrast Dannhauer's remark from the seventeenth-century in footnote 14.

present purposes, and those purposes are practical purposes. That an inerrant autograph once existed is a speculative assertion, interested in establishing a supposed perfection which no longer exists, and which may conceivably (and even probably) never be recovered (Smith 1893:144).

2. *Thomas Lindsay (1843–1914)*

The Scot, Thomas Lindsay, was even less forgiving:

But when all is said they are bound to admit [Warfield and his advocates] that the attribute of formal inerrancy does not belong to the Scriptures which we now have, but to what they call . . . the original autographs of Scripture. . . . It follows that the Scriptures as we now have them are neither infallible nor inspired in their use of these words. This is not an inference drawn from their writings by a hostile critic. It is frankly and courageously said by themselves, "We do not assert that the common text, but only that the original autographic text was inspired." The statement is deliberately made by Dr.Hodge and Dr. Warfield. This is a very grave assertion, and shows to what lengths the School are driven to maintain their theory, and it is one which cannot fail, if seriously believed and thoroughly acted upon, to lead to sad conclusions both in the theological doctrine of Scripture and in the practical work of the Church. . . . Where are we to get our errorless Scripture? In the *ipsissima verba* of the original autographs? Who are to recover these for us? I suppose the band of experts in textual criticism who are year by year giving us the materials for a more perfect text. Are they to be created by-and-by when their labours are ended into an authority doing for Protestants what the "Church" does for Roman Catholics? Are they to guarantee for us the inspired and infallible Word of God, or are we to say that the unknown autographs are unknowable, and that we can never get to this Scripture, which is the only Scripture inspired and infallible in the strictly formal sense of those words as used by the Princeton School? I have a great respect for textual and historical Biblical critics, and have done my share in a humble way to obtain a recognition of their work, but I for one shall never consent to erect the scholars whom I esteem into an authority for that text of Scripture which is alone inspired and infallible. That, however, is what this formalist theory is driving us to if we submit to it. I maintain, with all the Reformers, and with all the Reformed Creeds, that the Scriptures, as we now have them, are the inspired and infallible Word of God, and that all textual criticism, while it is to be welcomed in so far as it brings our present text nearer the *ipsissima verba* of the original autographs, will not make the Scriptures one whit more inspired or more infallible in the true Scriptural and religious meanings of those words than they are now (Lindsay 1895:291–293).

3. Henry Grey Graham (1874–1959)

I conclude my account of some responses to Warfield with a statement by an early twentieth century Scottish Roman Catholic Bishop. While the Bishop's remarks are not directed at Warfield specifically, they offer a cogent testimony to the fact that Warfield's appeal to the *autographa,* rather than to an ecclesiastical extant edition, brought the Protestant view of Scripture, as Lindsay argued, closer to the Roman Catholic view with but one difference: rather than depend on the mediation of an ecclesiastical hierarchy he now looks to the text critical community to fulfil the same role. The following quotation is all the more important because it came from the pen of a former Protestant Church of Scotland minister who held the distinction of being the only convert to the Roman communion from the Scottish Presbyterian Church ever to be made a bishop.[31] The Rt. Rev. Henry Grey Graham wrote the following in his popular essay on *Where We Got the Bible* (1911):

> Pious Protestants may hold up their hands in horror and cry out, "there are no mistakes in the Bible! it is all inspired! it is God's own book?" Quite true, *if you get God's own book,* the originals as they came from the hand of the Apostle, Prophet, and Evangelist. These, and these men only, were inspired and protected from making mistakes. . . . The original Scripture is free from error, because it has God for its author; *so teaches the*

---

[31]For a brief treatment of Graham see my entry on him as it appears in the *Dictionary of Scottish Church History and Theology.*

Catholic Church; . . . but that does not alter the fact that there are scores, nay thousands, of differences in the old manuscripts . . . and I should like any enquiring Protestants to ponder over this fact and see how they can possibly reconcile it with their principle that the Bible alone is the all-sufficient guide to salvation. Which Bible? Are you sure you have got the right Bible? . . . . You know perfectly well that you *must* trust to some authority outside of yourself to give you the Bible. . . . We Catholics, on the other hand, glory in having some third party to come between us and God, because God Himself has given it to us, namely, the Catholic Church, to teach us and lead us to Him (Graham 1924:64–65).

V. Conclusion

There was a general consensus among the Protestant dogmaticians of the seventeenth century that the *apographa* were inspired and authoritative. The seventeenth century Protestant dogmaticians located all the attributes of the sacred text in the extant MS tradition passed on by the Greek Orthodox Church and the Jewish synagogue and which prevailed during the Renaissance. This became the localised sacred text for Protestants. In the words of Richard Muller, the leading authority on this subject

By "original and authentic" text, the Protestant orthodox do not mean the *autographa* which no one can possess but the *apographa* in the original tongue which are the source of all versions. . . . The orthodox discussion of *autographa* and *apographa* was designed, therefore, to point toward a continuity of text-tradition between the original authors and the present-day texts (Muller 1993:433–434).

Moreover, this was an explicit response both to Tridentine Rome and its claims for the *Vulgata Latina* as well as a response to the early emergence of Biblical criticism amongst Protestants both on the continent as well as in Britain. This position was dogmatically maintained in the isogogics of the day as well as being codified in certain of the Reformed confessions. Moreover, it was also exegetically grounded within the text of Scripture itself. The extant, ecclesiastical recensions of the original language texts, the *apographa*, were, for the Protestant orthodox communities, the sacred text.

Futhermore, an assumed legitimazation of a genuine catholic ecclesiology was affirmed in this dogmatic stance: the Church was seen not only as the vehicle of received orthodox Christology and of the canonical books of the Bible, but also as the "witness and keeper of holy writ" (Thirty-Nine Articles, 29:6)

While the dogmaticians held to a verbal view of inspiration and regarded the *apographa* as infallible[32] this view was generally held in tension with all the phenomena in the *apographa* exhibiting a conflict with this notion. To appeal to a superior autographic text would have meant playing into the hands of the defenders of the Vulgate who argued that it was based on superior original language texts, closer to the original text.

In order to rescue Princeton (at the invitation of A.A. Hodge) at a time when her traditional view of verbal inspiration (inherited from the Protestant dogmaticians) was under severe attach from Biblical critics, Warfield shifted authority from the *apographa* to the *autographa*. To do this he demythologized the Westminster Confession, arguing that it taught the *autographa* alone were inspired and authoritative. In so doing, he allowed the Confession to continue to have relevance for the twentieth century. Part of the trade-off, though—and here contemporary Reformed and Lutheran confessionalists have been drawn in far too easily—was his important departure from not only the original, historical position of the Westminster Divines but from the paradigm of Biblical authority advanced by nearly all the

---

[32]Modern day advocates who have attempted to prove Warfield's thesis regarding the meaning of the confession on the Biblical texts have run into a brick wall when resorting to history to make their point: they have been forced to admit, "It is true that in the seventeenth century a good number of Christians esteemed that the Bibles they had in their hands were infallible" (Woodbridge/Balmer 1983:405, n.106); "Some Englishmen apparently did think that their Bibles perfectly reflected the originals" (Woodbridge 1982:187, n.64).

major seventeenth-century Protestant dogmaticians in response to Tridentine Roman Catholicism.[33] I give Muller the last word:

> It is important to note that the Reformed [and Lutheran] ortho-
> dox insistence on the identification of the Hebrew and Greek
> texts as alone authentic does not demand direct reference to *au-
> tographa* in those languages; the 'original and authentic text' of
> Scripture means, beyond the autograph copies, the legitimate
> tradition of Hebrew and Greek *apographa*. The case for Scrip-
> ture as an infallible rule of faith and practice and the separate ar-
> guments for a received text free from major (i.e., non-scribal)
> errors rests on an examination of *apographa* and does not seek
> the infinite regress of lost *autographa* as a prop for textual infal-
> libility (Muller 1993:433).

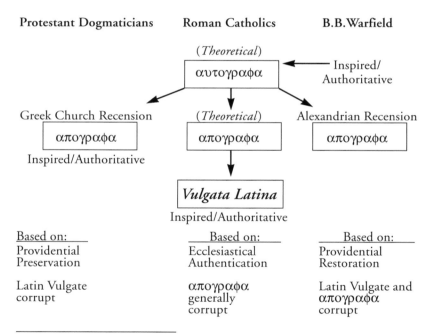

Protestant Dogmaticians	**Roman Catholics**	**B.B. Warfield**
	(*Theoretical*) αυτογραφα ← Inspired/Authoritative	
Greek Church Recension απογραφα Inspired/Authoritative	(*Theoretical*) απογραφα	Alexandrian Recension απογραφα
	Vulgata Latina Inspired/Authoritative	
Based on: Providential Preservation	Based on: Ecclesiastical Authentication	Based on: Providential Restoration
Latin Vulgate corrupt	απογραφα generally corrupt	Latin Vulgate and απογραφα corrupt

---

[33]One of the historical ironies of this development is the inescapable loss of awe and reverence for the existential Bible as sacred text in confessing communities and in the culture at large. David E. Timmer, in an editorial in the *Reformed Journal* treating the NIV's paraphrase of Genesis 2:8;19 took this occasion to note, "The principle of inerrancy, so often invoked to preserve Scripture from disrespect, has in this case led to flagrant disrespect for what Scripture actually is and says" (Timmer 1984:2–3).

CHAPTER THREE

The Language of Biblical Authority: From Protestant Orthodoxy to Evangelical Equivocation

INTRODUCTION

When the Church of England decided to turn in its credentials as part of historic Catholic orthodoxy, by voting to accept the ordination of women, it was only one profoundly disappointing defection in a long line of theological disasters witnessed this century. Nevertheless, this act was particularly heart-breaking because it meant that the previous triad of catholic consensus represented by Eastern and Western Catholicism, joined with Anglicanism, no longer had a major Protestant representative. In this the more ancient catholic traditions could now point a finger at the anticipated expiration of a sixteenth century movement which had spent its energy and then lost its way amidst the troubled seas of modernity.

To have been busy engaging exclusively the questions raised by the modern condition, with no reference to an established body of dogma as a normative precedent—certainly derived from Scripture but by means of the collective wisdom of the Church catholic—resulted in the silencing of the Sacred Text on this most vital issue of the role of women in the Church.[1]

I have just spent the better part of the last five years attempting to localize just what was the specific dynamic, or chain of

---

[1]It is a desperately tragic irony that those who have an appreciation for catholic consensus on such matters within the Church of England have lost all credibility in the public mind by declaring their willingness to accept the far worse error of papalism as their response to this apostasy.

events, that led to this bankrupt state within modern confessional churches. Obviously we all know that Biblical criticism lay at the heart of the matter, but what I wanted to discover is *how* and *why* so many well-armed and forewarned ecclesiastical bodies could all fall in time, one after another, without so much as knowing the process had taken place. Certainly everyone rightly feared and trembled at the German higher criticism, with its speculative theories about sources and carrying out an agenda dictated by the various philosophical schools of German Idealism.[2] But it was while everyone was staring steadfastly at this Philistine, would-be invader of the Church, that time and again an apparent out-flanking took place and the fall ensued. How and why?

I decided to use as my method over this well worn path of inquiry what is known as the phenomenological method: place the Bible side-by-side with all other sacred texts of other world

---

[2]This raises another issue I shall not be directly addressing here, namely, how did German Idealism come to replace the hermeneutic of the Church. Certainly the process of desacralization came first, dislodging confidence in the epistemological value of Biblical narrative and inviting an autonomous quest for certainty within the realm of human reason. Hence, the nineteenth century theological quest, based on the results of the German higher criticism, was an attempt to reconstruct a relevant meaning from the Bible for the new epistemological demands of Idealism, rather than an attempt to initialize the process of desacralization, a phase that had already been accomplished as witnessed by the invitation to higher criticism. According to the model I propose, Salvatorelli, in his detailed study, "From Locke to Reitzenstein: The Historical Investigation of the Origins of Christianity *HTR 22:4 (October, 1929): 263–369*, could not be more incorrect when he suggests, "The historical investigation of the origins of Christianity began with the English deists, who, being philosophers and not professional historians, were for that very reason able to give the first forward impulse to the historical study of Jesus and of primitive Christiantiy. *No purely historical interest could have induced Christian Europe to apply criticism to its sacred books . . .* (emphasis mine), p. 263. As a matter of fact all the Deists made appeal to historical evidence provided by Erasmus and Grotius regarding the Christologically significant interpolations found in the Greek and Latin MSS. of the N.T. thus showing their dependence on these sixteenth and seventeenth century scholars who were practicing textual critics, philologists as well as historians, doing to the text of Scripture what Valla had accomplished on the *Donation of Constantine*. In fact, it was such historical criticisms of these textual variants that opened the way for the Deistic project, which assumed a naturalistic view of the Bible as a result of the desacralization of the earlier text critics.

religions and see what it was that gave these texts their individual specialness as understood from within each faith community.[3] For the Sacred Text of the Judeo-Christian traditions, it was a belief in the inspiredness of every vocable; that every verbal unit had a sacred significance because it had as its source not the consciousness of man but the very consciousness of God.

This position has been *the* paradigm used to understand the sacred qualities of the Bible within both the Jewish as well as the Christian communities from the beginning, evidences of which are found embedded within the very text of Scripture itself: hence, for example, Yahweh is said to have composed the very words of the Decalogue with his very own finger.[4] How distorted the understanding of this paradigm has become in our own day by the modern world of Biblical criticism is typically stated in Richard Soulen's otherwise rather useful little: *Handbook of Biblical Criticism* (2nd ed. Atlanta:1981). Here he embarrassingly states:

> In reaction to the rise of historical criticism in the 18th and 19th cents. which, by discovering errors in Biblical fact and reason, threatened Scripture as the authoritative Word of God, there

---

[3]This as opposed to using the pre-critical dogmatic approach which assumes the nature of the Judeo-Christian Bible before hand. While the conclusions reached are basically the same how one arrives at them is quite different. Some have shown a nervous resistance to such an approach, such as Piepkorn who did not like what the word "inerrancy" was after: " . . . when we begin to take the term ["inerrancy"] literally of the Sacred Scriptures as such, a student of comparative religion might be impelled to observe that we are perilously close to the threshold of a tendency which exists in other world religions" (Piepkorn 1965:580). Barth showed the same reluctance, arguing that the seventeenth century dogmaticians had given the Judeao-Christian Sacred Text characteristics similar to other sacred texts of other world religions, characteristics he nevertheless admitted had been found in the valuation of Scripture in early catholic tradition as well: " . . . in this form [as understood by the Protestant dogmaticians] the Bible became so like the holy books of other religions, for which something similar had always been claimed, that the superiority of its claim could not be asserted in relation to them or to the many achievements of the human spirit generally" (Barth 1956 vol. 1, part 2:525–526).

[4]Abraham is simply wrong when he asserts: " . . . it is simply not the case that the Church has had an agreed account of inspiration throughout its past" (Abraham 1981:16).

developed a theory of Biblical inspiration in which every word
was defended as direct from God 1981:208).

This is a rather telling example of the danger of over-spe-
cilization: here an expert in Biblical studies reflects a profound
degree of ignorance about a rather significant theological consensus found within patristic literature, within mediaeval tradition, throughout the Reformation and picks up the theme late,
only in the eighteenth century where his own interests begin,
misinterpreting that era as the source of the doctrine.

The author was correct, however, in identifying historical criticism as what destroyed any possibility of viewing the Bible any
longer as a *sacred* text within the Academy. But here we come
upon a circle that must be broken: which came first, the historical criticism which negated the sacredness of the Text; or was
there a prior process of desacralization which then allowed a free
handling of the text, analogous to any other historical document. Various attempts to answer these questions have all made
their contribution: Peter Harrison has recently highlighted the
impact of eighteenth century English Deism in reducing the
unique quality of the Bible and Christianity, in his important,
Religion and the Religions in the English Enlightenment (Cambridge, 1990). Klaus Scholder, late Professor of Modern Church
History at the University of Tübingen has pushed the genesis
back even further, into the seventeenth century. He argues in his
The Birth of Modern Critical Theology (Eng. trans. SCM, 1990)
that it was the signing of the treaty ending the Thirty Years War,
which agreed to put religion to one side for the purposes of a political settlement, which then allowed for the sanctioning of various interpretations of the one Christian Faith.

My study, however, has pushed matters back even further. I
have argued that the process of desacralization began in earnest
not in the eighteenth, nor in the seventeenth, but in the sixteenth century when Desiderius Erasmus attempted to produced an improved edition of the *Vugata Latina* by means of an
appeal to Greek MSS. Here began the *quest for the historical text*
which I argue is always the precursor that inexorably leads to
that later development: the *quest for the historical Jesus.*

What I hope to establish in this lecture is that while everyone in confessional ranks attempted to resist to the death the invasion of the nineteenth century German higher criticism with its *quest for the historical Jesus,* they, nevertheless, unwittingly gave way to the process of desacralization by assuming the safe and "scientific" nature of the *quest for the historical text.* There is a sense in which the entire history of the influence of Biblical criticism on confessional communities is but a working out of this theme, with adjustment after adjustment taking place, until the original paradigm of verbal inspiration evaporates and no one is so much as aware that a change has taken place. What follows will be an attempt to outline this development within the nineteenth and twentieth century Anglo-American contexts.

I. History of the Problem

A. British Biblical Criticism and Adjustment

1. W. Robertson Smith

One of the most celebrated, but not the earliest crisis caused by Biblical criticism in the British Isles, is the famous heresy trial surrounding the views of W. Robertson Smith (1846–1894). Unlike his English counterparts who produced the landmark *Essays and Reviews* (1860), Smith had no taint of liberalism, or rationalist tendencies: his application of Biblical criticism was in the cause of promoting an evangelical view of the Faith. As Rogerson has put it, "It is difficult to think of a book that has so profoundly combined critical insights with a type of Evangelical belief, as Robertson Smith's *The Old Testament in the Jewish Church*" (Rogerson 1985). He is, therefore, an important example of one who provided a major adjustment to what he understood to be evangelicalism, as a result of his engagement with Biblical criticism.

In accepting the basic premises of the Wellhausen theory, denying the Mosaic authorship of portions of the Pentateuch and by negating aspects of the prophetic element he pushed to put a greater emphasis on the importance of personal religious experience over against the traditional understanding of verbal inspiration and dogma in general. In so doing he claimed that such a view of inspiration was late and had no sanction from the Presbyterian confessional standard governing the Scottish Calvinists, the Westminster Confession. Thus those who held to verbal inspiration were classed by him as *unconfessional* and as not rightly regarding the O.T. as the Word of God (Rogerson 277). When Wellhausen first appeared in English, it was Smith who wrote the Introduction. H.D. McDonald concluded in his mammoth work in 1963, *Theories of Revelation: An Historical Study 1860–1960* (Grand Rapids, 1979), "The fact . . . is that Robertson Smith's subjective understanding of revelation has remained and is specially influential at the present day" (McDonald 33).

2. James Orr (1844–1913)

Orr is important because he was and is still considered to be one of the most important apologetes ever produced by the Scottish Presbyterian Church. His view of Scripture, however, was also a departure from the dogmatic position of the seventeenth century confessionalists; but he claimed to be maintaining that same orthodoxy with integrity. Earlier models, he felt, had simply failed to take into account all the possible data (Hoefel 1986:45):

> Orr argued that one did not need a strict verbal view of inspiration in order to understand the gospel message. . . . He attempted to defuse critical accusations by pointing to the progressiveness of revelation, varying degrees of inspiration, the variety of literary devices used by writers, and the distinction between inspiration and providence, and the reality of diverse sources utilized in the accounts (Hoefel:48).

While holding to a "plenary" inspiration, he, nevertheless, rejected the traditional "verbal" inspiration model and so put further distance between the Scottish Presbyterians and their own pre-Enlightenment dogmatic tradition.

The adjustment option chosen in Scotland was not unlike that chosen by most in the Church of England by the end of the nineteenth century and most clearly spelled out in their ranks by William Sanday's *Bampton Lectures* for 1893: i.e. a clear move away from a verbal view of inspiration to a more dynamic view which would seem to be more accommodating to the evidence produced by the new critical methods.

B. American Biblical Criticism and Adjustment

1. Charles Briggs (1841–1913)

Charles Briggs, a contemporary of W. Robertson Smith, as well as a correspondent and supporter, was almost his perfect American counter-part. He was called up on heresy charges and suspended from the ministry in 1895 after delivering his inaugural address at Union Seminary in 1890. Titled ironically: "The Authority of Scripture," this address was an open advocacy of higher criticism and like the Scottish Presbyterians reaction to Smith, Briggs was denounced by the American Calvinists in like fashion.

Briggs's adjustment was different from either the English or the Scottish: rather than call for an up-front denunciation of the verbal view of inspiration with the claim that the Westminster Confession was silent on such matters, he used the confession in a different manner. He argued vigorously that the Confession did not teach a *verbal* inspiration, but an inspiration treating only those parts of Scripture dealing with faith and practice. To make his argument, however, he began by misrepresenting the historical data on the *consensus ecclesiae:*

> It is pretended that the Church doctrine of inspiration is in peril, and that the authority of the Scriptures is thereby undermined. If there were one clearly defined orthodox doctrine of inspiration to which all Christians agreed, as supported by holy Scripture and the creeds of the Church, our task would be easier. But, in fact, there are many various theories of inspiration, and several ways of stating the doctrine of inspiration that are without support in Scripture or symbol (Briggs 1899:110).

He then went on to posit what he believed to be the authentic teaching of the Confession, and I here quote from Trevor Morrow's Ph.D. dissertation treating Briggs and Warfield:

> Briggs sees the Bible as a human book which contains the Divine Word. It is therefore fallible in its humanity and infallible only when it speaks God's Word. The form and substance can be divorced. Every method appropriate to the humanity is therefore appropriate in our handling of the Bible in spite of the dangers of the phenomena bringing into question the substance of the faith which the holy spirit has spoken infallibly (Morrow 1984:374).

Here, for all his pretences at being an expert historian of the Westminster Standards, Briggs is completely off the mark. As heirs to the Protestant scholastic tradition the Westminster Divines knew of no such dialectic.

2. B.B. Warfield

Warfield was Briggs's antagonist during this time and he has since become the standard for many conservatives for how a high view of Scripture should be articulated. To quote William Abraham in his *The Divine Inspiration of Holy Scripture* (1981), "There is little doubt but that Warfield did more to shape recent Evangelical thinking on inspiration than any other theologian" (Abraham 1981:15). And since the debate raged between he and Briggs around the correct understanding of the Westminster Confession's statement on Scripture, Warfield, too, made attempts to master the history and interpretation of the Confession. He was determined to retain the authentic doctrine of *verbal* inspiration as taught by Charles Hodge before him at Princeton and by Turretin before that in Geneva. But he also wanted to legitimize aspects of the new criticism, namely, the *lower* or textual criticism, for which he actually received approbation from Charles Briggs.[5] To do this, however, he, too, had

---

[5]See my essay, "B.B. Warfield, Common-Sense Philosophy and Biblical Criticism *American Presbyterians* Vol. 69, No. 3 (Fall 1991):175–190; and Briggs, "The Greek Testament of Westcott and Hort," *Presbyterian Review* 3 (1882).

to work with an adjustment which also led him to erroneous conclusions regarding the teaching of the Confession.

Warfield's adjustment was different from that of Briggs. He wanted to assert not only verbal inspiration but that this inspiration demanded a corresponding "inerrancy," an innovative and originally an astronomical term which was only coming into vogue in that era. Even though all extant copies of the Sacred Text displayed no such "inerrancy"in the strict astrological sense—paradoxes, tensions and apparent conflicts in parallel narratives had always appeared in the text, as well as scribal errors, as all who surveyed the MS sources knew—the Scriptures, nevertheless, were always considered infallible by the Church. Warfield, however, felt the need to shift the locus of authority away from *extant* editions to a theoretical *autographic exemplar*, that is, exclusively to the *original* text of Scripture.[6] As with Briggs, to make the Westminster Divines teach such a modern, refined distinction was so obviously wrong that Briggs had a field day. In his reply to the formal charges brought against him which were based on Warfield's consensus (which had by this time become the accepted view within the American Presbyterian Church) as to what the Westminster Divines taught in their Confession, Briggs replied in the following defiant terms:

> It has been taught in recent years, and is still taught by some theologians, that one proven error destroys the authority of Scripture. I shall venture to affirm that, so far as I can see, there are errors in the Scriptures that no one has been able to explain away; and the theory that they were not in the original text is sheer assumption, upon which no mind can rest with certainty (Briggs 1899:615).

Elsewhere he decimated Warfield's theory, treating it as *reduc-*

---

[6]Abraham rightly called this the deductive method: "Where there was a strain . . . between the deductions as to what Scripture must be like if it is truly inspired and between what Scripture seems to be like when it is studied like other literature, the former was given logical priority. The deductions ruled" (Abraham:17). It was not Warfield's deductions which were wrong, however, it was his particular adjustment used to retain them that was historically, phenomenologically and theologically defective.

tio ad absurdum. Because it is a classic refutation of Warfield's position we quote here at length:

> The question in dispute is not whether there are errors in the present accessible texts of Holy Scripture, but whether or not these errors were in the original autographs. This Assembly attempted to define what were the original autographs: "Scripture as it came from them to whom and through whom God originally communicated His revelation." The Scripture in their opinion consisted of the writings as first written down by those to whom God communicated His revelation. We must go back of all the texts till we get to the original autographs of the authors before we have the inerrant Scripture. What has the criticism of the Canon to say to this astonishing dogma? . . . The Canonical Scripture was ever historically the Scripture in the text at the time recognized by the Synagogue and the church. No one ever thought of searching for the original autographs. And from the point of view of canonical criticism it is ever the text of Scripture in one's hands that is recognized as canonical or not. From this point of view, it is evident that what is canonical in Holy Scripture is entirely independent of any special form of the text or of the original autographs. It is true that the Protestant Reformers and the Puritans in their symbolical books made the Greek and Hebrew texts the final appeal in matters of religion over against the Roman Catholic Church, which made the Latin Vulgate the final authority; but even the Protestants did not think of making the original autographs their authority. They knew as well as we do that they had them not and could never have them. The Protestants appealed to the Greek and Hebrew texts that they knew, and devoted themselves chiefly to translating them into modern languages to give the Word of God to the people; and they used these translations as the Word of God of infallible, divine authority. No one in the time of the Reformation was so foolhardy as to affirm that "the Canon of Scripture is not the Latin Bible, is not in the Greek Testament of Erasmus, is not in the Hebrew Bible of Bomberg, but is solely and alone in the original autographs of the inspired authors," which have not one of them been in the possession of the Church since the second century A.D. It was a rational position for the Council of Trent to make the Latin Vulgate the authori-

tative Bible and to provide for a correct official text. It would be a reasonable procedure for a Protestant assembly to decide that the Massorectic Hebrew text of Ben Asher and the Greek Bible of the Vatican codex should be the final arbiter, as the most correct texts at present attainable. But it is altogether irrational to take the position that the inerrant Bible is solely and alone in the original autographs which no one has seen since the Church had a Canon, and which no one can ever see. . . . In point of fact, so far as the evidence goes, the original autographs of the Holy Scripture were never recognized as canonical. It was not until the Holy writings had been copied and circulated that they received that general recognition which is essential to canonicity. The copies, which in many cases were many degrees distant from the autographs, were recognized as canonical; and in no case, so far as we can determine, were the autographs recognized as canonical. . . . The question of the original autographs is not so simple and easy of solution as the majority of this General Assembly seem to have thought. The question emerges, Which autograph do you seek? What shall we say as regards the story of the resurrection of our Lord at the close of the Gospel of Mark?[7] There can be no doubt that it was not in the Gospel of Mark as that Gospel "came from him to whom and through whom God originally communicated His revelation." It was appended to Mark. And yet there can be no doubt that this story was attached to the Gospel of Mark at an early date, and that it has been recognized as no less truly canonical and divinely inspired than any other part of the Gospel. . . . But what shall we say of the editors and scribes who have made the editorial changes, which may be traced in the Hebrew text itself? Can we fix the time when the Divine Spirit ceased to guide the sacred scribes who edited and reedited, arranged and rearranged the writings of the Old Testament? . . . If inerrancy and certainty are only to be found in this way, they will never be found. Certainty has never been found in this way. Such autographs the Church and the Synagogue have never known. . . . Criticism can find no errorless scribe, no inerrant person (Briggs 616–620).

---

[7]Here Briggs is being disingenuous: he has already suggested the Vatican Codex is worthy of canonical sanction but this Codex does not have this account.

Here Briggs devastated Warfield with arguments and evidences Warfield himself knew well. But Warfield was determined to fight on, as a Knight in quest for the Holy Grail, arguing that

> The autographic text of the New Testament is distinctly within the reach of criticism in so immensely the greater part of the volumes, that we cannot despair of restoring to ourselves and the Church of God, His Book, word for word, as he gave it by inspiration (Warfield 1892:15).

Warfield was nothing if not tenacious about following his theory to the bitter end. Unafraid to denounce as *uncanonical* those texts sanctioned as canonical by the early Church (e.g. the last twleve verses of Mark containing the resurrection and ascension which Briggs the higher critic retained) in the quest for his "original" text. One need only look today at the NIV—the product of Warfield's evangelical, inerrancy advocating heirs—as one tangible result of Warfield's theory. Here Mark's account of the resurrection is treated as non-canonical.

The Scottish, too, brought down a barrage of criticism on Warfield's bold adjustment. Thomas Lindsay, no mean historian of the Reformation and post-Reformation eras, summarised Warfield's theory in the following terms:

> But when all is said they are bound to admit [Warfield and his advocates] that the attribute of formal inerrancy does not belong to the Scriptures which we now have, but to what they call . . . the original autographs of Scripture. . . . It follows that the Scriptures as we now have them are neither infallible nor inspired in their use of these words. This is not an inference drawn from their writings by a hostile critic. It is frankly and courageously said by themselves, "We do not assert that the common text, but only that the original autographic text was inspired." The statement is deliberately made by Dr. Hodge and Dr. Warfield. This is a very grave assertion, and shows to what lengths the School are driven to maintain their theory, and it is one which cannot fail, if seriously believed and thoroughly acted upon, to lead to sad conclusions both in the theological

doctrine of Scripture and in the practical work of the Church.
. . . Where are we to get our errorless Scripture? In the *ipsissima verba* of the original autographs? Who are to recover these for us? I suppose the band of experts in textual criticism who are year by year giving us the materials for a more perfect text. Are they to be created by-and-by when their labours are ended into an authority doing for Protestants what the "Church" does for Roman Catholics? Are they to guarantee for us the inspired and infallible Word of God, or are we to say that the unknown autographs are unknowable, and that we can never get to this Scripture, which is the only Scripture inspired and infallible in the strictly formal sense of those words as used by the Princeton School? I have a great respect for textual and historical Biblical critics, and have done my share in a humble way to obtain a recognition of their work, but I for one shall never consent to erect the scholars whom I esteem into an authority for that text of Scripture which is alone inspired and infallible. That, however, is what this formalist theory is driving us to if we submit to it. I maintain, with all the Reformers, and with all the Reformed Creeds, that the Scriptures, as we now have them, are the inspired and infallible Word of God, and that all textual criticism, while it is to be welcomed in so far as it brings our present text nearer the *ipsissima verba* of the original autographs, will not make the Scriptures one whit more inspired or more infallible in the true Scriptural and religious meanings of those words than they are now (Lindsay 1895:291–293).

Orr had a similar critique to offer:

It is urged . . . that unless we can demonstrate what is called the 'inerrancy' of the biblical record, down even to its minutest details, the whole edifice of belief in revealed religion falls to the ground. This, on the face of it, is a most suicidal position for any defender of revelation to take up (Orr 1909:197–198).

Instead of this approach, Orr put special stress on the ecclesiastical preservation of the original revelational content:

A first point . . . is, that if a revelation has been given by God, it is reasonable to expect that provision will be made for *the*

Preservation of the knowledge of the revelation *in some permanent and authoritative form*. Otherwise the object in giving the revelation would be frustrated. . . . It may not be possible now to trace all the links in this process of transmission; but the product may bear in itself evidence that the result intended has been surely accomplished (Orr 1901:156).

Here Orr localizes the final referent for ultimate Biblical authority in an extant, identifiable edition of the Sacred Text and in this he is in harmony with catholic tradition.

There is a profound irony in this criticism and in that of Briggs, Lindsay and Orr. Warfield, playing the role of the evangelical, the upholder of the Westminster Confession of Faith, has actually placed the Church and Her text in a perilous state while the advocates—to one degree or another—of higher criticism actually affirm a position which has much greater continuity with catholic consensus and who do not attribute to criticism the decisive task of reconstructing a lost original revelation. Hear to what extent Warfield has made the Church a bondservant of criticism:

So far from the Bible being less subject to criticism than other books, we are bound to submit its unique claims to a criticism of unique rigor. Criticism is the mode of procedure by which we assure ourselves that it is what it claims to be (Warfield 1892:595).

How to explain this irony that those who fully engaged Biblical criticism in all of its aspects—not just the lower, or textual criticism such as Warfield did—gave criticism an exceedingly modest place of authority within the structure of the Church, while the evangelical is quite willing to significantly alter the canon in defiance of Catholic consensus in his *quest for the historical text*?

The practitioners of historical criticism tend to have highly developed sensibilities regarding the actual phenomena of development, as well as a corresponding modesty regarding the actual results of criticism. That is, they are in a position to be honest about the limitations of criticism in terms of the tangible results realized by the project of pushing back the tradition further and further into the nether regions. Here all begins to dissipate and dissolve as the idealised *primitive* tradition becomes not just blurry and indistinct but illusory. This is why those critics who choose to remain in the murky waters of primeval sources become such profound sceptics in the end. Without reference to the later ecclesiastical ordering of the materials of Divinely inspired Revelation all one is left with are certain interesting fragmented parallels with other ancient Near-Eastern religious and philosophical traditions, the playground of most modern Biblical critics and historians of religion.

Warfield embodies, therefore, a paradigm of a kind of eclecticism, a half-baked approach to Biblical criticism, what Mark Noll calls "believing criticism." He chose to adopt only those elements of criticism which appeared to him to be capable of objectification, namely, *the quest for the historical text*, and believed that science would ultimately legitimize the transcendent Faith quite apart from the witness of the Church catholic. This project of reconstructing a primitivism was perceived by him to be of more value than that which had been believed "everywhere, at all times, by everyone" (Vincent of Lérins, *Commonitorium* 2). In Lutheran circles the counterpart to Warfield in this legacy has been carried on by the work of John Warwick Montgomery, a very *un*Lutheran apologete in my opinion.[8]

Because Warfield's approach has never fully engaged all aspects of Biblical criticism it has never played out to the end the disappointing and ultimately modest results of this endeavour, which would have underscored the utter bankruptcy of this discipline as an arbitrating aid to the Faith. Science never has come to the rescue of the Faith. Criticism certainly has its own indispensable place in the work of the Academy, but to view it as an auxiliary support in defense of Christianity's truth claims is to give it expectations outwith its intended design. It would be like asking a physician performing a post-mortem examination why he has spent all his time dissecting the corps rather than resuscitating it. Resuscitation is not one of the goals of an autopsy.

---

[8]For a thorough critique of Montgomery see, Kern Robert Trembath, *Evangelical Theories of Biblical Inspiration* (1987:27–37).

Warfield has had many critics over the years. Dewey M. Beegle (*Scripture, Tradition, and Infallibility* 1979) did a good job by first admitting that the Rabbinic view of inspiration "hinged on the precise wording of the text" (Beegle 1979:131), and that this was generally the view of the early Church, medieval Church and the Reformation churches. Because, however, Beegle was more interested in arguing against the specific doctrine of *inerrancy*, rather than against *verbal* inspiration *per se*, all his arguments were formulated to address this issue, making his treatment rather one-sided and ultimately an unhelpful treatment of the issue of inspiration. He is clearer, however, on the understanding of the Westminster Confession:

> With respect to autographs and manuscript transmission, Article VIII states that the Old Testament in Hebrew and the New Testament in Greek were "immediately inspired by God." Scripture in the original languages is "authentical" because God by his "singular care and providence" kept the manuscripts "pure in all ages." The stress is on the authenticity and purity of the extant manuscripts in Hebrew and Greek. The original writings were "inspired by God," but it does not say that this inspiration was characterized by an inerrancy that was lost during the process of transmission (Beegle:144).[9]

Beegle than goes on to make an important analysis of the Reformation stance on Scripture:

> . . . creedal statements on inspiration formulated during the sixteenth and seventeenth centuries were precritical in nature and . . . they neither elaborated nor reconciled the divine and human elements of Scripture in any systematic way (Beegle:145).[10]

---

[9]Beegle devotes an entire chapter admirably criticising the inerrant autograph theory, (150–174). His chapter on verbal inspiration, however, is considerably less helpful.

[10]Hence, Beegle contradicts himself by stating earlier that the Westminster Divines were working with a post-critical dialectic, claiming that Scripture was only infallible when addressing "faith and practice" and that "Since the Bible does not claim to speak authoritatively in the realms of Science, for example, one can allow for errors of fact in such areas" (Beegle:144). This most certainly was *not* the position of the Westminster Divines.

Rogers and McKim have also offered a major critique of Warfieldianism in their important *The Authority and Interpretation of the Bible* (1979). An important flaw in this work, however, was their assigning the origin of the inerrancy of the original autographs theory to the seventeenth-century Protestant scholastics. This I corrected in my essay, "B.B. Warfield, Common-Sense Philosophy and Biblical Criticism," found in the *Journal of the Presbyterian Historical Society* (1991). They stumbled a second time in ascribing infallibility to just faith and practice in the Reformers and the Westminster Confession of Faith. This I corrected in another essay, "The Protestant Dogmaticians and the Late Princeton School on the Status of the Sacred *Apographa*," *The Scottish Bulletin of Evangelical Theology* (1990).

John Vander Stelt offered another significant criticism of Warfieldianism in a dissertation he produced for the Ph.D. degree at the Free University of Amsterdam, titled: *Philosophy and Scripture: A Study in Old Princeton and Westminster Theology* (pub. 1978). This is a monumental work and simply cannot be ignored in any future work to be accomplished on this subject. It, too, however, falls down when it attributes a propositional understanding of truth as found in Scripture to the Scottish Common-Sense Philosophy supposedly cultivated at Princeton by John Witherspoon.

In concluding this section, therefore, we have determined that the British adjustment to Biblical criticism was in a direction away from a *verbal* view of inspiration to a more *dynamic* view which claimed infallibility only for those portions of the Sacred Text addressing faith and practice. Smith also claimed that he was not in breach of the teaching of the *WCF* because it did not address issues of mode of inspiration or Biblical criticism in general; he also put the defenders of verbal inspiration on the defensive for not accepting Scripture and its authority in the sense in which he understood it.

Charles Briggs in America also made an adjustment away from verbal inspiration but wanted to claim the *WCF* was on his side, teaching that the Bible was infallible only when addressing issues of faith and practice. Warfield, his theological opponent, made an adjustment in another direction, retaining verbal inspiration but locating it exclusively in the autographic text, rather than in an extant edition. While all of Warfield's critics, those of his contemporaries and those who have spoken in our own day, have all been correct in challenging his adjustment on historical grounds, they, on the other hand, were equally culpable on the same grounds when attempting to abandon a verbal view of inspiration. Neither party has been completely able to find an articulation that does justice to both the *consensus ecclesiae* as well as to the *consensus accademiae*.

II. The Language of the Protestant Dogmaticians and the Westminster Confession in Light of Catholic *Traditio*

A. Infallible

1. Meaning

Richard Muller's excellent *Dictionary of Latin and Greek Theological Terms Drawn Principally from Protestant Scholastic Theology* (1985), lists under the entry *authoritas Scripturae* the attribute of *infallibilitas*. This is in fact the term used by all the Protestant dogmaticians, Calvinistic and Lutheran alike, to affirm the complete truthfulness and trustworthiness of sacred Scripture. It is also the term explicitly used in the Westminster Confession:

> . . . our full persuasion and assurance of the infallible truth and divine authority thereof, is from the inward work of the holy Spirit. . . . The infallible rule of interpretation of Scripture is the Scripture itself (*WCF* I:5;9).

Reflecting the general consensus of the Protestant scholastic tradition such infallibility would have covered all narrative and propositional statements, with no selective applications to certain parts and not to others. This again is a tenet passed on from an earlier patristic consensus which found acceptance among Roman Catholics and Protestants alike.

2. Referent

Furthermore, the word *infallibilitas*, or infallible, as can be clearly seen in section 8 of this same chapter of the Confession, always had as its referent an extant edition then in the use of the Church:

> The Old Testament in Hebrew . . . and the New Testament in Greek . . . being immediately inspired by God, and, by His singular care and providence, kept pure in all ages, are therefore authentical (*WCF* I:8).

This is, after all, a text one can examine to discover its infallible judgements "so as in all controversies of religion, the Church is finally to appeal to them" (Ibid.), not to the consensus of the Academy, much less to non-extant autographs.

Certainly there were problems in these editions that were dealt with in one way or another by exegetes and ecclesiastical commentators; but because infallibility was localized, one simply could not run away from such difficulties.[11] Summary: the Bible was verbally inspired and infallible in extant editions. Simple enough. Muller, the leading authority on the theology of the orthodox Reformed dogmaticians of the seventeenth century, sums up this consensus in the following language:

> . . . Turretin and other high and late orthodox writers argued that the authenticy and infallibility of Scripture must be identified in and of the *apographa*, not in and of lost *autographa*. The *autographa* figure in Turretin's argument only insofar as they were written in Hebrew and Greek and are, therefore, best represented *quoad verba* and *quoad res* in the extant Hebrew and Greek *apographa*. The issue raised by the Protestant scholastic discussion of the relationship of the *autographa* and *apographa* is, in other words, one of linguistic continuiety rather than one

---

[11]Gerhard Maier well captured the attitude of the seventeenth-century dogmaticians—as opposed to the 20th century Warfieldians—as well as offering an intelligent, post-Enlightenment assessment of such phenomena in his classic *The End of the Historical-Critical Method* trans. by Edwin W. Leverenz (St Louis: Concordia Pub. House, 1977), pp. 71–72.

of verbal inerrancy. The orthodox do, of course, assume that the text is free of substantive error and, typically, view textual problems as of scribal origin, but they mount their argument for authenticity and infallibility without recourse to a logical device like that employed by Hodge and Warfield (Muller 1993:435)[12]

This consensus was formulated within a far reaching span of time from the early Church era until the Enlightenment. With the challenges of Enlightenment criticism many felt the need to forge a more well-defined and "scientific" defense of Scripture. Because Evangelicals lack an ecclesiology, they turned to "science" for their comfort. To suit such a purpose a new word was theologised: "inerrancy."

B. Inerrancy

1. Meaning and Usage

Arthur Carl Piepkorn produced a terribly useful study of the history of this term back in 1965.[13] He pointed out that the word was nowhere to be found in the confessional literature or the dogmatic tradition of the Lutheran Church.[14] Furthermore, it could not be located in the confessional literature of the early Church. Piepkorn combed the lexical literature and found it was a very recent word in theological parlance. Its *original* meaning was as a technical term for "fixed stars." It first appears in the *Oxford English Dictionary* as a term used in 1652, again as an astronomical term. It does not appear in a theological context until the nineteenth-century when Thomas Hartwell Horne

---

[12]How queer, indeed, then is a statement by Robert Godfrey that "B.B. Warfield became the most effective Reformed scholar in the Biblical presentation of inerrancy. . . . The witness of Reformed theologians from John Calvin down to the official synodical pronouncements of the Christian Reformed Church show that inerrancy [in the original autographs] is a Reformed doctrine" (W. Robert Godfrey "Fundamentalism and the Inerrancy of Scripture" *The Outlook* 44:4 (April 1994):4.

[13]Arthur C. Piepkorn, "What Does the Word 'Inerrancy' Mean?" *Concordia Theological Monthly* 36 (September, 1965):557–93.

[14]A survey of Reformed dogmatic literature from the seventeenth century would reveal its absence there as well.

first used it in the seventh edition of his *Introduction to the Critical Study and Knowledge of the Holy Scripture* (part 2 of volume 2, p. 81), where, ironically he says, "Absolute inerrancy is impracticable in any printed book." It is first used in a religious context when Edward Pusey referred in 1865 to "The old ultramontane doctrine of the inerrancy of the Pope, i.e., that of his preservation from error."

2. Referent

Its meaning need not be laboured but what is of interest is its referent: as soon as it enters theological parlance immediately it has reference to the original autographs exclusively. This is exceedingly important.

Most laymen and other non-theologically oriented folk have always sneered at how theologians can argue over such hair-splitting technicalities that they miss the big picture and the really practical side to life. As true as that may well be at times this criticism would not have carried any weight had it been used in the fourth-century in the presence of Anthanasius in an attempt to belittle the significance of the term ὁμοούσιος . And how willing would we be today to surrender the word ὁμοούσιος for ὁμοιούσιος, based on the argument that with computer technology we have now determined that the *latter* term is actually a *stronger* and therefore more *valuable* term. Perhaps some of you would have doubts and would feel more comfortable using *both* terms together so all possibilities would be covered. In reality what would happen is the negation of the value of both terms.

Or how many of you would be happy to have John 1:1 translated "in the beginning was Logic, Logic was with God and Logic was God," as a Reformed theologian, Gordon Clark, has advocated. Or perhaps you would be happy with the feminist rendering, "in the beginning was Wisdom and Wisdom was with God and Wisdom was God," because some feminist theologians feel this is one way of feminizing the Trinity?[15] The

---

[15]One of the earliest exegetical studies surveying the literature showing the possible link between the Johannine λόγος, σοφία and the ancient goddess tradition, was Hans Conzelmann, "The Mother of Wisdom," in *The Future of Our*

change of one landmark word in the theological terrain can alter the entire landscape! Such is what has happened with the substitution of the non-confessional word "inerrancy" for the catholic term *infallible*. Because "inerrancy" *always* and *only* has as its referent, the "original autographs," it always invites the *quest for the historical text,* which in turn always culminates in *the quest for the historical Jesus.* The change of but one word has resulted in the complete destruction of the classic Protestant view of Scripture and yet its would-be Reformation advocates continue to bow to the political pressure of non-Reformation, "evangelical" communities.

Don McKim has treated the reason for this development in the following terms:

> The preference of neo-evangelicals for the term "infallibility" of Scripture rather than "inerrancy" is reflected by their views of faith and reason, Scriptures' authority, and inspiration . . . Infallibility refers to Scriptures' complete trustworthiness and its reliability to accomplish its purpose (McKim 1985:93).

Moreover,

> The preference for the term "infallibility" when applied to Scripture is a distinguishing mark of those in the "moderate" and "left" wings of neo-evangelicalism (McKim:89).

Hence, because neo-evangelicals have co-opted "infallibility" and given it a *new* and *modern* meaning, those who would hold to a traditional, catholic view have recklessly abandoned this very important word and as a result have been forced into the lap of B.B. Warfield and his "inerrancy."

Two significant losses have resulted: 1) since the word "inerrancy" *only* and *always* refers to the "original autographs" ad-

---

Religious Past (Essays in Honour of Rudolf Bultmann) (1971):230–243. On treatments of both ancient and current interest in the goddess tradition see Larry Hurtado ed., *Goddesses in Religions and Modern Debate* (1990); Joan C. Engelsman, *The Feminine Dimention of the Divine* (1987); Riane Eisler, *The Chalice and the Blade: Our History, Our Future* (1987).

vocates of catholic orthodoxy have surrendered the bird in the hand—an extant infallible text—for the two inerrant foul in the bush, which turn out to be non-existent; 2) they have conceded a new definition for the word "infallible" which should never have been allowed. Thus they have permitted the moderns— neo-orthodox and neo-evangelical—to set the agenda and define the terms.

Finally, and perhaps most important of all, by surrendering the word infallibility one devalues and causes to become dated that great body of sixteenth and seventeenth-century dogmatic, exegetical and confessional literature, all of which used exclusively the word *infallible* and *never* "inerrancy."

A reclamation act is in order.

III. Adjustments: Good and Bad

A. The Legacy of Modernism

The modernist impulse of the nineteenth-century found its culmination in historicism's *quest for the historical Jesus.* I have argued that it was the *quest for the historical text,* begun as early as the sixteenth-century, that set this in motion. In Bultmann we reach the nadir of despair with little hope of ever discovering an historical Jesus; but, with some fairly major adjustments, namely, the demytholization of the New Testament, Christianity lives on in modern dress. Barth was uncomfortable with this option and so gave greater emphasis to an inward certainty provided by encounter with the Wholly Other and so creates what Cornelius Van Til called the new *modernism* rather than Neo-*orthodoxy,* the term given to Barth's project by the press. Warfield attempted to retain the old orthodoxy but by also making a major, largely unacknowledged concession to modernity, by abandoning the sacred text of the Church for a future scientific text reconstructed by the Academy.[16] William Arndt,

---

[16]Theoretically there is absolutely no difference between Warfield's project and that of the so-called "Majority Text Society." Both were/are still in a quest to restore a text that has been lost; both work(ed) from a primitivist, *restorationist*

within conservative Lutheran circles, followed Warfield's lead in adopting exactly the same adjustment.[17] In Baptist circles it was A.T. Robertson who made the shift (see the dedication page in his handbook on N.T. text criticism where his labours are presented in honour of the name Warfield).

While all of these options have found pockets of followers, by their very adjustments they have signalled to the modern culture the loss of consensus and the absence of timeless transcendence, qualities the Church alone is able to cultivate and retain. In the wake of this all that seems to be left is an ever growing secularity and public cynicism toward a religion ever in adjustment, never at rest. Like modern economics, while the gold standard may have been abandoned the printing of money continues, all the while being further and further debased.[18]

One of the major ideologies come to fill that gap is feminism, which brings us full circle to where we began. With no catholic consensus it is not surprising that it took an "evangelical" archbishop to cut Anglicanism forever free from her orthodox moorings, just as the evangelical Calvinist Warfield abandoned the notion of a Sacred Text in his *quest for the inerrant autographs*. Both developments were adjusting to modernity rather than addressing the modern situation with the timelessness of catholic truth. Such a task can only be accomplished by means of a post-critical orthodoxy.

---

principle, rather than a catholic *preservationist* principle; and neither has, or had, an ecclesiology that can (or could) account for the role the Church has played in configuring as well as canonising and transmitting the text of Scripture. The Dallas fundamentalists rallying around the Byzantine text do so because it is the "majority" text, without ever engaging the reason why it is such, i.e. because it was actually the text used in catholic ecclesiastical practice. Hence, one can only make sense of it's *majority* status by acknowledging its *Ecclesiastical* status, which explains *why* it is in the majority.

[17]See his "The Chief Principles of New Testament Textual Criticism," *Concordia Theological Monthly* 5 (1934): 503–515. I am indebted to Mr. Edward L. Boineau for assistance on this point.

[18]The application of this analogy to the problem of modern translations can hardly be missed. If the original autographs are the gold standard, and they are now gone, all that can be left is the free printing of "bibles" (like paper money), based on whatever standard of values a progressively cynical and secularised culture demands!

CONCLUSION

On the 28th of September in 1859, Constantine Tischendorf, the German text critic, stole the famous Codex Sinaiticus from St. Catherine's Monastery at the foot of Mt. Sinai in Egypt.[19] No single act could so wonderfully serve as a metaphor for what has happened to the Bible in the modern era. It has been lifted from its legitimate matrix within the bosom of the Church and has served countless students as a cadaver in the operating theatres of the world within the alien context of the Academy.

It certainly has a rightful place there, allowing students to gain the kind of knowledge necessary to be critical historians aware of all aspects of its constituent parts and able to discover the genius of its organic unity; just as a medical student can only gain a knowledge of the healing arts by taking up his scalpel and discovering first hand the wonder of the human body. But for many, the dirty business of examining the text of Scripture in such a clinical way desensitizes them from ever again being able to appreciate the Bible as a living, *Sacred Text*.

This is because they never move into the final phase where one steps back and rediscovers the Bible's true function within the ecclesiastical community, both historically and in the contemporary situation. What is needed is the critical awareness of the human circumstances involved in the compilation and transmission of Holy Scripture (it is the legitimate work of the Academy to provide this), and an equal awareness of its divine purpose and function (the Church alone, the only authentic matrix for the proper use of the Sacred Text, can provide this).[20]

---

[19]On the important historical recounting of this see, James Bentley, *Secrets of Mount Sinai: The Story of the World's Oldest Bible—Codex Sinaiticus* (1986).

[20]Brevard Childs has provided a method which would seem to allow for some exciting possibilities in this direction, see, T.P. Letis, "Brevard Childs and the Seventeenth Century Dogmaticians: A Window to a New Paradigm, *Churchman* 105 (1992): 261–277; and Mark G. Brett, *Biblical Criticism in Crisis?: The Impact of the Canonical Approach on Old Testament Studies* (Cambridge University Press, 1991.

This is analogous to Luther's understanding of the dual natures of God's work among his people: His *opus alienum* and His *opus proprium*. The former *alien* work is never an end in itself (as those who dwell exclusively in the Academy would maintain), but always a means to the latter, His *proper* work within the Church.[21] Prior to the Enlightenment all knew the latter and few the former; today most know the former but precious few the latter.

Historically, the Church has always held as sacred every verbal unit of Scripture, as scribal habits alone would indicate after the establishment of the canon.[22] So to be authentically Christian one cannot abandon such a model in favour of some modern adjustment, whether Barthianism (the Bible only *contains* the Word of God), or Warfieldianism (inspiration is only ultimately to be found in the *autographa*). R.P.C. Hanson has even insisted that verbal inspiration has always been the official doctrine of the Church and that,

> No alternative meaning of the word 'inspiration' when applied to the Bible has been produced which has any connection with the root meaning of the word itself. . . . We still cling to the word [inspiration], speaking of Scripture but we give no meaning to it which does not alter it into an entirely different concept unconnected with the traditional one (Hanson 1973:21).[23]

Historically, the Church has also always recognized this volume to be infallible in a localized and extant edition. This word, *infallible,* and its referent, should be retained and all modern

---

[21]The problem has entered when "Evangelicals" attempted to redeem Biblical criticism and bring it into the Church, a great sacrilege (Lev. 10:1–2), claiming they were practicing "believing criticism." Once the criteria of the *Academy* enters the *Church*, the battle is lost. The *New International Version* is the most pronounced and obvious result. One of the arguments of this essay is that the use of the word "inerrancy" is always an invitation to such sacrilege.

[22]On this point see Maurice A. Robinson, "Scribal Habits Among Manuscripts of the Apocalypse," unpublished Ph.D. Dissertation, Southwestern Baptist Theological Seminary, Fort Worth, TX, 1982.

[23]*The Attractiveness of God: Essays in Christian Doctrine* (1973).

adjustments abandoned, no matter how paradoxical it may appear to those caught in the tangled web of modern Evangelical Christianity and its transitory politics. If the Bible is not rediscovered as a Sacred Text, it will not be the fault of the Academy's Biblical criticism; it will be the failure of the confessing Church, into whose hands it was placed.

CHAPTER FOUR

Brevard Childs and the Protestant Dogmaticians: A Window to a New Paradigm[1]

Hans Küng and David Tracy have recently edited an important book. It reflects a groping about for a basic theological consensus, "in 'a time of troubles', a time when old certainties are breaking up, a post-modern era, an era post-Auschwitz and post-Hiroshima."[2] Employing Thomas Kuhn's now foundational category of paradigm,[3] they have titled this work: *Paradigm Change in Theology: A Symposium for the Future* (1989).

The book is the result of an international ecumenical symposium held in the University of Tübingen and attended by seventy men and women, mostly theologians, but also sociologists, philosophers and others. What brought them together was the self-evident loss of a theological consensus on how to approach the Bible in the post-modern world.

What I would like to suggest in this paper is that those who still regard themselves as in some sense confessional or catholic, need also to consider their own crisis. The reigning so-called *evangelical* paradigm of Biblical authority is crumbling. They, too, must look for a "paradigm change," in favour of an approach that has, in short, more integrity; an approach to "*The Bible Without Illusions*," to use the title of yet another recent work addressing the Bible in the modern world.[4]

---

[1]This essay was a lecture presented to the *Scripture and Theology Group* of the Rutherford House Fellowship, held in London, 24 October 1990.

[2]Hans Küng and David Tracy, eds., *Paradigm Change in Theology: A Symposium for the Future* trans. by Margaret Köhl (New York: Crossroad, 1989), p. xv.

[3]Thomas S. Kuhn, *The Structure of Scientific Revolutions* (Chicago: The University of Chicago Press, 1962; second edition enlarged, 1970).

[4]A.T. and R.P.C. Hanson, *The Bible Without Illusions* (London: SCM Press, 1989). The authors state, "This book has been written under the conviction that

Not all may be inclined to accept the pessimistic view of the popular author Francis Schaeffer, who assessed the *evangelical* terrain a few years ago in his final work, bemoaning what he called "*The Great Evangelical Disaster.*"[5] The serious criticisms of Bernard Ramm, however, in his *After Fundamentalism,* (1983);[6] or those of James Barr in his *Beyond Fundamentalism,* (1984 U.S.A.),[7] cannot be disposed of so easily. First, perhaps, I should define what I believe to be the dominant evangelical paradigm.

It is inevitable that we should turn first to J.I. Packer's book, *Fundamentalism and the Word of God* (1958). While there are many commendable facets to this work,[8] fundamentally, it is merely a restatement of the position of B.B. Warfield.[9]

As I have argued elsewhere,[10] it is my conviction that Warfield himself represented a paradigm shift at Princeton,

---

the interpretation of the Bible needs entire seriousness and scrupulous honesty. It is indeed the dishonesty of much contemporary treatment of the Bible that has largely impelled the authors to write it." p. 3.

[5]Francis A. Schaeffer, *The Great Evangelical Disaster* (New York: Crossway, 1984).

[6]Bernard Ramm, *After Fundamentalism: The Future of Evangelical Theology* (San Fransisco: Harper and Row, 1984).

[7]James Barr, *Beyond Fundamentalism* (Philadelphia: Westminster Press, 1984).

[8]I particularly appreciated his proper interpretation of Burgon's language on inspiration, pp. 179–80. Though, like Nigel Cameron's informed essays, "Inspiration and Criticism: The Nineteenth-Century Crisis," *Tyndale Bulletin* 35 (1984):129–59; "Dean Burgon and the Bible: An Eminent Victorian and the Problem of Inspiration," *Themelios* 7 (1982): 16–20, Packer's book does not make the necessary connection between Burgon's view of inspiration and its bearing on his approach to text critical issues.

[9]Packer saw, however, the weakness of Warfield's position in 1958: "How is it warrantable to treat the Bible as we actually have it as the Word of God, when we have no reason to think that any manuscript or version now existing is free from corruptions? It is sometimes suggested that the evangelical view of Scripture can have no practical application or significance, since the faultless autographs which it posits are not available to us, and that in practice we are involved in an inescapable subjectivism by the necessity of relying on conjectural reconstructions of the text," Packer, *Fundamentalism and the Word of God* (Grand Rapids: Eerdmans, 1958), p. 90.

[10]Theodore P. Letis, "The Protestant Dogmaticians and the Late Princeton School on the Status of the Sacred *Apographa,*" *Scottish Bulletin of Evangelical Theology* 8 (1990):16–42; "B.B. Warfield's Common-Sense Philosophy, New Testament Text Criticism and Inerrancy," a guest lecture presented to the annual meeting of the Evangelical Theological Society, Boston, 5 December 1987, pending publication in the *Journal of the Presbyterian Historical Association (American Presbyterian).*

away from the tradition of Archibald Alexander and Charles Hodge. In this I think it right to refer to Warfield's paradigm as the first "*neo*-orthodoxy," because while it differed from what Barth would propose a few years later, it was, nevertheless, a *new* orthodoxy. It was Warfield's neo-orthodoxy that made possible the final break with the Reformed dogmaticians who had provided Princeton with a paradigm that served confessional Calvinists since the seventeenth century.[11] In this break, Warfield anticipated Barth by at least a generation.

Warfield's wholly new paradigm, which relegated final authority to the *autographa*, rather than to the *apographa*, left Princeton vulnerable to the fragmenting effects of early twentieth century Biblical criticism. Warfield probably never foresaw that his quest for the historical *text* (for here alone is where he would find his *inerrancy*) would evolve into the quest for the historical *Jesus* at Princeton, just as it did in Britain in the eighteenth century and in Germany in the nineteenth century.[12] Eventually, even Prince-

---

[11]Warfield's *new* orthodoxy no longer recognized the *apographa* as the sacred text. For Warfield only the mythical autographs could now have such status, which he now insisted must also be viewed as *inerrant*. This word, *inerrancy*, betrays us, however, always promising more than any extant Biblical MS has ever been able to deliver. Furthermore, source criticism will not allow for one discoverable autographic exemplar for, say, any one Gospel, but recognises a series of oral and written sources culminating in an ecclesiastical recension. On this, see the classics F.C. Grant *The Gospels: Their Origin and Their Growth* (London: Faber and Faber, 1957) and B.H. Streeter, *The Four Gospels: A Study of Origins* (London: Macmillan and Company, 1936); and recently, William Stoker, *Extracanonical Sayings of Jesus* (Atlanta: Scholars Press, 1990) and Helmut Koester, *Ancient Christian Gospels: Their History and Development* (London: SCM Press, 1990).

[12]In my earlier treatments of Warfield I emphasised the neglected aspect of his introducing the German method of text criticism at Princeton. This I see as playing a major role in his paradigm shift. It softened extensively an inherent resistance at Princeton to all aspects of German criticism. Others, however, had earlier detected the extremes to which Warfield might be driven in his apologetic task, illustrating further his distance from the dogmaticians and his affinity with the modern age of science. Sandeen noted, "Warfield once stated: 'The verities of our faith would remain historically proven to us even had we no Bible.' These are remarkable words and have seemed to some to open up a possible area of compromise between criticism and conservatism, but I do not believe the hope was ever a real one. In these few passages we glimpse, as if through a partly

ton was reorganized to make way for the historical criticism and the next neo-orthodoxy, that of Karl Barth. This is a neglected aspect of the legacy of Warfield's paradigm shift.[13]

While Barth's paradigm was an attempt to retain orthodoxy in a post-critical way, like another mediating theologian, Schleiermacher, Barth imbibed too much of the prejudice of his age against the tradition of the Protestant dogmaticians. Like Schleiermacher, for Barth, Scripture was not a verbal revelation but merely a witness to a revealing God. In this Barth was not radical enough in his post-critical stance. Had he gone far enough he would have recognized what other scholars within the *Religionsgeschichtliche Schule* have come to see. Namely, considered phenomenologically, analogous to other sacred texts of other world religions, the Judeo-Christian Bible has always been revered just because of a belief in its *verbally* dictated inspiration. Because Barth was still locked in the polemical debates of the nineteenth century, his vision was hindered on this point.

For Barth, therefore, the dogmaticians' view of Scripture was, paradoxically, "naturalistic" because it presupposed that God had actually used human language as a vehicle for divine revelatory propositions. Consequently, Barth's final judgement was that "therefore we have to resist and reject the 17th-century doctrine of inspiration as false doctrine."[14]

---

opened door, a new side in Warfield's personality. . . ." Ernest R. Sandeen, "The Princeton Theology: One Source of Biblical Literalism in American Protestantism," *Church History* 31 (1962): 316. For a further perceptive analysis of Warfield in this vain, cf. Mike Parsons excellent treatment, "Warfield and Scripture," *Churchman* 91 (1977):198–220.

[13]Some have tended to stress a different interpretation of Warfield's legacy, crediting his paradigm with offering Evangelicals what Mark Noll called, "believing criticism" in his *Between Faith and Criticism: Evangelicals, Scholarship, and the Bible in America* (San Fransisco: Harper and Row, 1986). Rudolph Nelson's recent, *The Making and Unmaking of An Evangelical Mind: The Case of Edward Carnell* (Cambridge: Cambridge University Press, 1987), however, is a tragically sad but poignant tale reflecting in microcosm the broad intellectual schizophrenia produced by the Warfieldian paradigm in the latter half of the twentieth century.

[14]Karl Barth, *Church Dogmatics: The Doctrine of the Word of God* Vol 1, Part 2 ed by G.W. Bromiley and T.F. Torrance, trans, by G.T. Thomson and Harold Knight (Edinburgh: T and T Clark, 1956), p. 525.

In an unguarded moment, however, Barth frankly admitted that the position of the Protestant dogmaticians was "merely a development and systematisation of statements which had been heard in the Church since the first centuries."[15] John Barton, in his recent Bampton Lectures for 1988, confirms Barth's interpretation of the early Church:

> We have to acknowledge that the authority of the books in the "canon" was [for the early Church] clearly much greater than it is for most modern people. This authority was felt to inhere in the exact verbal form of the biblical text to an extent now scarcely believed even by fundamentalists.[16]

R.P.C. and A.T. Hanson have recently admitted the same point:

> The Fathers' treatment of the Bible is essentially atomic. It rests upon the assumption, of course, that there is a pretty similar level of inspiration and revelation to be found in every part of the text.[17]

Barth admitted, therefore, that it was not really the seventeenth century dogmaticians he opposed; it was the *catholic* doctrine of Scripture which they had retained. It was this he branded as "false doctrine." A high price to pay to play the role of the supreme mediating theologian of his day.

While Barth's own dogmatics were intended to replace that of the seventeenth century, we find they have not fully satisfied the modern sense of having lost a mother, that is, the mother Church—catholic tradition. It is my conviction that it is this *catholic* view of inspiration which must be reappropriated, in a post-critical, *post*-modern way, leaving behind the decidedly modern neo-orthodox paradigms of both Warfieldianism, as well as Barthianism. Furthermore, for Protestants, it is the posi-

---

[15]*Ibid.*

[16]John Barton, *People of the Book: The Authority of the Bible in Christianity* The Bampton Lectures For 1988 (London: SCM Press, 1988), p. 28

[17]R.P.C. and A.T. Hanson, *The Bible Without Illusions* (London: SCM Press, 1989), p. 30.

tion of the Protestant dogmaticians which must be creatively rediscovered, if they have any hope of maintaining continuity with authentic catholic tradition.

Presently, in The United States, we are witnessing a highly interesting development. Prominent Protestant theologians, scholars and ministers are going over to the fold of the Roman communion. A *New York Times* headline read on 9 September of this year [1990]: "*Citing Luther, A Noted Theologian Leaves Lutheran Church for Catholicism.*" The noted theologian was John Richard Neuhaus, author of *the Naked Public Square* and *The Catholic Moment*.[18] He was a former member of the Lutheran Church—Missouri Synod and until recently, a member of the Evangelical Lutheran Church in America.

A few years earlier, the well published, evangelical author, Thomas Howard, then Professor of English at Gordon College and author of *Evangelical is Not Enough*,[19] also became a Roman Catholic. Recently, Rev. Scott Hahn, a graduate of Gordon-Conwell Seminary in Boston and a pastor in the conservative P.C.A. (Presbyterian Church in America), converted to Rome and now teaches in one of their universities in Ohio. Hahn's significance goes far beyond his own conversion because as a popular and influential leader in his church he has also had considerable pull in bringing other conservative Presbyterian pastors and laymen over to Rome in the last few years. The one thing all these men had in common is that they were serious about theology and were all originally from conservative traditions.

Why the leap? Could this be one response to Schaeffer's "evangelical disaster"? Could it be that much of contemporary Protestantism, both liberal and conservative, bears little resemblance to the catholicity preserved in the seventeenth century Reformed, Anglican and Lutheran dogmatic traditions?

Neuhaus, like many others in the early seventies, felt be-

---

[18]J.R. Neuhaus, *The Naked Public Square: Religion and Democracy in America* (Grand Rapids: Eerdmans, 1984); *The Catholic Moment* (San Fransisco: Harper and Row, 1987).

[19]T. Howard, *Evangelical is not Enough: Worship of God in Liturgy and Sacraments* (San Fransisco: Ignatius Press, 1988).

trayed by the Missouri Synod's assimilation of American fundamentalism (by way of the un-Lutheran influences of John Warwick Montgomery) and along with Martin Marty, and Jaroslav Pelikan, he left the Missouri Synod in her time of upheaval in the mid-nineteen-seventies. He then left ELCA because he could find no echo for his catholic concerns. Howard admits he simply was not fed by the blandness of American evangelicalism. Scott Hahn was hungry for an identifiable body of dogmatic tradition which is so sorely lacking within a brand of Presbyterianism which is progressively assuming the character of the modern American corporate model, with church growth as the new bottom line.

But why the stress on the Protestant dogmaticians, such an antiquated and near impenetrable tradition (most of their works have never even been translated from the Latin)? It is because I have come to see that one cannot reappropriate the authentic legacy of the Protestant Reformation, in its catholic dimensions, except by way of the dogmaticians.

It is this tradition, with its refining definitions, though cumbersome at times, that prevents the sixteenth century Reformers from being lifted from their historical moment and forced to speak an alien discourse reflecting the *Sitz im Leben* of modernity. It is this alien discourse, I believe, that has driven at least some earnest folk toward Rome. Within the bosom of Rome one finds, even after Vatican II, a living continuity of dogmatic tradition, ironically, closer in kind to the seventeenth century Protestantism, than are most contemporary expressions of Protestantism.

Perhaps one lesson we should learn from Warfield, as well as from Barth, is not to despise, as they did, the wisdom of the Protestant dogmaticians, simply because the seventeenth century formulations were produced in a pre-critical age. Rather, we should see the seventeenth century context as an advantage. The dominant theological concern of that age was to develop dogmatics fashioned by the constraints of the Biblical data and secondarily, by catholicity. Dogmatics in the modern era, both liberal and conservative, tend to be fashioned as an apologetic response to the age of *scientia* (a discipline which proved to be subject to as many paradigm shifts as any other intellectual enterprise).

But is it realistic to think one can reappropriate the Protestant dogmaticians in a post-critical milieu? I believe the proposals of Brevard Childs offers just such an opportunity.[20] What are his proposals? I will begin with a brief historical sketch illustrating how the Bible lost its sacred text status. I will then propose how I believe Childs can provide the opportunity to rediscover the Bible on this basis, in a post-critical way.

Ninian Smart and Richard Hecht have provided what I think is the best definition, from a history-of-religions stand-point, of what constitutes a sacred text:

> We may look at sacred texts as being those which contain a power and authority and are given certain status within a given community. Such communities and traditions are held together most typically through liturgical acts, which help to focus life upon that which is ultimate and to which the sacred texts give testimony. The status of the sacred text is canonical: as well as being normative for a community or tradition, it is also that community or tradition's canon or canonical text. The term 'canon' has a variety of meanings, but in the context of sacred texts it means the defined grouping of texts for the community or tradition . . . one does not add to or subtract from them.[21]

The given community we have in view, of course, is the Christian Church; the liturgy is that, broadly speaking, reflecting catholic orthodoxy from the fourth century, which in turn, reinforced the sacred text standard.[22]

---

[20]Childs's most influential works have been, *Biblical Theology in Crisis* (Philadelphia: Westminster Press, 1970); *Introduction to the Old Testament as Scripture* (Philadelphia: Fortress Press, 1979); *The New Testament As Canon: An Introduction* (Philadelphia: Fortress Press, 1984). For a complete listing of his works through 1988 consult his *Festschrift*, Gene M. Tucker, David L. Petersen and Robert R. Wilson, eds. *Canon, Theology, and Old Testament Interpretation* (Philadelphia: Fortress, Press, 1988), pp. 329–336.

[21]Ninian Smart and Richard D. Hecht, eds. *Sacred Texts of the World: A Universal Anthology* (New York: Crossroad, 1982), p. xiii–xiv.

[22]That is, the orthodoxy arrived at by the early Councils reinforced a canonical configuration of the N.T. text which best reflected this orthodoxy from among the several floating textual recensions.

Since (and before) the emergence of catholic orthodoxy, until the Reformation, the Bible was forever to be found within the context of church use and so retained its status as a sacred text.[23] It was, in fact, ecclesiastical *use* that actually determined the *macro* canon (books) as well as the *micro* canon (the textual form of those books).[24]

Not only was the Bible regarded as a sacred text in liturgical or catechetical functions but also in the process of reproduction. We find that scribal habits became much more conservative from the fourth century onward—the century that witnessed the emergence of the canon—particularly within the Greek tradition, if not always in the Latin.[25]

---

[23]On the ecclesiastical use of the Bible in medieval times, the following standard works provide a good introduction, B. Smalley, *The Study of the Bible in the Middle Ages* (Oxford: Oxford University Press, 1952); *The Gospels in the Schools c.1100-c.1280* (London:The Hambledon Press, 1985); R.E. McNally, S.J., *The Bible in the Early Middle Ages* (Atlanta: Scholars Press, 1986 [reprint of 1959 edition]; G.W.H. Lampe, ed. *The Cambridge History of the Bible: The West From the Fathers to the Reformation* vol 2 (Cambridge: Cambridge University Press, 1969); G.R. Evans, *The Language and Logic of the Bible: The Early Middle Ages* (Cambridge: Cambridge University Press, 1984); K. Walsh and D. Wood, eds., *The Bible in the Medieval World: Essays in Memory of Beryl Smalley* (Oxford: Basil Blackwell, 1985).

[24]Adolf Jülicher spoke of *Anagnosis,* or public reading in the Church, as one of the earliest criterion for the developing canon. By the time of Justin Martyr (150 C.E.), Jülicher notes, "the first act in the worship of God on Sundays was to read aloud before the whole congregation a portion of Scripture, either from the 'Memoirs' of the Apostles or the writings of the Prophets. It seems to me that there is more here than a mere 'germ of the New Testament Canon,' . . . the Gospels and the writings of the Prophets are placed on an equal footing." *An Introduction to the New Testament*, trans. by J.P. Ward (London: Smith, Elder and Company, 1904), pp. 480; 484. Cf. also Hans von Campenhausen, *The Formation of the Christian Bible* (Philadelphia: Fortress Press, 1972). p. 331. There is yet resistence to this idea applying equally to the canonical books as well as to the canonical *text* of these books, by those still laboring within the Warfieldian paradigm. They can abide by the consensus of the church for the final form of the canon, but reserve the right to continue "the quest for the historical text" because only the autographic text will provide them with their theoretical inerrancy. Cf. Richard B. Gaffin, Jr., "The New Testament as Canon," in *Inerrancy and Hermeneutic: A Tradition, A Challenge, a Debate* (Grand Rapids: Baker, 1988), pp. 181 ff.

[25]The Latin Bible seemed to suffer more during the medieval era than did the Greek Bible. R. Loewe noted, "In the centuries following Jerome's death, the

As the Church divided into the Eastern (Greek) and Western (Latin) communities, the canonical dimensions of the sacred text experienced a diversity. A *Greek* vulgate became the standard in the Eastern Church, corresponding to a *Latin* vulgate in the West. Eventually the antagonism between these two bodies extended beyond doctrinal disputes to the belief that the canonical texts used to affirm each opposing community's distinctives, were themselves corrupted: the Greeks distrusted the Latin Biblical texts and the Latins were convinced the Greeks had altered their texts.[26]

Each textual standard continued to be authoritative, however, for their given community and constituted a sacred text. In both communities these texts were read, studied, interpreted, as well as conceptualized in icons and mosaics (in the East), or in images and stained glass (in the West).

Moreover, in an extended definition of sacred text, offered by Robert Detweiler, he includes the role of "privileged interpreters—priests, shamans, prophets, preachers, ayatollahs...enjoying a special relationship to the divinity . . . and thus able to disclose the text's 'true' meaning."[27] It was within the Christian communities that the Bible was interpreted, multiplied and

---

spread of both the new version [Jerome's] and the Old Latin remained ungoverned by self-conscious consistency or the canons of responsible textual criticism. . . . Heterogeneous interpolations would be included to meet the requirements of the immediate situation, and the text thus modified would become perpetuated as it was diffused in the course of missionary activity." "The Medieval History of the Latin Vulgate," in *The Cambridge History of the Bible* Vol. 2, p.109.

[26]The Greeks disparaged the *Vulgata Latina* because it was merely a translation from the inspired Greek of the New Testament and because Jerome abandoned the Greek LXX Old Testament text—thought to have the sanction of the apostolic Church—in favour of the Hebrew text. On the criticism that Jerome received for this, see his *Apologia contra rufinum* II, 24–25. On the other hand, the Latins came to regard Jerome's standard as sanctioned by the Pope and the usage of the Western Church and therefore distrusted the editions of the Eastern Church when they differed from Jerome. On this see, Theodore P. Letis, "The *Vulgata Latina* and the Council of Trent: The Latin Bible as Verbal Icon," a paper presented before the summer meeting of the Ecclesiastical History Society, 20 July, 1990, Chichester, England, pending publication.

[27]Robert Detweiler, "What is a Sacred Text?," *Semeia* 31 (1985): 214.

distributed as the unique possession of the Church, by church-men—monks, priests, and bishops—as a sacred text.

I say this lasted until the Reformation, which may seem surprising at first. Was not the Reformation just another form of ecclesial continuity? Was it not the Enlightenment that truly liberated Biblical texts from the domain of church and theology? Without wanting to engage the debate whether the Reformation was the beginning of modernity or a continuation of medievalism, in many respects the answer to these questions is, yes.

Nevertheless, I believe it was the Christian humanist, Desiderius Erasmus, himself a *disaffected* monk, who in a decisive way, disrupted the canon of the Western Church—putting in its place the Greek N.T. canon of the Eastern Church—and thus set in motion a process that by the nineteenth century, culminated in the loss of the Bible as a sacred text in the West. What emerged was the Bible as *religious* text.

By religious text I mean a text which still retains a "traditional specialness" but has lost its status as a sacred text. Once it was removed from the ecclesiastical matrix, its dimensions and interpretation were no longer determined by theologians who were preeminently churchmen. Leaving the context of the Church, the interpretation of the Bible became subject to a "new hermeneutic." Detweiler observes that the "history of secularization in the west is, in one important sense, the story of readers learning to read our sacred texts in a different way."[28]

To read the sacred text in a different way is to now read it within the matrix of the university, rather than the Church. Hans Dieter Betz has analyzed what this means:

> The function of the Bible in the University appears to be twofold. First, the Bible is recognized as a piece of world literature with a wide range of references to many disciplines. Second, the Bible is recognized sociologically as the holy scripture of living religious communities and traditions which exercise great influence in the contemporary society.[29]

---

[28]*Ibid.*, p. 225.
[29]Hans Dieter Betz, ed. *The Bible as the Document of the University* (Chico: Scholars Press, 1981), p. 2.

This is a new, detached, phenomenological view of the Bible as a religious text—important as religious genre, but not decisive to its reader as an authoritative and sacred text.[30]

Presently, a tension exists between the continuing use of the Bible as a sacred text within contemporary faith communities, and the phenomenological use of the Bible as a religious text within the university context. This tension, between the Bible as an ecclesiastical text and as the text of the university, reminds us of the words of Tertullian, "What indeed hath Athens to do with Jerusalem? What concord is there between the Academy and the Church?" Tertullian would be dismayed to learn that since the nineteenth century, the Academy has completely prevailed over the Church, resulting in "The Eclipse of Biblical Narrative," and the arrival of "The Strange Silence of the Bible in the Church."[31] Keegan has recently captured the present mood:

> The complaint is that biblical scholars have taken the Bible away from the people. Biblical scholars have rather successfully convinced many in the community of believers that only they, the biblical scholars, can really appreciate the Bible. They are the only ones who can determine what it means. The rest of the community must sit up and listen to the biblical scholars explain what the Bible means.[32]

No "community consensus" has emerged from the Academy explaining what the Bible means as a "religious text" (or, these days, even what are its boundaries), analogous to the great ecu-

---

[30]Detweiler observes, "A text becomes sacred when a segment of the community is able to establish it as such in order to gain control and set order over the whole community," *op. cit.,* p. 217. In like manner, once it loses such status it also loses the power to control human institutions and communities. Hence, the crisis in the modern Church.

[31]Hans Frei, *The Eclipse of Biblical Narrative: A Study in Eighteenth and Nineteenth-Century Hermeneutics* (New Haven: Yale University Press, 1974); James D. Smart, *The Strange Silence of the Bible in the Church: A Study in Hermeneutics* (Philadelphia: Westminster Press, 1970).

[32]T.J. Keegan, O.P., *Interpreting the Bible: A Popular Introduction to Biblical Hermeneutics* (New York: Paulist Press, 1985), p. 9.

menical or Reformation creeds of the Church. It is this vacuum that called forth the symposium mentioned at the beginning of this paper. This gaping open-endedness has invited Christian atheists to propose a project of "Deconstruction,"[33] while certain feminists seize the moment to offer a thorough-going "reconstruction,"[34] which happens to coincide with their revisionist view of history.

To be fair, however, it must be said that it never really was part of the design of the Academy's Biblical criticism to offer the Church a new certainty regarding Her long cherished belief that the Bible is a *sacred* text. Morgan and Barton have recently reminded us that it is not even a matter of the different *methods* used by Church and Academy to study the Bible; it is a matter of their different *aims.*[35] I believe the aims of both domains to be not only legitimate, but necessary within their given contexts.

What are the roots of these different aims? A few years back, Bernhard W. Anderson, in his Presidential Address to the Society of Biblical Literature in 1980, put his finger on Johann Philipp Gabler's inaugural address at the University of Altdorf in 1787 as holding a partial answer to this question. In Gabler's address, *De iusto discrimine theologiae biblicae et dogmaticae regundisque recte utriusque finibus,*[36] he called for a method that would make a distinction between the aims of *Biblical* theology and of *dogmatic* theology. Biblical theology would concern itself with what is "historical in nature," what "the sacred writers thought about the things of God."[37] While dogmatic theology, which is "didactic in nature," would treat "the philosophizing of a particular theologian concerning Godly things in terms of his

---

[33]See Thomas J.J. Altizer, *et al., Deconstruction and Theology* (New York: Crossroad, 1982).

[34]See Elisabeth Schüssler Fiorenza, *In Memory of Her: A Feminist Theological Reconstruction of Christian Origins* (New York: Crossroad, 1983).

[35]Robert Morgan and John Barton, *Biblical Interpretation* (Oxford: Oxford University Press, 1988), pp. 271–296.

[36]"A Discourse on the Proper Distinction between Biblical and Dogmatic Theology and the Boundaries to be Drawn for Each."

[37]Bernard W. Anderson, "Tradition and Scripture in the Community of Faith," *Journal of Biblical Literature* 100 (1981): 6.

own mode of thinking, historical situation, denomination and school."[38] This method led, contrary to Gabler's own wishes, to a

> separation between two disciplines, as it is to this day. Liberated from doctrinal controls and ecclesiastical management, biblical studies were pursued in the liberal atmosphere of *academia*, where historical methodology was refined and the larger theological questions were often ignored in the interests of specialization.[39]

Anderson attributes this method to Gabler's Enlightenment presuppositions. Surprisingly, however, one finds antecedents for this separation in the dogmaticians of the seventeenth century and earlier yet, in Melanchthon and Luther.

Robert Scharlemann emphasised a dual approach to theology in Luther and Melanchthon, corresponding to Church and Academy and to the realms of faith and reason. Melanchthon saw the difference between theology as *academic* (what did the text mean in its historical context) and *Kerygmatic* (what does it mean to the Church today).

> This distinction is contained in the difference Melanchthon saw between 'knowledge' and 'true knowledge' (*vera cognitio*) of the Scripture. Theological knowledge is the knowledge derived from Scripture and objectively seen by any competent scholar to be the content of Scripture. True theological knowledge is the knowledge which comes through the Scripture when concretely proclaimed and heard as the voice of God (*vox Dei*).[40]

For Melanchthon, the public, philological method, analogous to other university disciplines and refined by the humanist tradition, while not enough to arrive at the *vera cognitio*, was, nevertheless, the necessary first stage.

---

[38] *Ibid.*

[39] *Ibid.*

[40] Robert Scharlemann, "Theology in Church and University: The Post-Reformation Development," *Church History* 33 (1964):23. Luther held a similar distinction between a *theoretic* knowledge of the word and what Scharlemann calls the *acoustic* knowledge, "mediated by the word which is concretely heard as the voice of God" p. 23.

Johann Gerhard (1582–1637) of the University of Jena brought this distinction forward into the era of Protestant scholasticism. He recognized the difference between theology "considered systematically and abstractively" and theology "considered habitually and concretively" as "a divinely given habit conferred on a man by the Holy Spirit through the Word."[41] It is this distinction, Scharlemann judges, that determined the domain for each aspect of Bible study—the formal or objective suited for the university and the personal proclaimed *vox Dei,* in the Church.

Certainly, neither the Reformers, nor the dogmaticians like Gerhard, nor even Gabler, could have foreseen the secularization of the university. Nevertheless, in germ they each provided, in their own way, for the two separate domains. The clock cannot now be turned back to a more idyllic age when a theological world-view prevailed within the university. For many reasons, perhaps we should even be thankful for this.

The problem that has been with us since the nineteenth century, however, is that the Academy's criteria have entered the Church and sub-summed the prerogatives of the ecclesiastical use of the Bible.[42] Brevard Child's canonical approach provides, I think, an opportunity to once again place both approaches, with their different aims, back within their own *soevereiniteit in eigen kring.*[43]

---

[41]*Ibid.,* p. 25.

[42]It should not be neglected to add that even in the modern era a religious tyranny can enter the modern secular university as well, playing havoc with the sacred notion of academic freedom. Note particularly in the United States the religiously motivated, forced imposition of an ideological grammar on entire academic communities, resulting in the constriction of intellectual discourse by such predetermined linguistic boundaries. There should be no place for language in uniform within the academic community.

[43]This is a Dutch phrase used by Abraham Kuyper (1837–1920) which is translated "Sphere Sovereignty." It had reference to Kuyper's belief "that various distinct spheres of human authority . . . each have their own responsibility and decision-making power, which may not be usurped by those in authority in another sphere." L. Kalsbeek, *Contours of a Christian Philosophy: An Introduction to Herman Dooyeweerd's Thought* (Toronto: Wedge Publishing Foundation, 1975), p. 353.

There has been a revolt, (in the Academy itself!), over the loss of the *sacred* text. There have been many calls to recognize the Bible as a book *sui generis*. There is now a call to reconsider *The Bible as the Church's Book*,[44] and the *New Testament as the Church's Book*.[45] There are pleas for "Theological Hermeneutics."[46] Introductions are being written for "the Old Testament as Scripture" (Childs, 1979), and for "The New Testament as Canon" (Childs, 1985). This is no doubt the result, on the part of many of these new advocates, of wanting to recapture the loss of transcendence in the Church that has accompanied the loss of the Bible as a sacred text.

The Church has not, however, captured the high ground and fully reclaimed the Bible. The struggle continues to this very hour and is probably most focused in the current debate between James Barr (representing a *religious* text view of the Academy) and Brevard Childs (representing a *sacred* text view of the Church, but from an historical or phenomenological, post-critical perspective).[47]

For some years Childs, and others, have been arguing that since the Bible entered the domain of the Academy, "critical-

---

[44]Phyllis A. Bird, *The Bible as the Church's Book* (Philadelphia: Westminster Press, 1982).

[45]Willi Marxsen, *The New Testament as the Church's Book* trans. by J.E. Mignard (Philadelphia: Fortress Press, 1972).

[46]Charles M. Wood, *The Formation of Christian Understanding: An Essay in Theological Hermeneutics* (Philadelphia: Westminster Press, 1981); "Theological Hermeneutics," *Quarterly Review* 7 (1987): 91–100.

[47]It is true that Barr has addressed the issue of "The Bible as a Document of Believing Communities," in Hans Dieter Betz, ed. *The Bible as a Document of the University*, pp.25–47, but his concluding sentiment captures his real emphasis: "Openness to the world is gained for the Bible when the study and appreciation of it, as I have emphasized, are not limited by the traditional perceptions and methods of the believing community but are open to all the world and to its ways of thinking. And with this, starting out from the believing community, we come back to join hands with the thought of the Bible as the document of the university" p. 45. Barr's inaugural lecture at Oxford, *Does Biblical Study Still Belong to Theology?* (Oxford: Oxford University Press, 1978), gives a clear witness to Barr's emphasis and aims, answering "no" to this question. Childs is proposing a process the inverse of Barr's: from the historical-critical study of the Bible within the Academy to a post-critical appreciation of the Bible as the sacred canon of believing communities—both past and present.

historical scholarship has become capsulated within a methodology which has become incapable of handling the theological dimension of biblical texts."[48] For Childs, the first step in recognizing the *theological* dimension is to begin with the final ecclesiastical form of a Biblical textual standard:

> The canonical approach to text criticism applies a very different methodology in its use of the textual history in the pre-stabilization period. It does not attempt to establish a 'better' text than the Masoretic, but chooses to remain with the canonical text and thus identifies the level of literature with which it is concerned. Nevertheless, this canonical approach is vitally interested in all the evidence from the recensional history of the pre-stabilization period. It simply uses the evidence in a different manner towards achieving a particular goal, namely, the understanding of the canonical text.[49]

To finally return to the theme of this paper, this is perfectly in keeping with what served as sacred Scripture for the Protestant dogmaticians. The difference is that in Childs's method we approach the canonical texts in a post-critical way, fully informed that no *ur* text is necessarily discoverable.[50] Childs con-

---

[48]Paul D. Hanson, "The Theological Significance of Contradiction within the Book of the Covenant," in G.W. Coats and B.O. Long, eds., *Canon and Authority: Essays in Old Testament Religion and Theology* (Philadelphia: Fortress Press, 1977), p. 112.

[49]Childs, *Introduction*, p. 104. It is interesting to note that Barr, in his Croall Lectures at New College, Edinburgh, (1970) also accorded considerable significance to the final canonical form of the Biblical text: "But though in principle all stages of the tradition which went to make up scripture are relevant, a certain basic character attaches to the text of the literary units as they now are...all others are a matter of historical reconstruction, however probable. From the point of view of modern literary appreciation also, the final form of the text has the first importance.... The form as it stands is, from the point of view of the tradition, the definitive form, the state in which the tradition ceased to modify the text and agreed that it should stand. Thus both the theological motivation of the tradition and the scholarly techniques of modern investigation agree in according a certain fundamental character to the final state of the text." James Barr, *The Bible in the Modern World* (San Fransisco: Harper and Row Publishers, 1973), pp. 163–64.

[50]In Childs's words: "My understanding of canon was offered as a major criticism of late seventeenth and eighteenth century Reformed orthodoxy which

trasts this with the model that both Warfield and Barth would have employed:

> The usual method of text criticism results in each successive generation of critics offering fresh suggestions regarding the form of the original text. This highly individualistic model seems unaware of the continuing and enduring role of the canonical text, held in common by ongoing religious communities, which serves an authoritative function. The point is not to defend unreflected tradition, but at least to remain in conversation with it.[51]

Childs is concerned that the Academy's near exclusive preoccupation with biblical criticism causes it to lose sight of the hermeneutical significance of the canonical configuration of the traditional Church texts. In a post-critical way, Childs has been calling for a reconsideration of the Bible as a sacred text, for ecclesial, religious purposes, as it functioned for the communities that produced this final form. In this way we gain insights into their hermeneutic.[52]

---

tended to place the authority in a divinely inspired book apart from its reception by the communities through the work of the Spirit. By defining canon as those sacred writings which were received, treasured, and shaped by a community of faith, I proposed a very different dynamic from that, say, of Charles Hodge, but one which was akin to the early Church Father's view of a rule-of-faith" review by Childs of *Holy Scripture: Canon, Authority, Criticism* by James Barr, in *Interpretation* 38 (1984): 67. For the purpose of my thesis, however, I must also stress that while the dogmaticians may not have had a fully informed historical understanding of the process leading to the final form of the text, they did purposefully perpetuate the rule-of-faith consensus arrived at by the orthodox fathers when they affirmed the same ecclesiastical recensions as did the early Church—the Greek N.T. text of the Eastern Church and the Hebrew text underlying the Latin Church text, a unique Protestant blend of both catholic traditions.

[51]Childs, *Introduction*, p. 105.

[52]This extra *aim* of canonical hermeneutics would appear to have next to no relevance for those whose exclusive domain is the Academy. I think this lies behind much of the antagonism between Barr and Childs. In an early response to Childs, Barr remarked, "An exegesis which would work strictly within the confines of the canon is certainly a possibility that could be added to other forms of exegesis, but it is doubtful how it could be the basic theological form of exegesis." Barr, s.v. "Biblical Theology" in *The Interpreter's Dictionary of the Bible* (Supplementary Volume) (Abingdon: Nashville, 1976), p. 110. I believe that be-

Childs believes a post-Enlightenment "Biblical theology" can be discovered if one attends to the fact that

> a religious reading of Israel's traditions arose early in its history and extended in different ways throughout the oral, literary, and redactional stages of the growth of the material until it reached a fixed form of relative stability. This religious interpretation involved a peculiar construal which sought to give the developing material a shape which could be appropriated by successive generations.[53]

By successive generations Childs means the Bible can, even in our modern era, be reappropriated as the Church's book, after the rigours of all aspects of Biblical criticism—indeed, not until such criticism has been performed.

James Barr disagrees. He has seen too much misconstruing of data in the area of Biblical semantics, in the name of theology, to turn the Bible back over to the Church.[54] He in fact sees himself as a key figure in accepting the role of a gadfly, preventing the theologians from quietly stealing the Bible away from the Academy, only to again shroud it in medieval-like canonical authority, in the name of "biblical theology." While he is willing to grant that the Bible will continue to have its use within the context of the Church,

> It also has a context in a wider academic community, and it can fully serve the context of the church *only* in so far as it respects also the integrity of modes of study and interpretation, valid within that community, over which theology as theology cannot pronounce [emphasis mine].[55]

While these remarks are intended for Childs and his advocates, certainly Childs would whole-heartedly agree! In fact, Barr himself freely acknowledges of Childs,

---

cause Childs's aim is mostly irrelevant to Barr's own concerns, Barr is unwilling to consider sympathetically how Childs's method could provide such a theological exegesis.

[53]Childs, Review of *Holy Scripture,* p. 67.

[54]James Barr, *The Semantics of Biblical Language* (London: SCM Press, 1961).

[55]Barr, *Does the Bible Still Belong to Theology*, p. 16.

> Childs entirely accepts in itself the historical principle, that one can validly and must necessarily consider previous stages of the books [of the Bible], that one must consider their relations with writings outside the biblical canon, and that the books can be understood in terms of their origins and background.[56]

Furthermore, in the same article, Barr admitted that Childs's method, in the final analysis, is really a legitimate aspect of historical criticism:

> Traditional biblical scholarship has had a bias toward *origins*, toward explaining things through what they had been *beforehand*. Childs wants us to look with equal interest at what came afterwards. . . . Biblical scholarship, in its claims to be historical, has often been historical in one direction rather than in the other: it has looked for antecedents, but been unable to deal with after-effects.[57]

Nevertheless, it is the project of rediscovering the Bible as *canon* that disturbs Barr, because this

> accords with much popular religious sentiment: biblical studies are hideously complex, they require technical expertise, they are full of divergent sources, periods, and hypotheses: the canonical principle leaves the believer at peace, alone with his Bible.[58]

Barr's more recent criticism reflects an unhappiness with Childs's additional canonical approach and sees this as too concessive, a method that finds its justification in a "valuation of traditional critical scholarship...almost exactly the same as the valuation attached to it by conservative/fundamentalist cir-

---

[56]James Barr, "Reading the Bible as Literature," *Bulletin of the John Rylands University Library* 56 (1973–74): 24.

[57]*Ibid.*

[58]James Barr, *Holy Scripture: Canon, Authority, Criticism* (Philadelphia: Westminster Press, 1983), p. 169. Barr's most recent critique of Childs appears in the latter's *Festschrift*, "The Theological Case Against Biblical Theology," *Canon, Theology and Old Testament Interpretation*, pp. 3–19.

cles."[59] While this is clearly an over-statement, it nevertheless reveals Barr's true concern: Childs aids and abets the theologians.

The struggle between the Church and the Academy continues. What Childs provides is an opportunity not to have to take sides. The canonical approach takes seriously all aspects of Biblical criticism—something neither the Warfield nor the Packer model will allow for—and yet permits the Bible to retain its sacred text status at the canonical level, something Barth disparaged. The implications of this are varied and promising.

It means that the Academy retains her right of full autonomy, doing authentic Biblical criticism with integrity, not bound by any individual community's model of a "believing criticism," (which amounts to doing Biblical criticism with one hand tied behind one's back).

Furthermore,—and as a Lutheran, I speak in terms of a Protestant catholicism—the Church has an opportunity to rediscover, in a creative and discerning way, the rich, theological corpus of the Protestant dogmatic traditions, which operated with Scripture at the same level as does the canonical approach. This time, however, it can be in a fully informed and post-critical way.

---

[59] *Ibid.*, p. 148. In reality, this charge proves to be little more than a strawman. I know of no fundamentalist who has endorsed Childs. In fact, just where one would expect endorsement, if Barr's charge had merit, one finds instead disapprobation, cf. Dale A. Brueggeman's rather typical fundamentalist antagonism against Childs, "Brevard Childs' Canon Criticism: An Example of Post-Critical Naiveté," *The Journal of the Evangelical Theological Society* 32 (1989): 311–326. Moreover, Carl Henry has recently placed Childs on the index of works unacceptable to evangelicals, "Canonical Theology: An Evangelical Appraisal," *Scottish Bulletin of Evangelical Theology* 8 (Autumn 1990): 76–108. Here Henry continues to display both a resistence to Biblical criticism and a nervous jealousy for the inerrant autographs theory, a preoccupation of his critique.

CHAPTER FIVE

The Prologue of John and the Egyptian Manuscripts: John 1:18 as a Case Study in the Canonical Approach

I. INTRODUCTION

This essay has as its goal a very specific application of the method of exegesis advocated by Brevard Childs, and termed by him the "canonical approach." As a post-critical means of explicating "Biblical theology," I will be applying the method to a rather controversial text critical problem in John's prologue by which means I hope to give a concrete demonstration of how I see the method possibly operating within the New Testament regarding textual variants specifically .

Because the canonical approach supposes, rather demands, a full interplay with all applicable methods of historical criticism, prior to offering a canonical solution, I will provide a thorough-going text critical analysis of the pertinent data pertaining to Jn. 1:18. This will prove to be the least interesting dimension of the paper, but is obviously the foundation on which the remainder of the essay will build. I will then offer an history of exegesis of the passage in question, which should provide a much greater insight into the how and why of contemporary text critical consensus on the possible variants at this place (a method, I might add, not always employed in a traditional text critical study). Only then will I make application of the canonical solution. At the end of the exercise one will either more fully understand the method, and appreciatively take its benefits; or else one will have all the more reason to disapprove of it as an aspect of modern Biblical exegesis. I doubt that there will be much room for indifference.

II. Text Critical Data and Analysis

It will not be the purpose of this study to broach the topic of source criticism,[1] or the relationship of proto-Gnosticism/ pre-Christian Gnosticism[2] to the author, or composition of the fourth Gospel.[3] Although I acknowledge the impossibility of separating source from text criticism,[4] this study will deal exclusively with possible Gnostic influences on the transmitted text of the favourite Gospel within the Gnostic faith communities.[5] In the Greek MSS. the variants are as follows[6]:

μονογενὴς θεός
ὁ μονογενὴς θεός
ὁ μονογενὴς υἱός[7]

---

[1]The classic work in this area is still Rudolph Bultmann, *The Gospel of John: A Commentary* Trans. by G. R. Beasley-Murray (Philadelphia: The Westminster Press, 1971).

[2]On these definitions see Edwin Yamauchi, *Pre-Christian Gnosticism* (London: Tyndale Press, 1973); R. McL. Wilson, "Slippery Words II: Gnosis, Gnostic, Gnosticism," *Expository Times* 89 (1977/78), pp. 296–301; *Gnosis and the New Testament* (Oxford: Basil Blackwell, 1968). Kurt Rudolph, "'Gnosis and 'Gnosticism'-the Problems of Their Definition and Their Relation to the Writings of the New Testament" in *The New Testament and Gnosis*, ed. by A. H. B. Logan and A.J.M. Wedderburn (Edinburgh: T. & T Clark, 1983).

[3]See Edwin Yamauchi, "Pre-Christian Gnosticism, The New Testament and Nag Hammadi in Recent Debate," *Themelios*, Vol. 10, No. 1 (September 1984): 22–27, for a good up-date on this issue.

[4]Although there seems to be a resistance to this in the N.T. Textual Criticism Section of the SBL. Note Frank Wheeler's disapprobation of combining source and text criticism, "The Text of Mark 14:65 (Matt. 26:68; Lk. 22:64)-Markan Priority and Text Critical Methodology" Paper presented to SBL November 22, 1986.

[5]An earlier study addressing this variant, Paul R. McReynolds, "John 1:18 in Textual Variation and Translation", in *New Testament Textual Criticism: Its Significance for Exegesis* (Oxford: Oxford University Press, 1981), took no note at all of possible Gnostic influences on this variant.

[6]Paul R. McReynold's essay, *op. cit.*, provides the most comprehensive listing of the evidence and I freely employ it here, while also supplementing it with the UBS[4] critical apparatus.

[7]There are two other readings, μονογενὴς υἱός θεοῦ found in the old Latin q, the co[sa], and in Irenaeus[lat] and Ambrose[vid]; and ὁ μονογενὴς, found in the vg[x gat] and in the Diatessaron. Here I must be quick to add, that on a purely the-

The first two readings are found in the old Egyptian witnesses (e.g. μονογενὴς θεός: p⁶⁶ ℵ* B C* L; ὁ μονογενὴς θεός: p⁷⁵, ℵ², 33), while the last reading, ὁ μονογενὴς υἱός, is that found in the Ecclesiastical, or Byzantine witnesses, i.e. the vast majority of the Greek manuscripts and all the lectionaries used in the liturgy of the Eastern Church.

What I shall call the θεός readings have, indeed, early Greek manuscript attestation. Moreover, while μονογενὴς θεός also has early patristic evidence (Valentinians c.170, Irenaeus[lat] 202, Clement d. 215, Origen d. 254, Eusebius 339, Serapion 361, Basil 379, Didymus 398, Gregory-Nyssa d. 394, Epiphanius d. 403, Cyril-Alexandria d. 444: *a total of eleven writers with thirty-nine citations*, though some show a knowledge of the υἱός reading as well), and versional evidence (cop[bo], syr[p], [hmg], eth[ro]),[8] ὁ μονογενὴς θεός has neither, and so will not demand further attention. Hence, the debate is between ὁ μονογενὴς θεός, and ὁ μονογενὴς υἱός.

The υἱός reading also has early and wide-spread patristic evidence ([Irenaeus] 2nd cen., Hippolytus d. 235, [Clement] d. 215, [Origen[lat]] d. 254, Hymenaeus c.270, Alexander-Alex. d. 328, Eustathius d. 337, Ps-Dion. Alex. 3rd c.?, Eusebius d. 339 Serapion d. 362, Julian d. 363, Athanasius d. 373, Basil d. 379, Pseudo-Basil 4th c.?, Gregory-Naz. d. 390, [Gregory-Nyssa,] late 4th c., Pseudo-Athanasius 4th c., Chrysostom d. 407, Theodore-Mops d.428, Hadrian 5th c., [Cyril-Alex.] 5th c., Proclus d. 446, Nestorius d. 451, Theodoret d. 446: *twenty plus fathers with forty plus citations*.[9]

The υἱός reading has witnesses nearly as early as θεός (most scholars agree both readings go back to the second century),

---

oretical basis, I must grant my rigorous eclectic friends the possibility that such minority readings could be original.

[8]While McReynolds has the cop[bo] reading μονογενὴς θεός, UBS⁴ has it reading ὁ μονογενὴς θεός.

[9]The reason the Egyptian reading has less patristic support, but nearly as many citations as the received reading, is because McReynolds has allowed allusions and non-direct references to this reading to be counted while disallowing this for the received reading, but provides his rationale for doing so. This was a major point of contention during the nineteenth-century stage of the debate surrounding this passage, *op. cit.*, p. 107–08, n. 9.

and twice as many fathers have υἱός as have θεός. Of the number of twenty supporting υἱός, seventeen "support no other reading" (the vast majority).[10] But what I should like to stress at this point is the pedigree of the witnesses. While the θεός reading has the earliest patristic witness, it happens to be among the Valentinian Gnostics. While the θεός reading is used exclusively by Athanasius.

The versional evidence for the υἱός reading is rather impressive: it^{pl}, vg, syr^{c,h,pal}, arm, eth^{pp}, geo., slav. That is, it is found in one of the very earliest Syriac versions and is at the very heart of Western catholic ecclesiastical usage, as witnessed by nearly all of the old Latin and all of the Vulgate witnesses, but two. Added to the witness of the Byzantine Greek MSS and lectionaries of the Greek Church, one finds in this variant the comprehensive and exclusive affirmation of both Eastern and Western ecclesiastical traditions. This was, in fact, the "received reading," in the very widest sense of the concept.

III. GNOSTIC USE OF THE GOSPEL OF JOHN

In light of the recently discovered Coptic Nag Hammadi Library[11] we now have an entire corpus of texts, many of which are "gospels,"[12] attempting to expand the original, mostly Jewish influenced *Kerygma,*[13] to encompass what has been referred

---

[10]McReynolds, *op. cit*, p. 110.

[11]*The Nag Hammadi Library in English*, trans. by members of the Coptic Gnostic Library Project of the Institute for Antiquity and Christianity (San Francisco: Harper and Row, 1977, rev. ed. 1988).

[12]On types of Apocryphal Gospels see Edgar Hennecke, *New Testament Apocrypha*, ed. by Wilhelm Schneemelcher, Vol. 1, (Philadelphia: The Westminster Press, 1963, rev. ed. 1991), pp. 80–531; and J.K. Elliott's valuable *The Apocryphal New Testament: A Collection of Apocryphal Christian Literature in an English Translation based on M.R. James* (Oxford: Clarendon Press, 1993) for fresh translations at times based on more recent critical texts with an excellent, up-to-date bibliography on apocryphal literature.

[13]See Raymond E. Brown, *The Gospel According to John*, 2 Vols. (Garden City: Doubleday and Company; 1966) for an important source stressing Jewish influ-

to as "the acute Hellenization of Christianity" (Harnack), more of the *Zeitgeist* of the age (Jonas), or, the disenchanted, Jewish, apocalyptic expectation (Robert Grant)—in short, what has come to be known as the various schools of Gnosticism. And while much has been said regarding the possible Gnostic sources employed in the composition of John's Gospel, little has been said regarding the Gnostic influences on the finished, canonical book as it was employed within Gnostic communities, along side the Coptic Gnostic corpus.

Extant Gnostic sources revealing the prominent place John the son of Zebedee played within Gnosticism are: *The Apocryphon of John*;[14] portions of the earliest commentary on John by the Valentinian Heracleon as found in Origen's commentary of the same Gospel; another Valentinian commentary on John's prologue by Ptolemy, some of which can be found in Irenaeus's *Against Heresies*; and finally, Hippolytus preserves the fact that the Valentinian Naassenes and Peratae referred to John to the near exclusion of the synoptics. Elaine Pagels noted that the Valentinians "used [John] so extensively that Irenaeus says that to refute their teaching he has been compelled to refute their false exegesis of John. . . ."[15]

If, however, the canonical Gospels—even John—were not enough to capture the full Gnostic myth, thus precipitating the distinctively Gnostic Coptic literature, certainly we might expect the Gnostics to modify the canonical books bringing them into line with their major motifs.[16] Short of explicit statements

---

ences on John's Gospel. Also, see D.A. Carson, "Recent Literature on the Fourth Gospel: Some Reflections," *Themelios*, Vol. 9, No. 1 (September, 1983): 8–18, for a good survey of much literature on this and other aspects of John's Gospel.

[14]*Nag Hammadi*, pp. 98–116; *New Testament Apocrypha*, pp. 314–331.

[15]Elaine H. Pagels, *The Johannine Gospel in Gnostic Exegesis* (Nashville: Abingdon Press, 1973), p. 16.

[16]There are studies showing the possible *de*-Christianizing of originally Christian Gnostic texts, as well as the *Christianizing* of purely Gnostic texts. See Martin Krause, "The Christianization of Gnostic Texts," in *The New Testament and Gnosis*.

from the heresiologists how would one know a Gnostic-created variant if one saw one, especially in John?

As a matter of fact we do have evidence from Origen[17] that Heracleon[18] altered John's Gospel in the Prologue:

> It was, I consider, a violent and unwarranted procedure which was adopted by Heracleon, the friend as it is said, of Valentinus, in discussing this sentence: "All things were made through Him." For he says that the aeon (age) and the things in it, were not made by the Logos; he considers them to have come into existence before the Logos. He deals with the statement "without Him was nothing made," with some degree of audacity, nor is he afraid of the warning [Proverbs 30:6]: "Add not to his words, lest he find thee out and thou prove a liar," for to the "nothing" he adds: "Of what is in the world and the creation."[19]

Here we find Heracleon emending the text before him in order to differentiate the Logos from the Ultimate Creator (ὁ θεός). This incensed Origen (who was not above offering rather dramatic conjectural emendations when it suited his own theological *a priori* beliefs),[20] because clearly, Heracleon's emendation is "obviously very much forced and in the face of the evidence . . . has no inner probability to recommend it."[21]

Is it possible that there are other Gnostic emendations not detected by Origen (or by the heresiologists); or perhaps just not contested by them, either because they caused no problem theologically, or because they became familiar by their early entry into certain MSS? A look at the Coptic MSS may provide a clue.

---

[17]Origen's, Commentary on John in *The Ante-Nicene Fathers*, Vol. 10, P. 331.

[18]The extant comments of Heracleon on John can be found in Robert M. Grant, ed., *Gnosticism: A Source Book of Heretical Writings from the Early Christian Period* (New York: Harper and Brothers, 1961), pp. 195–208.

[19]Origen, *op. cit.* This could have been a mere gloss on the part of Heracleon, but Origen's invoking of Proverbs 30:6 seems to indicate that at least Origen interpreted this alteration as an actual conjectural emendation on the part of Heracleon.

[20]See his comments on Matt. 19:19 *Origenes Werke*, Vol. 10, pp. 385–388.

[21]Origen, *Commentary on John*, p. 331.

IV. COPTIC MANUSCRIPTS OF THE GOSPEL OF JOHN: THEIR INFLUENCE ON THE GREEK MSS

It was once thought that there was no N.T. text in the Bohairic dialect of northern Egypt until the seventh century, but with the discovery of a semi-Bohairic fragment of the book of Philippians and the Bodmer papyrus of the Gospel of John, we now know that such translations existed by the fourth century. Of interest in this inquiry is the fact that this Bodmer MS of John's Gospel is believed to have been produced by a Gnostic scribe, and as such probably served in a Gnostic community.[22]

The Sahidic version is dated by most critics at the third or fourth century. If others are correct that it is as early as the second half of the second century, it is certainly one of our earliest versional witnesses of an early form of text found in the southern part of Egypt.[23]

Herman C. Hoskier, who provided the world with the most exhaustive collation ever attempted of the two oldest Greek uncials (Codices B and Aleph, both of the mid-fourth century), came to the conclusion that both uncials were produced in Egypt and were much affected by bilingual texts containing a Coptic translation.[24] Hence, based on this first-hand data, while everyone else before him was pushing the date of the Bohairic version up into the seventh century, Hoskier, standing nearly alone, made bold to claim it was much earlier, a claim now accepted with the discovery of the Bodmer MS of John.[25]

Hoskier provides examples of no less than 78 places, in the Gospel of John alone, where he believes either B, or Aleph, or both, have been brought into conformity to the Coptic versions.[26] One interesting example is at 16:19, regarding the influence of the Sahidic on the old Egyptian Greek papyrus frag-

---

[22]Bruce M. Metzger, *The Early Versions of the New Testament* (Oxford: Clarendon Press, 1977), p. 125.

[23]*Ibid.*, p. 127.

[24]Herman C. Hoskier, *Codex B and Its Allies: A Study and an Indictment* Vol. 1 (London: Bernard Quaritch, 1914), p. 7

[25]Metzger, *op. cit.*, p. 125. n.9

[26]Hoskier, *op. cit.*, pp. 317–325.

ment, p^{75}. The Greek papyrus says the Rich Young Ruler's name was Neves.[27] The Sahidic says his name was Nineve, probably from an old Egyptian folk-tale, with a character whose name was Nineve, which in Sahidic means, "nobody."[28] In John 8:57, p^{75}, along with Aleph and the Sahidic, reads ἑώρακέν σε, rather than as the vast majority of other witnesses which read ἑώρακας.

Examples of possible Gnostic influence on the Coptic Bodmer Papyrus of John have been detected by its editor.[29] Note the Gnostic-like use of the word "Truth" (Jn. 5:33; Jn 18:37; Jn 8:34) and the substitution of the word "Truth" for the word "righteousness" (Jn 16:8 and 16:10), in this document.

Ruffis L. Moretz, in an important dissertation written under K.W. Clark, discovered no less than six hundred variants in the oldest Coptic MSS which find no corresponding reading in any Greek MS.[30] Furthermore, Moretz discovered that while the oldest Coptic texts have an affinity with B and p^{75} when they do agree, the Coptic has a slightly greater affinity with p^{75}, which is even earlier than the Egyptian B. This may mean a nearer and earlier link with the Coptic. Moretz seems not to draw the same conclusion, perhaps because he is uninformed regarding Hoskier's data.[31]

There are further examples illustrating a possible Gnostic influence on the old Egyptian uncials and papyri, via the use of

---

[27]See NA^{26} at Lk. 16:19.

[28]K. Grobel, "Whose Name Was Neves," *New Testament Studies*, Vol. 10 (1964): 381–382. Note also Metzger's theory, *The Text of the New Testament*, p. 42.

[29]Metzger, *The Early Versions*, p. 125. This should not seem unusual given the strong Egyptian tendency toward religious syncretism. Furthermore, C.J. Bleeker and others, maintain, "Christian gnosticism arrived there [in Egypt] earlier than the orthodox church." "The Egyptian Background of Gnosticism" in *Le Origini Dello Gnosticismo*, (Leiden: E.J. Brill, 1967), p. 229. Moreover, Bleeker has shown that Gnosticism itself is quite indebted to ancient Egyptian religion. Hence, Coptic, the language native to Egyptian religion, would have priority in giving expression to a belief system, just as Latin took primacy in the Western Church. See also Birger Pearson's *Gnosticism, Judaism, and Egyptian Christianity* (Minneapolis: Fortress, 1990).

[30]Rufus L. Moretz, *The Textual Affinity of the Earliest Coptic Manuscripts of the Gospel of John*, unpublished Ph.D. dissertation, Duke University, 1969, pp. 182–184.

[31]Moretz does not list Hoskier's valuable study in his bibliography.

Coptic versions by Gnostic communities. In the Gospel of John there appears to be a collusion between the Coptic texts of John and the Greek Egyptian witnesses, especially regarding Aleph, which Hoskier felt had been produced in an Egyptian scriptorium.[32] For example, the Valentinian Gnostics did not regard Jesus as the Son of God; rather, he was the Logos come to manifest the Father and the Son in the material world. In the following places in John (and once in Mark) the reading "Son of God" has been altered to "God's Chosen One," "Holy One of God," "Son of Man," or the words are just left out all together (Mk.1:1; Jn. 1:34; Jn. 6:69; Jn. 9:35).

At these places Aleph and p^{75} are in agreement with the Sahidic version, but for Mk. 1:1 and Jn. 1:34, where Aleph stands alone.

The reason Gnostic scribes would have altered these passages in their scripture, whether the Coptic MSS, or the Greek, can be found in the Gnostic understanding of the prologue of John's Gospel.

V. GNOSTIC EXEGESIS OF JOHN'S PROLOGUE

Elaine Pagels published a detailed study of the extant Gnostic exegetical works on John's Gospel.[33] She notes that while some Gnostics formulated new Gospels to down-play the significance of the earthly Jesus, others used "their spiritual exegesis to demonstrate the 'error' of literal reading and to raise the reader's consciousness to the level of symbolic interpretation."[34] Still others, as we have already shown from Origen's comments on Heracleon, did not always find a "symbolic interpretation" enough, and so emended the text to make it conform to a Gnostic theme.

Jacqueline A. Williams has produced another important study treating specifically the Valentinian interpretation of the

---

[32]H.C. Hoskier, *Concerning the Date of the Bohairic Version* (London: Bernard Quartch, 1911), p. 14.

[33]See footnote 15 for reference.

[34]Pagels, *Gnostic Exegesis*, p. 14.

Gnostic *Gospel of Truth*, in her *Biblical Interpretation in the Gnostic Gospel of Truth from Nag Hammadi*, (Atlanta: Scholars Press, 1988). She, too, came to the same assessment as Pagels on Valentinus's exegetical practice: "Valentinus' use of texts is intriguing because he never quotes them verbatim. . . ." Furthermore, in answering the question, has he been faithful to his texts, she answers,

> On one level the answer is obviously no. Characteristic changes, such as a shift of topic from Christ to Father, demonstrate the degree of liberty which Valentinus has taken with texts. Thus, the nature of the changes made by Valentinus precludes a faithful understanding of the intentions of their authors.[35]

Pagels notes a very important theme within Valentinian Gnosticism, alluded to already. For the Valentinians, "not only is the visible logos *not* the Monogenes, but he is separated from him by whole realms of being.[36] That is, the logos of John's prologue *is not* the only begotten Son of God.

The *Excerpta Ex Theodoto* expands on this theme:

> And he who remained "Only Begotten Son in the bosom of the Father" explains Thought to the Aeons through Knowledge, just as if he had also been put forth from his bosom; but him who appeared here, the Apostle no longer calls "Only-Begotten," but "as Only-Begotten," "Glory as of an Only-Begotten."[37]

And as for the mystical significance of the term, "Son" (or by

---

[35]Jacqueline A. Williams, *Biblical Interpretation in the Gnostic Gospel of Truth from Nag Hammadi*, (Atlanta: Scholars Press, 1988), p. 189. She treats a parallel with John 1:18 on pp. 75–77, but makes no comment regarding the origin of the variant μονογενής θεός. She in fact prefers the reading μονογενής υἱός because she finds an otherwise insignificant parallel with *The Gospel of Truth* 24:9–14 (A²). Ironically, she seems to be oblivious to the theological significance of the two variants. In fairness it must also be pointed out that while not everyone will accept all of his examples Bart Ehrman has, nevertheless, demonstrated that the orthodox, too, were not always faithful to the documents before them and that alterations were made that were doctrinally motivated, *The Orthodox Corruption of Scripture*, pp. 275–283.

[36]*Ibid.*, p. 37.

extension, "Son of God") Valentinus's own *Gospel of Truth* makes this explicit:

> Now the name of the Father is the Son. It is he who first gave a name to the one who came forth from him, who was himself and he begot him as a son. He gave him his name which belonged to him; he is the one to whom belongs all that exists around him, the Father. His is the name; his is the Son. It is possible for him to be seen. But the name is invisible because it alone is the mystery of the invisible which comes to ears that are completely filled with it. For indeed the Father's name is not spoken, but it is apparent through a son.[38]

Hence, we see the prohibition on speaking the Father's name, i.e. "Son," which is reserved for the ears of those initiated.

Clearly, then, two decisive themes for the Valentinians were (1) to differentiate, especially in the prologue, between the Son, who remains in the bosom of the Father and never becomes incarnate, and the Logos, who enters the material world to communicate the Father and the Son; (2) the name of the Father, i.e. "Son of God," was not to be spoken and so was a mystery reserved for the initiated only. This certainly could explain the kind of changes noted above.

Furthermore, one of the major points defended by both Clement and Irenaeus[39] was the *identification* of the Son and the Logos as the same person. Yet, they make no attempt to challenge μονογενὴς θεός, the variant at 1:18 which, I will argue, allows for a separation between the Logos and the Son. Why?

In Clement's case the answer is simple. His Christology was in some ways not that different from the Valentinians, holding to a subordinationist position. Pagels notes that for Clement, "The

---

[37]The *Excerpta Ex Theodoto of Clement of Alexandria*, Trans. and ed. by Robert Pierce Casey, (London: Christophers, 1934), p. 45.

[38]*Nag Hammadi*, p. 47. Note also William Judson Vaughan III, *The Concept of Seeing God in the Gospel of John*, unpublished Ph.D. dissertation, The Southern Baptist Theological Seminary, 1971, "Unlike the Gospel of John, in which Father and Son are clearly differentiated, *The Gospel of Thomas* and *The Gospel of Truth* present the Son as but the emanation of the Father," p. 20.

[39]Pagels, *op. cit.*, pp. 38–46.

logos's very definition as logos-theos involves his distinction from 'the God' (ὁ θεός)."[40] The same holds true for Origen. Irenaeus may have found a way to give an orthodox twist to the otherwise peculiar reading. Hence, none of them draws attention to the variants at Jn. 1:18. But eventually the reading became suspect and was deleted from the ecclesiastical texts and lectionaries.

VI. JOHN 1:18 AND THE HISTORY OF EXEGESIS IN THE PATRISTIC ERA

Is it possible that the language wholly uncharacteristic of John (or, one should say, uncharacteristic of the entire N.T.), μονογενὴς θεός, could be a Valentinian emendation to protect both the distinction between the Son and the Logos—both of which were divine, the latter to a lesser extent—and perhaps to also preserve the name "Son" from public use (Pagels tells us that Heracleon's commentary was "to be read by 'non-initiates'")?[41] Neither Clement nor Origen would have balked at the reading, although both of these fathers employ both variants and sometimes, as Origen, within the same work.[42] According to both Irenaeus and Clement, however, the Egyptian reading, μονογενὴς θεός, was that used by the Valentinians.[43]

Furthermore, this was the reading preferred by Arius. In fact, Ezra Abbot, the Unitarian who did a great deal of research on this reading in the nineteenth-century, notes:

> The Arians who laid great stress on the fact that the Father was "unbegotten" and "without beginning," ἀγέαητος and (ἄναρχος, were fond of calling the Son "the only-begotten God," because, while the term expressed his high dignity, it

---

[40]*Ibid.*, p. 39.

[41]*Ibid.*, p. 18.

[42]Origen's *Commentary on John.*

[43]Irenaeus, *Adversus Haereses* I, 8,5; *cf.* also I, 9, 1–5. Clement, *Excerpta Ex Theodoto* 6, 2.

brought into view his derived existence. Begotten by an act of God's will, he could not, they argued, be eternal.[44]

Abbott also noted that some "orthodox" also employed the Egyptian reading on occasion, but Faustinus and Victorinus-Rome resorted specifically to the received reading in their disputes with the Arians. Athanasius himself is never found employing the Egyptian reading, but exclusively the received reading.[45] Abbott assesses the evidence for these two readings as follows:

> On a review of the external evidence it will be seen that the MSS which reads [sic] θεός are of the highest rank, though few in number, weighty authorities, but not decisive; while the testimony of the ancient versions and the quotations of the passages of the Christian fathers, decidedly favor υἱός. We trace both readings to the second century; but we find θεός supported almost wholly by one class of authorities, the Alexandrian or Egyptian; while the witnesses for υἱός are far more widely diffused as well as far more numerous, representing all quarters of the Christian world. The whole Western Church seems to have known no other reading.[46]

What saith Bultmann on this score? Bultmann is the one scholar in the twentieth-century who has perhaps done the most in discussing the relationship of Gnosticism to the N.T. and he has devoted a commentary to John's Gospel. On this point, however, Bultmann is sadly perfunctory and less than helpful. He sees no theological import to the Egyptian variant within Gnostic exegetical understanding of the prologue. He

---

[44]Ezra Abbot, "On the reading 'only Begotten God,' in John 1:18; with particular reference to the statements of Dr. Tregelles," *Bibliotheca Sacra* Vol. 18, (1861): 840–872. Note also H.A. Blair's argument that it was in fact, Valentinus's Christology that precipitated the classic Arian Christology, H.A. Blair, "Valentinus and the Arian Christ," *Church Quarterly Review* Vol. 148 (1949): 1–16. I find this study much more historically compelling than Robert Gregg's and Dennis Groh's *Early Arianism—A View of Salvation* (Philadelphia, 1981), *cf.* p. 93.

[45]UBS[4] Jn. 1:18.

[46]Ezra Abbot, "On the reading 'an Only Begotten God' or 'God Only-Begotten,'" John 1:18, *Unitarian Review*, (June 1875): 567.

dismisses the Egyptian reading in a footnote because "υἱός is what the Evangelist always writes."[47] He feels the Egyptian reading was simply the result of an error of dictation.

The question arises, if the Egyptian reading fell out of use in the Greek texts produced from about the 4th century on (after the ascendancy of Nicene christology), how is it that the reading was revived in the 19th century, thus prompting Ezra Abbott, the Unitarian, to crusade against the Egyptian reading, which one would expect him to be defending if it had a history of offering support for a heterodox, or, indeed, an heretical, non-Trinitarian christology?

VII. THE NINETEENTH CENTURY DEBATE REGARDING JOHN 1:18

With the discovery and/or collation of the old Egyptian uncials during the nineteenth century, the debate regarding the correct reading of Jn 1:18 was begun in earnest. Ironically, however, it was not the radical German critics who cried to have the Egyptian reading restored to the text. It was the mild, and pious Plymouth Brethren disciple, Samuel Prideaux Tregelles.[48] Prior to Tregelles's edition of the Greek NT, produced in six parts during 1857–1872, not one edition of the published Greek New Testament, since the invention of printing, had printed the Egyptian reading as the correct text. Why did this conservative evangelical want to restore the Egyptian reading?

To go into great detail on this here would take us far afield. To summarize a conclusion I arrived at in my own Ph.D. dissertation research treating Tregelles should, however, help to throw light on this question.[49] By the mid-Victorian era the two old

---

[47]Rudolf Bultmann, *The Gospel of John*, p. 81, n. 2.

[48]Samuel Prideaux Tregelles, *An Account of the Printed Text of the Greek New Testament* (London: Samuel Bagster & Sons, 1854.), pp. 234–35.

[49]*From Sacred Text to Religious Text: An Intellectual History of the Impact of Erasmian Lower Criticism on Dogma as a Contribution to the English Enlightenment and the Victorian Crisis of Faith*, unpublished Ph.D. dissertation, the University of Edinburgh, 1995, pending publication. See chapter 9, "Samuel P.

Egyptian uncials which Tregelles and nearly all other text critics were following, offered the most ancient evidence to that date of a very early form of the Greek N.T. Both MSS conspired between them in omitting two of the *loci classici* in defense of the deity of Christ, namely, I John 5:7–8, and I Timothy 3:16. This left the ranks rather thin in this department. The Egyptian variant at John 1:18 referred to the "only begotten god," and so Tregelles, and other orthodox, believed that what the old uncials had taken away with one hand, they had also given back with the other, in this apparent fresh proof text for Christ's deity. It took the Unitarian Abbot to remind Tregelles, and others, of the second to fourth-century exegetical tradition surrounding the Egyptian variant.

No doubt Tregelles's conservative theological tradition prompted the Unitarian Abbot to challenge Tregelles's arguments supporting the Egyptian reading, since the latter was certain that the θεός reading served the cause of orthodoxy.[50] Abbot, on the other hand, seemed not to be aware of the reading's possible link to Gnosticism since Gnostic studies were still in their infancy at this time, though he was aware of an Arian connection. Yet, Abbot is also aware that some orthodox used the Egyptian reading (e.g. Clement, Origen, Irenaeus, *et al.*) which gave some degree of comfort to Tregelles's cause. So, Abbot launched a major attack on Tregelles's interpretation and grasp of the data.

This challenge by Abbot was met by an even more astute advocacy of the Egyptian reading, coming from the orthodox Fenton John Anthony Hort's "On ΜΟΝΟΓΕΝΗΣ ΘΕΟΣ in Scripture and Tradition," (1876).[51] Here Hort showed himself

---

Tregelles, Constantine Tischendorf and Samuel Davidson: Mid-Century, Non-Conformist Adjustments and the Dismantling of the Second Phase of the Ideology of Harmless Engagement."

[50]See Abbot's rather self-serving disclaimer not to be questioning Tregelles's dogmatism, *Bibliotheca Sacra*, p. 844.

[51]F.J.A. Hort, *Two Dissertations* (Cambridge and London: Macmillan and Co., 1872) pp. v–72. Patrick, in a recent biographical sketch of Hort says these two essays were exercises produced for the two degrees, B.D., and D.D., which Hort received in 1875. Graham A. Patrick, *F.J. A. Hort Eminent Victorian*

an authority on this particular controversial passage. His inquiry on the subject was prompted by another essay he wrote at about the same time "*On the 'Constantinopolitan' Creed and other Eastern Creeds of the Fourth Century*" (1876).[52]

In the latter essay his goal was to establish that μονογενὴς θεός was found in the earliest form of the emerging Nicene Creed, which he argued came from Caesarea. If this were the case it would then also prove that μονογενὴς θεός was original to John's prologue.[53] His desire to prove this point led him into the most tendentious treatment of the evidence.

Fully aware that the Valentinian association is the earliest association with the θεός reading, rather than offer a plausible explanation for why this is the case by refuting the possibility that it originated in this community, he is content merely to assert to the contrary. In fact, the degree of his sensitivity to the strength of the case against his own position can be measured by the equal force of the emphatic tone he employs in his numerous assertions to the contrary:

> The always questionable suggestion of dogmatic alteration *is peculiarly out of place here* . . . (emphasis mine).[54]
>
> . . . among [the Valentinians] whom *by mere accident* we first meet with this and other important verses of John, θεός could be *only an awkward appendage* . . . (emphasis mine).[55]
>
> . . . the Valentinians of Clement take it up *for a moment*, make a *kind of use of it* as a *transitional step* [emphasis all mine] explaining how St. John came to give the predicate θεός (in i 1) to *Logos*, whom they anxiously distinguish from *Monogenes (Arche)*, and then pass on to their own proper view, in which Sonship alone appears as the characteristic mark of *Monogenes* . . .[56]

(Sheffield: The Almond Press, 1988), p. 66. This information was in turn derived from I.M. Bubb's *The Theology of F.J.A. Hort, in Relation to Nineteenth Century Thought*, unpublished Ph.D. dissertation, University of Manchester, Manchester, England, 1956.

[52]Hort, *ibid.*.

[53]*Ibid.*, pp. 54–72.

[54]*Ibid.*, p. 9.

[55]*Ibid.*

[56]*Ibid.*

. . . the Valentinians of Irenaeus...[believed that St. John used θεός in Jn. 1:1 to distinguish] *Arche* (=*son*) and *Logos* . . .[57]

Nevertheless, in spite of all that Hort is here forced to concede against his own position, he concludes,

> [n]either in the Valentinian nor in any other known Gnostical system *could there have been any temptation to invent such a combination as* μονογενὴς θεός (emphasis mine).[58]

The fact that the very old evidence for θεός is exclusively Egyptian, is met with the assertion that:

> No . . . suspiciousness attaches to the combination of authorities which read θεός. . . . [T]heir concordance marks a primitive transmission uncorrupted by local alteration.[59]

The fact that υἱός is found in one of the earliest Syriac versions and in nearly all of the old Latin, and certainly in nearly all the *Vulgata*, is interpreted by Hort in the following manner:

> That the Old Syriac has υἱός is quite natural, when it has so many early 'Western' readings. . . . Among early versions . . . the invaluable Memphitic [the Coptic Bohairic version] more than balances the Old Latin and Old Syriac, which so often concur against BCL Memph. in *wrong readings of high antiquity*" [emphasis mine].[60]

One could go on to draw attention to the fact that this

---

[57] *Ibid.*

[58] *Ibid.*

[59] *Ibid.*, p. 8. Here we have the seedling of what would become Hort's theory of a "Neutral Text" having been preserved in the Egyptian uncials. Hort's remarks here are simply not tenable in light of Origen's comments, highlighted earlier, regarding intentional regional corruptions, which Hort would have known, and in light of the earlier mentioned studies surveying Valentinus's textual practices. Moreover, Bart Ehrman's magisterial study, *The Orthodox Corruption of Scripture*, alluded to earlier, has forever silenced the debate regarding the possibility of the transmission of a "neutral text."

[60] Hort, *Ibid.*, p. 7.

"Western" corruption is further substantiated, in Hort's argument, by the fact that fathers "with a predominantly Western type of text,"[61] support the υἱός reading; but why the Latin edition of the Western father Irenaeus supports θεός once (and once as μονογενὴς υἱός θεός), he does not venture to answer.

While all of this has the feel of question begging and special pleading the real weakness of this aspect of his position is further compounded by the fact that the contemporary discipline of text criticism has given up Hort's notion that all but the "Western non-interpolation" "Western" readings are corruptions, thus leaving his arguments sounding painfully dated.[62]

Just prior to the publishing of Hort's essay on the subject, another Unitarian, James Drummond, entered the debate, adding further support to Abbot's arguments.[63]

From all appearances it looked as though the orthodox text critics were all holding to the Egyptian reading simply because the word "θεός" appeared in the text as a referent to Christ.

For this reason, though the Unitarians could not convince the orthodox of the dubious nature of the latter's new proof text, they felt the need, nevertheless, to challenge this apparently misappropriated text now being used in the service of orthodoxy. They did this by rallying the cause of the theologically weaker (from the orthodox perspective) variant υἱός. The Unitarian preference for υἱός then only reinforced orthodoxy's defenders of the rightness of their exegesis of μονογενὴς θεός, thus bringing the received reading into a negative "guilt-by-as-

---

[61]Hort, *Ibid.*

[62]In 1942 Büchsel made the argument in Kittel's *Theologisches Wörterbuch,* s.v. "μονογενής," that Hippolytus's use of υἱός means it could not have been a product of the Latin Bible. He went on to conclude that μονογενὴς θεός could only be rendered as "an only-begotten God," a Gnostic-influenced emendation, intended to soften monotheism within Gnostic circles. I am indebted to, I.M. Bubb's *The Theology of F.J.A. Hort,* for this reference. Finally, Hort seems also to have lost his argument regarding the Nicene Creed coming from Caesarea, see Bubb, *op. cit.* pp. 293–302.

[63]James Drummond, "The Reading μονογενὴς θεός 'The Only Begotten Son', in John 1:18," *The Theological Review* Vol. 8, No. 35 (October 1871): 468–495. Also note Adolf Harnack's affirming review of Hort's essay as found in *Theologische Literaturzeitung* (1876): 541 *ff.*

sociation" relationship with those who did not hold to the high orthodoxy of the Nicene era. All of this is highly ironic.

The greater irony still, however, is that the father who was the architect of this high orthodoxy, Athanasius, never employed the Egyptian reading; his followers responded to the Arians with the received reading; and the Egyptian reading itself, in light of modern Gnostic studies, seems to have arisen from the Valentinians, who did not even believe the Son and the Logos to be the same entity.

Some of the nineteenth-century orthodox did resist the Egyptian reading, such as Henry Alford, whose edition of the Greek N.T. appeared over the years 1849–71;[64] Christopher Wordsworth in his edition of the Greek N.T. (1860–1869);[65] Frederick Henry Ambrose Scrivener (1813–1891);[66] and finally, John William Burgon (1813–1888).[67]

Burgon, in fact, so far as I can tell, was the first English scholar to suggest openly the connection between the Egyptian reading and the Valentinians.[68] Because his other arguments, however, appeared to most to be hopelessly biased with a theological agenda, his data were little noticed over the years. Nevertheless, he became one of the leading patristics scholars within N.T. text critical studies during the nineteenth century. He compiled the largest index of patristic scripture citations ever amassed (though the citations are obviously not always from the most critical editions of the Fathers). In the words of F.F. Bruce, no friend of Burgon's opinions,

> Dr. [sic] John William Burgon, Dean of Chichester from 1876 till his death in 1888 . . . was an able textual scholar in his

---

[64]Henry Alford, *The Greek Testament* 4 vols. (London: Rivingtons, 1849–71), vol. 1, p. 622.

[65]Christopher Wordsworth, *The New Testament of Our Lord and Saviour Jesus Christ in the Original Greek* (London: Rivingtons, 1860–1869), p. 273.

[66]F.H.A.Scrivener, *A Plain Introduction to the Criticism of the New Testament* 3rd ed. (Cambridge: Deighton Bell and Co., 1883), p. 605.

[67]John William Burgon, *The Causes of the Corruption of the Traditional Text of the Holy Gospels Vindicated* (London: George Bell and Sons, 1896), pp. 215–218.

[68]*Ibid.*

own right, and was actually ahead of his time in his appreciation of the importance for textual criticism of biblical citations in early Christian lectionaries. In both the areas of study he did much valuable pioneer work.[69]

Nevertheless, these few voices were silenced by the epochal edition of Westcott and Hort.[70] In turn, the Princetonian, B. B. Warfield, brought the Egyptian reading acceptance among the orthodox in America by way of the first handbook on the discipline published in North America, which was based on Westcott and Hort's *Introduction*.[71]

VIII. THE CONTEMPORARY DISCUSSION

During this century the Egyptian reading has prevailed within text critical circles, but not without its dissenting voices. While the original U.B.S. Greek New Testament Committee was meeting to edit a critical edition, in parallel with the German Nestle/Aland edition, a healthy debate ensued regarding this passage. The majority of the committee, led by Bruce Metzger, opted for the Hortian explanation for how the υἱός reading was a later emendation, substituting an easier reading for a harder, Egyptian reading. Allen Wikgren, however, dissented from the majority, opting for the υἱός reading. This appears as one of the very few minority notes found in the *Textual Commentary*.[72]

---

[69] F.F. Bruce *The English Bible* (Oxford: Oxford University Press, 1970), p. 14.

[70] *The New Testament in the Original Greek,* ed. by B.F. Westcott and F.J.A. Hort, 2 Vols.(Cambridge: Macmillan and Co., 1882).

[71] B. B. Warfield, *An Introduction to the Textual Criticism of the New Testament*, 3rd ed. (London: Hodder and Stoughton, [1886] 1890), pp. 189–192. For a study of Warfield's influences on the American academic community via his text critical work see, Theodore P. Letis, "B.B. Warfield, Common-Sense Philosophy and Biblical Criticism," *Journal of the Presbyterian Historical Society (American Presbyterians)* vol. 69, no. 3 (Fall, 1991), pp. 175–190.

[72] The note reflecting Wikgren's opinion reads as follows: "It is doubtful that the author would have written μονογενὴς θεός, which may be a primitive, transcriptional error in the Alexandrian tradition . . . At least a D decision would be preferable. A.W." *A Textual Commentary on the Greek New Testament* ed. by B.M. Metzger, *et al.* (London: United Bible Societies, 1971), p.198.

When I attempted to discover the specifics of the debate by consulting the rather extensive notes that were kept of the committee's discussions on such textual variants, I was instructed by Professor Metzger in the following terms:

> In response to your query about further information concerning the debate that took place between the committee and Wikgren concerning John 1:18, I am sorry to report that the notes on this discussion (like the notes on many other such discussions by the committee) were very brief. This is reflected in the laconic way in which I reported his dissenting vote in the *Textual Commentary* on the passage. The very fact that Wikgren himself cannot recall the argument(s) he used indicates to me that, rather than making a counter proposal supported by an elaborate discussion, Wikgren probably merely indicated that he demurred from the majority of the committee at this point. In other words, I am not able to supply any specific information that could be used in printed form, supplementing what is already mentioned in the *Textual Commentary*.[73]

But in an earlier letter to me from Wikgren, responding to my request for information regarding the committee's debate on this issue, he offered the following comments:

> I'm sorry that I have not been able to locate any notes on the passage, but I remember that my vote was based on more than just "accidental" evidence, e.g. the Latin and possible theological influence. We had a secretary for the committee who made copious notes on the discussion, and of course Metzger had to reduce these drastically. But I feel that justice was not always done to various viewpoints.[74]

---

[73]Letter from Bruce M. Metzger to the Author, 10 May 1996.

[74]Letter from Allen Wikgren to the Author, 19 April 1994. Metzger's remarks in the *Preface* to the *Textual Commentary*, would seem to be in accord with Wikgren's recollections that there was "for most sessions, more or less full notes of the discussions that proceded the voting." But later Metzger says: "More than once the record of the discussion proved to be incomplete because, amid the lively exchange of opinions, the Committee had come to a decision without the formal enunciation of those reasons that appeared at the time to be obvious or self-evident. In such cases it was necessary for the present writer to supplement, or even

And so we see the twentieth-century debate has lost none of the heat from the original nineteenth-century discussions.

IX. John 1:18 and the Canonical Approach

Childs explains in his *The New Testament as Canon,* Excursus I, titled: "The Hermeneutical Problem of New Testament Text Criticism," the following guidelines for arriving at the "canonical" variant:

1) *Abandon the notion of an "original" text:*
". . . the process of canonization did not insure an uninterpreted 'neutral' text. Clearly, Hort seriously underestimated the element of intentional change."[75]
This is because "The earliest levels of textual witness reveal a state of wide multiplicity, indeed, the model of a reservoir of tradition from which different streams flow is far more accurate than that of an ideal autograph at the source."[76]

2) *Look for the reading that became exegetically and hermeneutically sanctioned, or canonized:*
"Important things happened between the writing of the epistles and the formation of a canonical collection, a process which modern literary critical research has sought to clarify. Again the implications for text criticism move away from the model arrived at by Hort to one which reckons with the best received text rather than that of the author's autograph. . . . In spite of the excessive rhetoric Burgon sensed that a theological dimension of the *textus receptus* was not being properly handled in the critical approach of Hort. He queried whether the Holy Catholic Church could have been misled from its inception by its use of a corrupt text. Could one discount the continuous witness from antiquity, the church fathers, the versions and lec-

---

to reconstruct, the tenor of the committee's discussions" p.*v*. A pity someone did not keep a journal for such a momentous occasion.

[75]Brevard S. Childs, *The New Testament as Canon: An Introduction* (Philadelphia: Fortress Press, 1985), p. 523.

[76]*Ibid.,* p. 524.

tionaries for a discarded text (Sinaiticus) which a German found in a waste basket?"[77]

Hence,

"Theoretically, the goal of text criticism, which is commensurate with its canonical role, is to recover that N.T. text which best reflects the true apostolic witness found in the Church's Scripture."[78]

The actual praxis requires:

STEP ONE: *work within the proper canonical context.*
"Because the text-critical goal has been defined as recovering the best received text, one begins by a self-positioning within the framework of actual ecclesiastical textual traditions, the outer parameter of which has usually been set by the Byzantine (*koine*) text. (For the Latin tradition the role of the Vulgate as a starting-point from within an inclusive ecclesiastical tradition would be roughly analogous)."[79]

STEP TWO: *use traditional text critical methods within this tradition.*
"Moreover, the criteria by which these judgements are made are precisely those which critical scholarship has developed over the last two hundred years."[80] The goal is simply different: one

---

[77] *Ibid.*, pp. 523–524.

[78] *Ibid.*, p. 527. But never let this language be misunderstood: "Burgon badly misunderstood the real theological issue at stake. . . . He turned the debate into a misconstrued historical issue, arguing that the *textus receptus* represented the oldest text which was closest to the original apostolic autographs. . . . Burgon's defence of the Byzantine text was as historicist as Hort's. . . . Burgon's error has, unfortunately, continued among those scholars who have in recent times once again sought to defend the 'majority text' as the most historically accurate (Hodges, Pickering, Fuller)" p. 524.

[79] *Ibid.*, p. 528.

[80] *Ibid.* Is there a tension in this process? "Is there any means of locating a text which is by definition different from the original author's autograph and at the same time is not to be identified with an uncritical text represented by the last stages of a stabilized *koine* tradition? No one should be deceived as to the difficulties involved in escaping the horns of this dilemma" pp. 527–528.

is no longer looking for an idealized, perhaps imaginary 'auto-graphic' text; one is now trying to discover the reading that fits the canonical context, in its kerygmatic role, within the entire N.T. corpus, as determined by the apostolic community who gave final shape to the sacred text."

How do the data for John 1:18 fit into the canonical approach?

1) The oldest *Greek MS* evidence (p^{66}, ℵ*, B: 3rd and 4th cen.) witnesses to μονογενὴς θεός and (p^{75}, ℵ$^{1,2,3?}$ 3rd and 4th cen.) to ὁ μονογενὴς θεός. The latter reads like the Coptic and so may well have been influenced very early by a bilingual text (used possibly by a Gnostic community). The former eventually became the "received" *Egyptian* reading. The oldest evidence of all is *patristic*: the Valentinians (c. 170) for μονογενὴς θεός. The oldest *versional* evidence, however, apart from the Coptic (i.e. syr^{c,h,pal}, it^{pl} : 3rd–4th cen.), and the vast majority of the Greek MSS as well as all of the lectionaries—thus reflecting the reading sanctioned by ecclesiastical usage—witnesses to ὁ μονογενὴς υἱός.

CONCLUSION

With the arguments I have offered regarding the *earliest* evidence (the Valentinians), there is more than an excellent *prima facie* case for μονογενὴς θεός having been an alteration of the text for theological reasons. Bart Ehrman has already conceded that this was most probably the case. He believes, however, that it was altered by the orthodox during the adoptionist controversy. But it could have just as easily arisen at the hands of the Valentinians and was consequently put to use in a different way later by the orthodox.[81] This would then also explain the oldest

---

[81]Ehrman, *The Orthodox Corruption*, pp. 78–82. Ehrman concedes that the MS pedigree of this reading was "among a variety of Alexandrian writers, both orthodox and Gnostic" (p. 82), and then offers the interesting analysis that both had an high christology, by the standards of adoptionism. In light of the first appearance of the Egyptian reading among the Valentinians, and in light of their

extant MS evidence, i.e. the Greek Egyptian MSS., as having been influenced regionally, perhaps first by an altered Coptic version used within a Gnostic community along side a Coptic Gnostic library such as was found at Nag Hammadi. In the words of Abbot again:

> We trace both readings to the second century; but we find θεός supported almost wholly by one class of authorities, the Alexandrian or Egyptian; while the witnesses for υἱός are far more widely diffused as well as far more numerous, representing all quarters of the Christian world. The whole Western Church seems to have known no other reading.[82]

While Irenaeus, Clement, and Origen used the phrase for a time, indeed, the Church, both in her Eastern and in her Western Catholic dimensions made a deliberate determination *not* to allow μονογενὴς θεός to stand as the words of the apostle, by not reproducing this variant once Nicene orthodoxy was in place. The Arian use of the Egyptian reading would have provided enough reason for this, even if the possible Gnostic origins of the phrase were by now no longer evident to most. Hence, my argument is that on a purely traditional text critical basis—and we have barely touched on the internal evidence, namely, the style of the author of the prologue—μονογενὴς θεός, while early, is not original.[83] On a *canonical approach basis,* it certainly was never sanctioned as a received, or canoni-

---

particular exegesis of John's prologue, added to the later use of the passage by the Arians, and Athansius's complete disinclination to use it, seems to makes a stronger case for the post-Nicene orthodox to have eventually perceived it—in spite of its use by various earlier orthodox fathers—as representing a different and lower christology than the received reading allowed. But I agree totally with Ehrman in his explanation for why the change was found only in the prologue of John's Gospel (n. 175). To this I will add in support of my own argument that the Gnostics no doubt co-opted this as a quite separate bit of material and it may have even had a life of its own as a separate pericope from the rest of the Gospel, in their ranks.

[82]*Op. cit.*

[83]For those who would say the Egyptian reading is the harder reading and for that reason it should be seen as the original reading, we need only point out that for a Valentinian Gnostic, μονογενὴς υἱός is decidedly the harder reading.

cal reading within the ecclesiastical texts of either the Eastern, or Western Catholic traditions, probably because it was perceived to offer, at the very least, a subordinationist christology which the early church must have felt was not in tenor with the dominant christology of either the post-Nicene era or the N.T. itself.[84]

---

[84]D.A. Fennema has made a gallant effort to give the Egyptian reading an orthodox interpreation that Tregelles would have applauded: "For the theme of the Prologue, summed up in 1.18 and explicated throughout the Gospel, proves to be this: He who has revealed God the Father is none other than 'God the only Son,'" "John 1.18: God the Only Son," *New Testament Studies* 31 (1985), p. 131. But this smacks of reading Nicaea back into the text of the Gospel and ignores the Arian use and interpretation of the phrase. Furthermore, if the early church had seen that the phrase bore such a meaning, effortlessly in tenor with Nicaea, surely the Egyptian reading would have triumphed and not the "received" reading instead.

CHAPTER SIX

The Reformation and the Philosophy of Vernacular Translations of the Bible

Many will be surprised to learn that it was not Luther, nor Calvin, nor Tyndale in the sixteenth century who first advocated that the Bible should be made available to all in their own language. It was a Roman Catholic and Dutch humanist, Desiderius Erasmus (ca. 1466–1536).[1] In his *Paraclesis* (Greek for "exhortation"), a foreword published in his Greek *Novum Instrumentum* (1516) a year before Luther had even posted his *Ninety-Five Theses*, Erasmus had said:

> I absolutely dissent from those people who don't want the holy scriptures to be read in translation by the unlearned—as if, forsooth, Christ taught such complex doctrine that hardly anyone outside a handful of theologians could understand it, or as if the chief strength of the Christian religion lay in people's ignorance of it. Perhaps the state secrets of kings have to be concealed, but Christ wanted his mysteries to be disseminated as widely as possible. I should prefer that all women, even of the lowest rank, should read the evangelists and the epistles of Paul, and I wish these writings were translated into all the languages of the human race, so that they could be read and studied, not just by the Irish and the Scots, but by the Turks as well, and the Saracens. . . . I would hope that the farmer might chant a holy text at his plow, the spinner sing it as she sits at her wheel, the traveller ease the tedium of his journey with tales from the scripture. . . . Let each individual grasp what he can, and give expression to what he feels.

If the last remark sounds like the formula for a charismatic

---

[1]Of course, Wycliffe was earlier than Erasmus, but his effort predated the age of printing and so his influence was much more limited than that of Erasmus.

prayer meeting, it is not far from Erasmus's goal. While all the Reformers were profoundly indebted to Erasmus's inspiration and nearly all of them put his recommendations into practice, none of them would have been happy with the reductionistic, non-dogmatic, lay Christianity Erasmus envisioned and hoped that popular translations of the Bible might produce. But in twentieth century America, certainly it is Erasmus who has triumphed over the Reformers.

In the sixteenth century, however, it was only the many Anabaptist communities who most radically caught Erasmus's vision to disempower the structures of catholic Christianity—both Protestant as well as Roman—by means of vernacular translations of the Bible. Against hierarchy and creed, these free church traditions were keen to replace received dogmatic and ecclesiastical consensus with a religion by democratic consensus. In seventeenth and eighteenth-century England this simple, Erasmian Christianity resulted in the emergence of various non-conformist, antitrinitarian groups—Socinians, Sabellians, and Unitarians—and eventually Deism. All of these developments were, in one way or another, the result of putting the Bible into the hands of the common man without reference to how the Church had interpreted Her sacred text.

The magisterial Reformers advocated a different strategy. While they agreed with Erasmus that the Bible should be translated into the vernacular they never assumed it would be studied outside of the ecclesiastical context, that is, outside of the catholic dogmatic consensus which all Protestants retained while rejecting the unbiblical accretions of Romanism developed during the middle ages. Hence, Luther produced the *Small Catechism, the Larger Catechism,* and the Lutheran Church as a whole produced the confessional standard, *The Book of Concord.* Calvin in Switzerland produced the *Geneva Catechism* (1541), and in Germany, Hungary, Belgium and the Netherlands the Reformed produced the *Heidelberg Catechism* (1563). In England the Presbyterians produced the *Westminster Standards.* Finally, the Reformed Anglicans had their matchless *Prayer Book* and the *Thirty-Nine Articles,* the twentieth of which recognized the Church as "the witness and keeper of Holy Writ."

Each Protestant community had its own confessional standards, all of which assumed the validity of the orthodox standards of the ancient Catholic Church.[2] As James Moffatt put it,

> Calvinists and Lutherans amid all their differences have been agreed, from the outset, that the Church is not a mere conventicle, a self-started body of "pious variers from the Church," gathered round some "heated pulpiteer" or of provincial religionists who belong to one class in the main. The spirit of the authentic creeds, confessions, and testimonies of the Presbyterian Churches may be summed up in the words of the apostle, "I speak of Christ *and the Church*."[3]

Therefore, the study of the Bible was always prefigured in confessional Protestant traditions by the received orthodoxy contained in the catechisms, creeds and confessions.

One of the tenets one learned during catechesis within these confessional traditions was a belief that the Bible was alone the inspired Word of God. And because every word of it was inspired and sacred, it could only be authoritative in a final sense in the *original* languages in which it had been given by inspiration. In the words of the *Westminster Confession of Faith*:

> The Old Testament in Hebrew . . . and the New Testament in Greek . . . being immediately inspired by God, and, by His singular care and providence, kept pure in all ages, are therefore authentic . . . so as in all controversies of religion, the Church is finally to appeal to them (*WCF* 1:8).

So for confessional Protestants while vernacular translations certainly had their place, ultimately the Greek and Hebrew texts were decisive on matters of belief. This had a definite effect on how these texts were translated. Calvin, for example "favoured a

---

[2]On the place of creeds within the history of the Church a very accessible work is Gerald Bray, *Creeds, Councils and Christ* (Downers Grove, 1984). Although, I find myself at odds regarding Dr. Bray's strange advice advocating that the creeds and confessions should be in modern language, which goes counter to the very idea of static phraseology which accompanies the finality of confessional literature.

[3]James Moffatt, *The Presbyterian Churches* 2nd ed. (London, 1928), p. 4.

literal translation, even to the extent of preserving the word order where no difference between Greek and Latin syntax forbade."[4] Therefore it is not surprising that when Reformers, such as Tyndale, decided to take Erasmus's advise seriously by Englishing the inspired Hebrew and Greek texts, they tended to keep very close to a literal translation, as close as possible to one English word for each inspired word from the Hebrew and Greek texts.

Even then, however, because the Protestant Reformers were all learned men they knew it was impossible to convey *all* of the meaning found in the Greek and Hebrew texts in another language by way of translation. Hence, Francis Turretin, the orthodox Protestant scholastic and heir to Calvin's Geneva Academy, argued—as did all Protestant divines—that although translations

> are of great value for the instruction of believers, no other version can or should be regarded as on par with the original [language texts], much less as superior. Because no other version has any weight which the Hebrew or Greek source does not posses *more fully*, since in the sources not only the content . . . but also the *very words*, were directly spoken . . . by the Holy Spirit, *which cannot be said of any version*. . . . The translations are all streams; the original [language] text the source whence they take their lasting quality. One is the *rule*, the other the *ruled* which has merely human authority (emphasis mine).[5]

Therefore, all the qualities that accompany divine inspiration only fully apply to those original language texts in which Scripture was given by inspiration: "a given translation made by human beings subject to error is not to be regarded as divine and infallible verbally," although "it can be properly so regarded *in substance* if it faithfully renders the divine truth of the [original] sources . . ." (emphasis mine).[6]

That no translation, no matter how carefully or literally rendered can fully communicate word for word *all* the meaning of

---

[4]T.H.L. Parker, *Calvin's New Testament Commentaries* (Grand Rapids, 1971), p. 102.

[5]Francis Turretin, *The Doctrine of Scripture* trans. by J.W. Beardslee III (Grand Rapids, 1981), p.152.

[6]Ibid., p. 154.

the original languages can be most clearly seen in the historic and official Bible of the Reformed Church of England, the *Authorized Version*. Though the translators sought to retain Tyndale's masterful, literal, word for word rendering from the Greek and Hebrew, when this was not possible and more words were needed in English than were used in the original sources the additional words were placed in italics. This did not mean that these words were unnecessary, unimportant or superfluous (I once was handed a Bible by someone who believed they had arrived nearer the truth by crossing out all the italicized words in the book of Genesis). Rather, these italicised words signalled what Turretin was at pains to make clear: no translation can fully convey all the meaning from the original languages, which is why the Greek and Hebrew alone must be final.

Where translations failed, preaching was to offer additional clarity. Within historic Reformation churches liturgy and preaching, in Beardslee's words, "continues the work of Bible translation; hence the importance of an educated ministry."[7]

What happens when the ministry is no longer fully educated as were the Reformation pastors of the sixteenth, seventeenth, eighteenth and even the nineteenth centuries; and what happens when creeds and confessions are jettisoned in favour of "the Bible alone"? The answer is found in two impulses cultivated most fully in the American religious context: 1) *restorationism* and 2) *demytholization*.

Restorationism argues that historic orthodoxy as found in the creeds and confessions of Reformation Christianity reflect a degenerative and defective form of the Faith and what is necessary is a *return* to a more primitive form of Christianity.[8] This conviction is held by two groups of moderns 1) those who are interested in reconstructing earlier recensions of the New Testament than that which was preserved and used within historic orthodoxy since the fourth century (sometimes called the Byzantine text but

---

[7]Ibid., p. 154, n. 3.

[8]A wonderful introduction to this phenomenon is Richard T. Hughes, ed. *The American Quest for the Primitive Church* (Urbana, 1988).

here I will refer to this as the *Ecclesiastical text* since it became normative outside as well as inside of the Eastern or Byzantine Church); 2) Those Anabaptist communities who reject creeds and confessions believing their churches alone have retained the primal Christian tradition. Oddly enough, many fundamentalists in this group have clung to the old Anglican Bible because of a defective historiography which claims this Bible represents a now lost MS tradition reaching back to the earliest, first century, Anabaptist communities.[9] Both groups are menacing because the former are never able to arrive at a consensus, thus they continue to offer approximation after approximation while the data remains in flux; while the later have in a misinformed and confused way instilled in the English of the Anglican Bible all the qualities which Reformation scholars attributed exclusively to the original language texts.

The Demythologizers are those who are not interested in either *preserving* catholic consensus in Bible translation, nor are they interested in *restoring* a more primitive and alien, ancient, Near-Eastern religious tradition—they simply want to communicate in contemporary idiom.[10] These are the pragmatists bred in business schools and in mass-media journalism and communication departments in many American universities. They have little scholarly interest but know how to make the Bible sell. Hence, everything that would be a barrier to communicating the bare essentials of the Bible so that, in Erasmus's words, "each individual [can] grasp what he can, and give expression to what he feels" is demythologized, that is, made contemporary. One demythologizes the Bible in translation, that is, casts its message in terms that are relevant to various special interest groups, to certain ideologically oriented communities (e.g. feminists), or to those seriously deficient culturally or intellectually, for purposes of culti-

---

[9]For a brief study of this see, Theodore P. Letis, *The Revival of the Ecclesiastical Text and the Claims of the Anabaptists* (Fort Wayne, 1992).

[10]I cannot take credit for this analysis concerning Bultmann's project as it applies to modern Bible translations since I am indebted to Jakob Van Bruggen's observation on this point in his important, *The Future of the Bible* (Nashville, 1978). This is soon to be reprinted by the Institute for Renaissance and Reformation Biblical Studies.

vating diversified markets. Here we discover the very inversion of Turretin's principle: the ruled (translations) now become the rule (the true standard for what is the essence of Christianity) and the verbal content of the original languages is left behind. Gerald Hammond put it this way:

> The basic distinction between the Renaissance [and Reformation] and modern translators is one of fidelity to their original. Partly the loss of faith in the Hebrew and Greek as the definitive word of God has led to the translator's loss of contact with it, but more responsibility lies in the belief that a modern Bible should aim not to tax its readers' linguistic or interpretive abilities one bit. If this aim is to be achieved then it seems clear that a new Bible will have to be produced for every generation—each one probably moving us further away from the original text, now that the initial break has been made.[11]

This is a major, neglected theme in American religious studies which could go a long way in explaining the state of much of modern American Christianity.

The only antidote to this plight is for those small remnant Reformation communities who still retain confessional and catholic integrity to act as salt and light in this insipid and ever dimming age. With little promise of success they must walk by faith and not by sight and celebrate their distinctives with intelligence, dignity, and winsomeness[12] in hopes of attracting with the full fragrance of the old classic translations those whose senses have been dulled by the pollutants of modernity (II Cor. 2:14–17).

---

[11]Gerald Hammond, *The Making of the English Bible* (New York, 1983), pp. 12–13.

[12]I should like to thank my friend, Wallace Bell, for teaching me the value of a "Winsome Christianity."

CHAPTER SEVEN

The Ecclesiastical Text Redivivus?

The English New Testament text critic, F.C. Burkitt, once said of the Christian Religion, "we do not know why it lived and lives, any more than we know why we ourselves are alive."[1] Since E.J. Epp announced fifteen years ago the mystifying fact that there was a revival underway of the views of J.W. Burgon, text critics have been saying the same thing about the Ecclesiastical Text.[2] Two recent assessments of this phenomenon are those by Professor Daniel B. Wallace, of Dallas Seminary and the late Professor Kurt Aland, of the *Institute für neutestamentliche Textforschung*. Both essays are windows to how scholars are responding to this development.

Daniel Wallace

Daniel Wallace's brief essay, "Some Second Thoughts on the Majority Text," *Bibliotheca Sacra* (July–September 1989), is primarily an in-house discussion directed to the Dallas Seminary constituency. Wallace points out, as I have,[3] "in the last several years some if not most of the leading advocates of the majority

---

[1]F.C. Burkitt, *The Gospel History and its Transmission* (Edinburgh, 1911, 3rd ed.), 75.

[2]E.J. Epp, "New Testament Textual Criticism in America: Requiem for a Discipline," *Journal of Biblical Literature* 98 (1979), 94–98.

[3]"For some years now a small group of conservative evangelicals, affiliated mostly with the American dispensational institutions of Dallas Seminary and Moody Bible Institute, has sought to circumvent all detracting criticisms lodged against the *Textus Receptus*, or the King James Version, by producing a 'critical' edition of the majority Greek text." T.P. Letis, *The Majority Text: Essays and Reviews in the Continuing Debate* (Ft. Wayne, IN, 1987), 1.

text view have received their theological training at Dallas Seminary."[4] This is an important point.

Why did Dallas interest so many in the textual views of a nineteenth century, High Church, Anglican divine (John William Burgon), with whom they hold next to nothing in common theologically? Strangely, Wallace raises the point but never attempts to address it. I believe, to do so, would call attention to his own "Dallas theology."

To those of us outside of American fundamentalism the connection between Dallas' theology and the rise of Majority Text advocates at Dallas is all too obvious. Dallas's doctrine of inerrant autographs has largely informed the Majority Text project of Hodges and those influenced by him over the years. His scheme of statistical probability, which Wallace has done a fine job in criticizing, seems to offer, on *a prima facia* basis, a more objectified, scientific approach. This is in keeping with the post-Enlightenment desire on the part of some to give Scripture a scientific aura, claiming it was *inerrant* in the original autographs.[5] In truth, it is ultimately a more simplistic means[6] for claiming a closer approximation to these autographs, rather than the more demanding, and at times more subjective, ap-

---

[4]D.B. Wallace, "Some Second Thoughts on the Majority Text," *Bibliotheca Sacra* 143 (July–September 1989), 271.

[5]For a survey of the development from the view of the continental Protestant dogmaticians, to the mostly American view of inerrant autographs, see T.P. Letis, "The Protestant Dogmaticians and the Late Princeton School on the status of the Sacred *Apographa*," *Scottish Bulletin of Evangelical Theology*, Vol. 8, No. 1 (Spring 1980), 16–42.

[6]One Majority Text advocate recently seemed to suggest that certain data on textual variants do not merit a place in the textual apparatus because such data are irrelevant to the Majority Text theory: "Both groups of critical [Greek text] editions contain a good number of notes which ought to be considered irrelevant because they are readings found in only one, or some very few MSS." W.G. Pierpont, "Modern Critical Editions of the Greek New Testament and Their Critical Notes," a paper distributed by the Majority Text Society, n.d., n.p. Also, another member of the Majority Text Society, Dr. Maurice A. Robinson, has remarked in response to another essay distributed by the Society, "Such continues to make it appear as though a preference for the Byzantine (or Majority/Traditional) textform is somehow tied to a severe inerrantist harmonization of differences

proach of the eclectics.[7] Wallace omits this neglected influence of the inerrant autographs theory, I believe, simply because on this point there is complete agreement between himself and the Majority Text advocates from Dallas. Nevertheless, I think it offers one explanation for why this school has produced an abundance of Majority Text defenders.

That there is a larger world of scholarship, outside of Dallas Seminary, which does not hold to the doctrine of inerrant autographs, and yet sees value in retaining the received texts for canonical purposes, is ignored.[8]

It is important for Wallace to continue stressing that Hodges's Majority Text is *not* the *Textus Receptus*. By making this point he claims that scholars like the Alands and others have misunderstood Hodges. As I have stated elsewhere,[9] I simply do not believe this to be the case. Hodges' critics see his project as an attempt to produce a *critical* addition of the text-type represented for the last four hundred years in the Protestant *Textus Receptus*.

---

among parallel passages. Such a hermeneutic could thus use the Majority Text issue as a convenient vehicle for a wider-ranging agenda." "Majority Affirmations and Peter's Denials: On Keeping Critical Issues Distinct," an unpublished lecture presented before a regional meeting of the Evangelical Theological Society, 1990.

[7]It should be pointed out that many of the American reasoned eclectics— namely, those involved with the Evangelical Theological Society—are also interested in inerrant autographs. They find a high degree of satisfaction in the Codex Vaticanus/p[75] witness, believing it to be the closest link to the objective certainty they are striving after. On the other hand, the British, who generally seem never to have been affected by this doctrine of inerrant autographs, have developed a more rigorous eclecticism. Unconcerned by such theological considerations they are not as confident of the near exclusive quality of the B/p[75] witness. I.A. Moir expresses this when he judges, "there were probably several 'Ur-texts' of the NT derived from oral tradition and thus we are no nearer the autographs than we were a century ago," "Can We Risk Another 'Textus Receptus'?" *The Journal of Biblical Literature* 100 (1981), 618.

[8]See the works of B. Childs. Also, recall the position of M.M. Parvis, "The *textus receptus* is not *the* 'true' text of the New Testament but it is one text. It was the Scripture of many centuries of the Church's life. It cannot today displace our so-called critical texts, but it is worthy of a place, a very special place, beside them," "The Goals of New Testament Textual Studies," *Studia Evangelica* 6 (1973):406.

[9]Letis, *The Majority Text*, 11, 12, 14, 19.

The *Textus Receptus* is simply the generic term used to refer to this ecclesiastical text-type and tradition.[10] It is only Wallace and other Dallas folk who think the *Majority Text* edited by Hodges, *et.al.*, has made a dramatic break with this ecclesiastical tradition. No one else seems impressed by their claims.

There are a few other points Wallace should have considered. He will have to re-evaluate the generality that the Byzantine text is overly harmonistic[11] in light of Dr. W.F. Wisselink's recently published research on this subject.[12]

Furthermore, Wallace needs to qualify his statement, "Hoskier's work [*Concerning the Text of the Apocalypse*] stands out as the only complete collation of the Greek witnesses for any New Testament book."[13] Dr. J.K. Elliott has pointed out that Hoskier did not consult all available MS. evidence in his project.[14]

Regarding Wallace's critique of Hodges proper, it is here that their common theological tradition helps. Wallace is the rare critic who perhaps alone truly understands Hodges' position— Wallace studied under him at Dallas. He addresses the specifics of Hodges' method and demonstrates its failure, point by point. Wallace has done a good job here and has performed an important service in his analysis of the *Dallas* Majority Text School.

---

[10]Wallace, *op. cit.*, 275. Parvis's is typical of a score of examples that could be cited. I give his quotation without context merely to illustrate his usage of the phrase: "A third option which we may mention is to edit a late Koine text, to reproduce, in fact, the *textus receptus*, if we may use that phrase to designate the 'received text' of the Greek Church as opposed to the Stephanus and Elzevir texts derived from it," *op.cit.*, 405.

[11]*Ibid.*, 279, n. 39.

[12]*Assimilation as a Criterion for the Establishment of the Text: A Comparative Study on the Basis of Passages from Matthew, Mark and Luke,* Ph.D. dissertation, The Reformed Theological College, Kampen, 1989. I was happy to be invited to participate in the defense of this dissertation and to provide some editing assistance on the English translation. For a brief abstract see *The Bulletin of the Institute for Reformation Biblical Studies I* (Fall 1989):11. The published form of this dissertation can be purchased from Kok Publisher BV, P.O. Box 130, 8360 AC Kampen, the Netherlands.

[13]Wallace, *op. cit.*, 284, n. 61.

[14]Dr. Elliott's recent study of Hoskier's work on the MSS. of the Apocalypse led him to point out, "It is to be noted that Hoskier did not collate every manuscript of Revelation available to him." "Manuscripts of the Book of Revelation Collated by H. C. Hoskier," *Journal of Theological Studies* 40 (1989), 111, n. 2.

Nevertheless, in this essay my own position is seriously misrepresented as a pre-critical advocacy of the *textus receptus*. This also served Wallace's purposes of wanting to conveniently dismiss alternatives to his own highly selective American fundamentalist approach to text critical theory and method. Almost to the man American fundamentalists who engage text criticism do so searching for that method which will provide the most satisfying sense of objective certainty.[15]

This as a goal is commendable enough but when this desire for certainty leads to the distorting of other options which do not confirm the presuppositional *a priori* belief in the "inerrant autographs" theory held to by Wallace, then it becomes a problem. Even after personally communicating with Wallace and citing journal publications by me that made clear mine was not a pre-critical advocacy of the *textus receptus* he ignored such data and in a more recent incarnation of this same essay by him he continues to erroneously class me in this category.[16]

---

[15]This always results in advocating the "reasoned eclectic" approach which canonizes the fourth-century Egyptian recension. This approach provides American fundamentalists with the same sense of certainty that pre-critical advocates of the *textus receptus* find in excluding text criticism altogether in favour of the Ecclesiastical text. On the source of this fundamentalist approach to text criticism see my "B.B. Warfield, Common-Sense Philosophy and Biblical Criticism," *American Presbyterians* 69:3 (Fall 1991), 175–190. Wallace is just more selective in which aspects of text criticism and Biblical criticism in general, that he disallows. I have also dealt with the pre-critical advocates of the *textus receptus* but Wallace again conveniently leaves this material unacknowledged, *i.e.*, my *The Revival of the Ecclesiastical Text and the Claims of the Anabaptists* (Fort Wayne, IN, 1992).

[16]Daniel B. Wallace "The Majority Text Theory: History, Methods, and Critique," in Bart D. Ehrman and Michael W. Holmes, eds., *The Text of the New Testament in Contemporary Research: Essays on the* Status Quaestionis (Grand Rapids: William B. Eerdmans, 1995). Furthermore, Wallace has — and I can say this only in disbelief—even misrepresented specific statements, twisting them in directions that are nearly preposterous. Here he claims I "erroneously assumed Dallas Theological Seminary's confessional stance . . . include[d] a belief in the traditional text," 301–302, n.25. What I actually said was that "Dallas Seminary (and Moody Bible Institute) held very rigorously to *the old Baconian position of Warfield, although they rejected his Calvinism*" (emphasis mine), and that "a new hybrid arose *within* some fundamentalist-dispensational institutions, mixing Warfield's inerrancy position with Hill's advocacy of the Byzantine text" (emphasis mine), Letis, *Edward Freer Hills' Contribution to the Revival of the Ecclesi-*

Here Wallace's claim that I do not accept the Majority Text theory "precisely because their resultant text is not the TR"[17] could not be more misleading. In this introduction by me which he cites I compiled a general consensus of misgivings about the Hodges/Farstad *The Greek New Testament According to the Majority Text* (1982), from every major journal review article written by American and British text critics and New Testament scholars at the time, and demonstrated that on purely technical grounds the Majority Text theory could not stand.

Finally, how ironic it is that Wallace is keen to highlight the fact that there are few text critics among advocates of the Ecclesiastical Text (a point I first brought out in 1987 regarding the Dallas Majority text advocates specifically) when I know of no substantial text critical work produced by Wallace, who had, in fact, required the assistance of a British text critic to produce a book review of a text critical treatise.[18]

In short, Wallace's own unacknowledged predispositions as an American fundamentalist leave him less than capable of accurately assessing the various schools advocating the Ecclesiastical Text. What is required is someone trained more in the scientific study of religion and with a genuine pedigree as a text critic and less oriented by one's own unacknowledged sense of advocacy.

Kurt Aland

The translation of Kurt Aland's important essay, "The Text of the Church?"[19] is yet another response to the revival of the

---

astical Text, 167–168. Pertinent literature is then cited in a footnote to document this movement *within* these institutions. Even cited is a review by a Dallas Seminary journal reviewer denouncing the Byzantine text theory. At no point can my language be used to bear the meaning given it by Wallace.

[17]Wallace, "The Majority Text Theory," 304.

[18]In reality a post-critical advocacy of the Ecclesiastical Text is a theological decision, not a text critical one, though, as with the canonical approach as advocated by Brevard Childs, it is clearly predicated upon the historical circumstances of actual ecclesiastical use as opposed to attempting to reconstruct either a theoretical *ur* text, or "inerrant" autographs.

[19]K. Aland, "The Text of the Church?, "*Trinity Journal* 8 (Fall 1987, 131–144.

Ecclesiastical Text. Several of Professor Aland's remarks are exceedingly helpful in focusing the issues as understood by some of us outside of the Dallas orbit.

Professor Aland admits forthrightly that,

> it is undisputed that from the 16th to the 18th century orthodoxy's doctrine of verbal inspiration assumed . . . [the] Textus Receptus. It was the only Greek text they knew, and they regarded it as the "original text."[20]

Furthermore, he asks the question "who in the German-speaking countries today would seek to revive the arguments of 18th century orthodoxy? . . . and yet in the United States Burgon is enjoying a considerable revival."[21]

In response to this development, Aland, like Wallace, goes after Hodges, the most visible, but perhaps the easiest target (passing by Edward F. Hills, the scholar who truly initiated this revival.)[22]

In his criticism of Hodges, Aland actually wants to go so far as to suggest we have no real evidence for the Egyptian origin of Codices Vaticanus and Sinaiticus.[23]

Elsewhere though, Aland puts the state of the debate in very helpful terms, noting,

---

[20]Aland, *op. cit.,* 131. One could certainly challenge Professor Aland's assertion that the T.R. "was the only Greek text they knew." I have highlighted T.H.L. Parker's study of Calvin's N.T. commentaries, where Parker admits, "there existed even in the sixteenth century an alternative to the *textus receptus* which already ruled" but it "was largely disregarded as an eccentricity." Letis, *Majority Text*, 136.

[21]*Ibid.*, 135.

[22]*Ibid.*, 136. Professor Aland has, perhaps unkindly, pointed out a typographical error in the first edition of Hills' *The King James Version Defended* (1956). This, however, was corrected in subsequent editions, *e.g., The King James Version Defended* (Des Moines, 1984, 4th ed.), 115, 116, actually making reference to Professor Aland's own excellent essay, "The Greek New Testament: It's Present and Future Editions," *The Journal of Biblical Literature* 87 (1968).

[23]On the clear connection of these uncials with Egypt see the references to Hoskier as they appear in, "The Gnostic Influences On the Text of The Fourth Gospel: John 1:18 in the Egyptian Manuscripts, "*The Bulletin of the Institute for Reformation Biblical Studies* (Fall 1989), 4–7.

Hodges asserts for the Egyptian text that "its existence in early times outside of Egypt is unproved." But this statement can easily be turned about to read: the existence of the Majority Text in early times is unproved.[24]

Ironically, for Aland, the way out of this impasse is to invoke the data of patristic citations: this was the decisive argument for Burgon in the nineteenth century, used to get around the absence of hard data for the Ecclesiastical Text in Greek MSS. before the fourth century. Now, one presumes, Aland invokes statistics from *critical* editions of the fathers which seem to overturn the patristic evidence compiled by Burgon and employed by Miller.[25] Who will arbitrate the conflict between these two interpretations of patristic data? Is it really necessary to await an arbitration before one comes to a conclusion on this issue?

For those who find the received texts of the Jewish/Christian ecclesiastical traditions sufficient for religious, canonical purposes, it is enough to know that by the sixth century,

> Every Church had a Gospels manuscript on its altar. . . . Their use of the Majority text indicates clearly that it was the choice of those in authority as the text to be recognized officially and propagated. . . . In the age of Justinian as in the 9th century the Majority text consolidated the position it had clearly claimed in the 4th century as the official, proper, and correct text of the developing Byzantine Church.[26]

Aland continues,

> This Byzantine text was regarded as "the text of the church"— to return to the title of this essay. It was the text of the official

---

[24]Aland, *op, cit.*, 103. Historically speaking, among the Greek witnesses, Professor Aland's assessment is certainly correct.

[25]J.W. Burgon, *The Traditional Text of the Holy Gospels Vindicated and Established*, Arranged, Completed, and Edited by Edward Miller (London, 1896), 90–122. To see how this data can be mishandled at times, consult Pickering's response to Gordon Fee, Letis, *Majority Text*, 33–41.

[26]Aland, *op. cit.*, 140–141.

Byzantine church, and the church in its striving for uniformity
did all that it could to make it the common text.[27]

Aland concludes, saying the claim for the Majority Text as the
"text of the Church," is "the most impressive and effective claim
of its proponents."[28]

Aland, however, personally opts for an earlier MS. tradition:
B/p[75]. Believing it comes closest to the autographic exemplar(s),
Aland seems to echo Hort's old belief that B/Aleph represented
a "Neutral text."[29] Aland prefers *this* "church text" to that of the
Byzantine Church.

Contrary to the Alands' sanguine view of the Egyptian textual tradition (B/p[75]), Dr. Johnston, an authority on the Syriac
text, has demonstrated that the alleged agreement in these two
witnesses, supposedly linking the second century with the
fourth century, is anything but certain.[30]

Furthermore, Professor J.C. O'Neill has shown that Codex
Vaticanus probably does not represent a pure line of careful,
Alexandrian transmission from the second century. Instead, it is
probably a fourth century recension, the project of an Egyptian
scriptorium.[31] In fact, there seems to be no criteria that would
qualify the Egyptian recension as an *ecclesiastical* text, with any
hint of catholicity. Note the words of Parvis in the early seventies
regarding the state of the current critical text, "When we recon-

[27]*Ibid.,* 143.

[28]*Ibid.,* 144.

[29]Aland seems to have merely substituted the less emotive word "strict" for
neutral, his protestations to the contrary notwithstanding, cf. K. Aland and B.
Aland, *The Text of the New Testament* trans. By E.F. Rhodes (Grand Rapids,
1987), 14. If strict means a text which transmits "the text of an exemplar with
meticulous care (*e.g.,* p[75]) and depart[s] from it only rarely," (*ibid.,* 64) surely this
is what Hort meant by *neutral*—a good copy of an exemplar resembling the autographic text, not seriously contaminated by either extant or original deprava-
tions. Certainly Hort also acknowledged that Codex Vaticanus was a "living
text" when he rejected certain of its singular readings.

[30]See his essay, "Codex Vaticanus (B) plus P[75]—The 'Best' Text of the New
Testament?," *The Bulletin of the Institute for Reformation Biblical Studies"* I (Fall
1989), 2–4.

[31]J.C. O'Neill, "The Rules Followed by the Editors of the Text Found in the
Codex Vaticanus," *New Testament Studies* 35 (April 1989), 219–228.

struct the 'original' text, we are not reconstructing but rather we are constructing something that never before existed in heaven and earth."[32] J.K. Elliott made a similar assessment in 1988,

> The recent printed editions of the Greek New Testament, which we can buy give a text which never existed as a manuscript of the New Testament. They are all reconstructions based on their editor's choice of readings from Manuscripts they had at their disposal, or which they elected to concentrate on.[33]

The *Textus Receptus* at least has the continuity and sanction of catholic usage to commend it to faith communities.

Was there development on the way to Ecclesiastical Text? No doubt there was, although to what extent is still greatly debated. There simply is not always a clear-cut distinction in the relationship between source criticism, redaction criticism, and textual criticism.[34]

Analogously, we know there was *canonical* development which terminated in the fourth century. There was also *christological* development, beginning in the fourth century and culminating at the seventh century, Council of Constantinople (680-1). Is it so surprising, therefore, if the shape of the text developed as well?[35]

A contemporary example of how various pericopes could have been present in an early form of the text, then were omitted during a period of controversy, and then were reinserted at a later canonical stage, can be seen in the recent history of the debate surrounding the long ending of Mark's Gospel. Kurt and Barbara Aland have observed that,

> The practice of concluding the gospel of Mark at 16:8 . . .

---

[32]Parvis, *op. cit.,* 397.

[33]J.K. Elliott, "The Original Text of the Greek New Testament," *Fax Theologica* 8 (1988), 6.

[34]Cf. John Wenham, "Why Do You Ask Me About the Good? A Study of the Relation Between Text and Source Criticism," *New Testament Studies* 28 (January 1982), 116–125.

[35]Regarding the hermeneutical and theological significance of this, again, consult the works of Childs.

continued to be observed in some Greek manuscripts as well as in versional manuscripts for centuries, although the "longer ending" of Mark 16:9–20 was recognized as canonical. . . .[36]

From the Reformation to the late nineteenth century this ending retained its canonical status. With the discovery/collation of the early Alexandrian uncials it was then thought to be a late interpolation, and on this basis it was therefore considered to be non-canonical (recall the first edition of the R.S.V. relegated these verses to very small, italicized print at the foot of the page). Recently, however, Bruce Metzger has acknowledged that while the ending may not be Mark's, nevertheless, because of its very early appearance in the second century, "the passage ought to be accepted as part of the canonical text of Mark."[37]

Furthermore, the lesson learned only this century about so-called *late* interpolations, found in third century papyri, has not yet had its full effect on some.

We are indebted to Kurt and Barbara Aland for the crucial work they have done while directors of the *Institute für neutestamentliche Textforschung*. In the present essay, however, we are particularly indebted to Kurt Aland's rare command of church history. It is this that informs his analysis of the *Majority* Text as the *Ecclesiastical* Text, first of the Eastern Orthodox Church and then of the Protestant Reformers and their heirs in the seventeenth and eighteenth centuries. Both Burgon and Parvis made this their argument. Parvis summarizes,

> We may recall the reliance which Dean Burgon placed on what he styled the "traditional text." "Speaking generally," he wrote, "the Traditional Text of the New Testament Scriptures, equally with the New Testament Canon, rests on the authority of the Church Catholic." This text is, in fact, "neither more nor less than the probate of the orthodox Greek Christian bishops, and those, if not as we maintain of the first and second, or third, yet unquestionably of the fourth and fifth, and even subsequent centuries."[38]

---

[36]Aland/Aland *op. cit.*, 69.

[37]B.M. Metzger, *The Canon of the New Testament: Its Origin, Development, and Significance* (Oxford, 197), 270.

[38]Parvis, *op. cit.*, 406.

Parvis then offered his concurring sentiment,

> The *textus receptus* is the text of the Church. It is that form of text which represents the sum total and the end product of all the textual decisions which were made by the Church and her Fathers over a period of more than a thousand years.[39]

Currently we are experiencing a renewal of both pre-critical and a post-critical interest in reviving the Ecclesiastical Text. But perhaps it is closer to the truth to say the Ecclesiastical Text never really died. Certainly in light of the unbroken usage within the Greek Church one cannot properly speak of a *return* to the Ecclesiastical Text. Furthermore, the Alands' attempt to project the impression that there is now but one *Standard Text* (what others are calling the new *Textus Receptus*) will not make a horizon filled with a multiplicity of theoretical *original* texts go away. Parvis observed,

> Each one of these critical texts differ quite markedly from all of the others. This fact certainly suggests that it is very difficult, if not impossible to recover the original text of the New Testament.[40]

One of the reasons no agreed upon original text has emerged —the recent harmony between NA[26] and UBS[3] notwithstanding—has been addressed by many studies suggesting there never was one original, in the strict sense. It can be unsettling for those who have invested these *originals* with the quality of inerrancy when someone as safe as F.F. Bruce claims,

> If we appeal to the "autographic" texts, we should consider the implications of the fact that for some of the most important books of the Bible autographs never existed. There was no autograph of the Epistle to the Romans in the proper sense—that is, no copy written by Paul himself. Paul dictated, and Tertius copied. Indeed, the early textual history of the epistle suggests that more copies than one may have been made at Paul's direc-

---

[39] *Ibid.*
[40] *Ibid.*, 397.

tion—not only the primary one, naturally lacking the personal greetings at the end, for other churches that would be glad to have this definitive exposition of the gospel. When a letter was intended to go to a number of different places, it is conceivable that several simultaneous copies were made by as many amanuenses at one dictation.[41]

This no doubt explains in a large measure why the elusive original still haunts us. Still short of such objective certainty, Parvis recognized that the various attempts at approximation,

> Further suggests that that which we look upon as Scripture may be determined by our own theology—by whether or not we are Protestants or Roman Catholics, for example. Why do we have so many critical texts, that is, so many "original" texts? Which one of them is my Scripture? Which one of them is your Scripture?[42]

It was in the face of this same development in the early Church, no doubt, that the Greek Ecclesiastical Text emerged in the fourth century for the Eastern Church. Certainly we know from Jerome that this was the case in the fourth century for the Western Church, which resulted in the *Vulgata Latina*.[43] That same climate, as it currently exists, probably offers some explanation for why the Ecclesiastical Text lived, and lives today.

---

[41]F.F. Bruce, *Foreword,* 8–9, in Dewey M. Beegle, *Scripture, Tradition, and Infallibility* (Grand Rapids, 1973). Furthermore, W.A. Strange, *The Problem of the Text of Acts,* unpublished D. Phil., Oxford University, 1988, has given new life to an old thesis, namely, that Luke produced two separate recensions of the book of Acts which accounts for the differences between the Western text and other text-types of this book.

[42]Parvis, *op. cit.,* 397.

[43]The same holds true for the Greek Old Testament text, as summed up by P. Kahle in his Schweich Lectures: "We may try to edit the Jewish standard text of the Greek Tora. But can we possibly regard such a text as an 'Urtext'—a text from which all existing texts have to be derived? A standard text of the Targum of the Pentateuch, the Targum Onkelos, was preceded by different forms of the old Palestinian Targum of the Pentateuch, of which some valuable fragments have been found in the Cairo Geniza. The standard text of the Latin Bible, the Vulgate, was preceded by different forms of the *Vetus Latina.* . . . It is always so, and there can be no doubt that the standard text of the Greek Tora was preceded by divergent forms of earlier translations" *The Cairo Geniza* (London, 1947), 175.

CHAPTER EIGHT

The Revival of the Ecclesiastical Text
and the Claims of the Anabaptists

INTRODUCTION

Controversies surrounding translations of the Bible have been with us since the dawn of the Christian Faith itself. While many of the New Testament authors relied on a form of the Hebrew Old Testament when making allusions or quotations, some used a translation of the Old Testament in Greek.[1]

While this does not seem to have been a problem for the early Church, eventually the Hellenization of Christianity resulted in the near exclusive use of the Greek Old Testament, to the eclipse of the Hebrew text, the Greek having "assumed priority as early as the first century."[2]

---

[1]For a most useful treatment of all such places in the New Testament see, T. Horne, *An Introduction to the Study and Knowledge of Holy Scripture* 4 vols. 12th ed. (London, 1869), vol. II, pp. 114–178. For treatments of the LXX and the Old Testament Text in general the following are useful, H.B. Swete, *An Introduction to the Old Testament in Greek*, rev. by R.R. Ottley (London, 1914, reprt. 1989); *A Handbook to the Septuagint* (London, 1920); S. Jellicoe, *The Septuagint and Modern Study* (Oxford, 1968); P. Warters, *The Text of the Septuagint: Its Corruptions and Their Emendations* (Cambridge, 1973); E. Würthwein, *The Text of the Old Testament* trans. by E.F. Rhodes (Grand Rapids, 1979); S. Talmon, "The Old Testament Text," in *The Cambridge History of the Bible* vol. 1 (Cambridge, 1970); B. J. Roberts, "The Old Testament: Manuscripts, Text and Versions," in *The Cambridge History of the Bible* vol. II, pp. 14–22; E. Tov, *The Text-Critical Use of the Septuagint in Biblical Research*, Jerusalem, 1981.

[2]B. J. Roberts, "The Old Testament," p. 14. Cf. also, R. Beckwith: "Manuscripts of the Hebrew Bible are virtually all of Jewish not Christian origin, and the Christian manuscripts most likely to reflect Jewish influence are those of the two ancient versions made direct from the Hebrew, the Septuagint and the Peshitta, the former of which was translated by Jews in the pre-Christian period and the latter partly by Jews, partly by Syrian Christians, from about the first

This can be seen most clearly in the oldest extant uncial copies of the Christian Bible, Codices *Sinaiticus* and *Vaticanus*, both from the forth century; and Codex *Alexandrinus* (a Byzantine text in the Gospels), from the fifth century, all of which have the Greek version as their Old Testament text.

The *Vulgata Latina* and St. Augustine

By the fourth century, however, Latin translations from these types of Greek uncials were so numerous and their texts so divergent from one another that Jerome was commissioned to produce one authoritative ecclesiastical recension in the Latin language. Jerome completed the Gospels by 384 and after spending some fifteen years producing a Latin translation from the Hebrew (but for the Psalms which were taken from the Gallican Psalter, and some of the Apocrypha which remained in the old Latin) he received a great deal of criticism for "altering" both testaments, but particularly for abandoning the Greek Old Testament in favour of the Hebrew Bible of the Jews. The reason for this criticism was the perceived violation of the commonly held belief that the Septuagint translation was an *inspired* translation:

> A more potent cause for dissatisfaction with change was the fact that, as regards the Old Testament, the Septuagint . . . had come to be accepted as the bible of the Church, with a supposed miracle accompanying its production to guarantee its quality of verbal inspiration.[3]

Even the greatest orthodox theologian of the Western Church, St. Augustine, felt betrayed at Jerome's abandonment of the LXX, which Augustine described in his *De doctrina Christiana* in the following terms:

---

century AD onwards. . . . The order of the books in these [LXX] manuscripts is generally similar to that in the Greek patristic lists." *The Old Testament Canon of the New Testament Church: Its Background in Early Judaism* (Grand Rapids, 1985), pp. 192–193.

[3]R. Loewe, "The Medieval History of the Latin Vulgate," in *The Cambridge History of the Bible*, vol. 2, p. 107.

The seventy translators enjoyed so much of the presence and power of the Holy Spirit in their work of translation, that among the number of men there was but one voice.[4]

Moreover, in his *De civitate Dei XVIII:* 42–43, he insisted further that,

the agreement in the words of their versions was marvellous, amazing, and plainly inspired by God. . . . There was such a unity in their translations that it was as if there had been one translator; for in truth there was the one Spirit at work in them all. And this was the purpose of their receiving such a marvellous gift of God; that in this way the authority of those Scriptures should be emphasised, as being not human but divine. . . . The Church has accepted this Septuagint as if it were the only version. . . . For the very same Spirit that was in the prophets when they uttered their messages was at work also in the seventy scholars when they translated them. . . . The task of translation was achieved not by servile labour of a human bond-servant of words, but by the power of God which filled and directed the mind of the translator.[5]

It should be mentioned that Augustine knew no Hebrew and so was not able to make judgements concerning the accuracy of the LXX. Nevertheless, to this day, the LXX is regarded as the inspired, authoritative version of the Old Testament in the East-

---

[4]A.D.R. Polman, *The Word of God According to St. Augustine* (Grand Rapids, 1961), p. 185.

[5]St. Augustine, *Concerning the City of God Against the Pagans* trans. by H. Bettenson (London, 1972), pp 820–821. Here Augustine also makes a veiled criticism of Jerome, first referring to him as "a man of great learning and a master of all three languages," who has "translated these Scriptures into Latin not from the Greek but from the Hebrew," but then goes on to say in the next paragraph, "Nevertheless, it is the judgement of the churches of Christ that no one man should be preferred to the authority of so large a body of men [i.e. the LXX translators] chosen for this important task by Eleazar, the high priest at the time" (p. 821). For a brief treatment of Jerome's work on the *Vulgata Latina* and the criticism he received, see, J.N.D. Kelly, *Jerome: His Life, Writings and Controversies* (London, 1975), pp. 86–90; 153–170. For a more extended treatment of Jerome's contribution to Biblical studies see, A. Kamesar, *Jerome, Greek Scholarship, and the Hebrew Bible* (Oxford, 1993).

ern Church, while the *Vulgata Latina,* much of which had been produced by Jerome, is still regarded as the authoritative edition within the Roman communion.[6]

Humanism and the Reformation

During the Reformation era the magisterial Reformers were much influenced by Erasmian humanism. Had there not been the Renaissance humanists, there would never have been a Reformation of the Church.[7] The Reformers came to agree completely with Erasmus and other humanists that the corruption of the Christian religion during the medieval era was the direct

---

[6]This must be qualified slightly, because while Trent was unambiguous about the *Vulgata Latina* being authoritative over all extant Greek and Hebrew editions, this has been cast in a different light as of the papal encyclical, *Divino Afflante Spiritu* (1943). On the significance of this encyclical for modern Roman Catholic Biblical studies see, R.B. Robinson, *Roman Catholic Exegesis Since* Divino Afflante Spiritu: *Hermeneutical Implications* (Atlanta, 1988). For a study treating what Trent meant at the time of the original decree treating the Latin Bible, cf. T.P. Letis, "The *Vulgata Latina* and the Council of Trent: The Latin Bible as Verbal Icon," a lecture presented before the Summer meeting of the Ecclesiastical History Society, Chichester, England, 19 July 1990, pending publication.

[7]On the influences of the Northern Renaissance on the Reformation see, L. W. Spitz, *The Religious Renaissance of the German Humanists* (Cambridge, 1963), which is still of great value. Another important but neglected study is H.A.E. Van Gelder, *The Two Reformations in the 16th Century: A Study of the Religious Aspects and Consequences of Renaissance and Humanism* 2nd ed. (The Hague, 1964). J. K. McConica's *English Humanists and Reformation Politics Under Henry VIII and Edward VI* (Oxford, 1968) is still valuable for the English Reformation. For a work treating the humanist influences on later Puritanism see, M. Todd, *Christian Humanism and Puritan Social Order* (Cambridge, 1987). Other useful general studies are, B. Hall, *Humanists and Protestants, 1500–1900* (Edinburgh, 1990); L.W. Spitz, *Renaissance and Reformation* 2 vols. (St. Louis, 1971); *The Protestant Reformation* 1517–1559 (New York, 1985) S. Ozment, *The Age of Reform, 1250–1550: An Intellectual and Religious History of Late Medieval and Reformation Europe* (New Haven, 1980); R. L. DeMolen, *The Meaning of the Renaissance and Reformation* (Boston, 1974); Q. Breen, *Christianity and Humanism: Studies in the History of Ideas* (Grand Rapids, 1968); A.E. McGrath, *The Intellectual Origins of the European Reformation* (Oxford, 1987); *Reformation Thought: An Introduction* (Oxford, 1988); L. Grane, ed. *University and Reformation* (Leiden, 1981).

result of losing contact with classical tradition[8] and the primary texts of the Christian faith. Hence, all the most important leaders of the Reformation began as the off-spring of Erasmus, demanding a return, *ad fontes,* to the original language texts of Scripture as the theological foundation of the Church and to the exegetical tradition of the early fathers.[9]

Theirs was an attempt to return to ancient catholic orthodoxy.[10] David Steinmetz reminds us of what this meant:

---

[8]On the influence of pagan classical traditions on the early church see J. Pelikan's definitive, *Christianity and Classical Culture: The Metamorphosis of Natural Theology in the Christian Encounter with Hellenism*, the Gifford Lectures at Aberdeen for 1992–1993, (New Haven: Yale University Press, 1993.

[9]Good introductions to the thought and influence of Erasmus are, P.S. Allen, *The Age of Erasmus* (Oxford, 1914); J. Huizinga, *Erasmus and the Age of Reformation* (New York, 1924); M.M. Phillips, *Erasmus and the Northern Renaissance* (London, 1949, rev. 1981); R.H. Bainton, *Erasmus of Christendom* (New York, 1969); J. D. Tracy, *Erasmus: the Growth of a Mind* (Geneva, 1972); R. L. DeMolen, ed. *Erasmus* (London, 1973); R.J. Schoeck, *Erasmus of Europe: The Making of a Humanist 1467–1500* (Edinburgh, 1990); J. McConica, *Erasmus* (Oxford, 1991); C. Augustijn, *Erasmus* (Toronto, 1993). On Erasmus's contribution to Reformation Biblical studies, see, J.H. Bentley, *Humanists and Holy Writ: New Testament Scholarship in the Renaissance* (Princeton, 1983); A. Rabil, Jr., *Erasmus and the New Testament: The Mind of a Christian Humanist* (San Antonio, 1972); A. Reeve, *Erasmus' Annotations on the New Testament: the Gospels* [with an important *Introduction* by M.A. Screech] (London, 1986); *Erasmus' Annotations on the New Testament: Acts, Romans, I and II Corinthians* [again with an *Introduction* by M.A. Screech] (Leiden, 1990); E. Rummel, *Erasmus as a Translator of the Classics* (Toronto, 1985); *Erasmus'* Annotations *on the New Testament: From Philologist to Theologian* (Toronto, 1986); A. Brown, "The Date of Erasmus' Latin Translations of the New Testament," *Transactions of the Cambridge Bibliographical Society* vol. 8, no. 4 (1984). On the impact of Hebraic studies in the sixteenth century, two interesting and beneficial studies are, J. Friedman, *The Most Ancient Testimony: Sixteenth Century Christian-Hebraica in the Age of Renaissance Nostalgia* (Athens, 1983); G. L. Jones, *The Discovery of Hebrew in Tudor England: A Third Language* (Manchester, 1983).

[10]Useful surveys on the rise of this ancient catholic tradition are, H. H. Milman, *The History of Christianity from the Birth of Christ to the Abolition of Paganism in the Roman Empire* 3 Vols. 2nd ed. (London, 1863); R. Rainy, *The Ancient Catholic Church* (Edinburgh, 1902); R. M. Grant, *Augustus to Constantine: The Rise and Triumph of Christianity in the Roman World* (San Francisco, 1990). An interesting probing of this early catholic tradition and its demise is, Robert Markus, *The End of Ancient Christianity* (Cambridge, 1990).

Hence, the attempt of the Protestant reformers to recapture ancient doctrine and discipline is labelled innovation by a Church which has lost contact with its own past and which identifies modern belief and practice with the faith and discipline of the early Church. . . . In point of fact, the Protestant reformers are attempting to keep faith with the ancient teaching of the apostles as understood by the fathers against the later unwarranted innovations and novelties introduced by the medieval Catholic Church.[11]

In short, the magisterial Reformers were as interested in retaining contact with ancient *catholic* tradition—Lutheranism and Anglicanism more so than Reformed Christianity—as they were keen to develop all the implications of *sola scriptura*.

Returning to the original language texts was as much a part of this ancient catholic tradition as it was a logical outworking of *sola scriptura*. If the Bible was to be the supreme authority in the Church, then one must use the very best editions possible and read them in their original languages; and one must be acquainted with those fathers whose conversational speech was the very language breathed upon by God in giving the New Testament documents.

This meant that not only were the Reformers concerned to use the editions of the Greek text produced by Erasmus and the Hebrew texts preserved by the Jewish synagogues, but this meant also that all their ministers had to be trained in the trilingual tradition, *trium linguarum gnarus*, "expert in three languages," the classical and Biblical languages of Greek, Hebrew and Latin. This requirement prevails today in most of the conservative representatives of the three major Reformation traditions, Lutheran, Reformed and Anglican, but sadly has been lost in many of the more mainline seminaries.[12]

---

[11]David C. Steinmetz, *Luther in Context* (Bloomington, 1986), p. 92.

[12]On the teaching of Greek and Latin in American Universities through the turn of the century, see, F.W. Kelsey, ed. *Latin and Greek in American Education: With Symposia on the Value of Humanistic Studies* (New York, 1911).

Such training was in order to lead the Church properly and to avoid once again succumbing to the great darkness of yet another "Babylonian captivity of the church."[13]

The Protestant clergy were then, as the Reformers themselves, in the best humanist tradition, profoundly learned

---

[13]On the humanist tradition in Luther and church and university life at Wittenberg and in Germany in general see, Spitz, *The Religious Renaissance,* pp. 236–266; E.G. Schwiebert, "The Reformation From a New Perspective," *Church History* vol. 17 (1948): 3–31; *Luther and His Times* (St. Louis, 1951); H. A. Oberman, *Luther: Man Between God and the Devil* (New Haven, 1989), pp. 113–124; A.G. Dickens, *The German Nation and Martin Luther* (Glasgow, 1976), pp. 21–71; S. Ozment, "Introduction: Religion and Culture in the Renaissance and Reformation," in S. Ozment, ed. *Religion and Culture in the Renaissance and Reformation*; in S. Ozment, *op. cit.,* pp. 43–64; H.A. Oberman, *Die Gelehrten die Verkehrten:* Popular Response to Learned Culture in the Renaissance and Reformation," in Ozment, *op. cit.* F. Painter, *Luther on Education* (Philadelphia, 1889); H. J. Grimm, "Luther and Education," in *Luther and Culture* (Decorah, 1960), pp. 73–142; C. Bergendoff, *The Church of the Lutheran Reformation* (St. Louis, 1967); S. Karant-Nunn, "Luther's Pastors: The Reformation in the Ernestine Countryside," *Transactions of the American Philosophical Society* vol. 69, no. 8 (Philadelphia, 1979); J.M. Kittelson, "Humanism and the Reformation in Germany," *Central European History* 9 (1976): 303–322; "Luther on Education for Ordination," *Lutheran Theological Seminary Bulletin* 65 (1985):27–40; "Luther's impact upon the Universities—and the Reverse," *Concordia Theological Quarterly* 48 (1984): 23–38; G. Strauss, *Luther's House of Learning: Indoctrination of the Young in the German Reformation* (Baltimore, 1978). On Calvin and his reform movement in Geneva see, Q. Breen, *John Calvin: A Study in French Humanism* 2nd ed. (Grand Rapids, 1968); B. Hall, *John Calvin: Humanist and Theologian* 2nd ed. (London, 1967); A. Ganoczy, *The Young Calvin* trans. by D. Foxgrover and W. Provo (Philadelphia, 1987), esp. pp. 178–181. W.J. Bouwsma, *John Calvin: A Sixteenth Century Portrait* (Oxford, 1988), pp.113–130; 191–229; "The Peculiarity of the Reformation in Geneva," in Ozment, *Religion and Culture,* pp. 65–80. K. Randell, *John Calvin and the Later Reformation* (London, 1990); G.R. Potter and M. Greengrass, *John Calvin* (New York, 1983), pp. 57–127; A. McGrath, *A Life of John Calvin* (Oxford, 1990), pp. 21–128; G. Lewis, *"Calvinism in Geneva in the Time of Calvin and Beza, 1561–1608,"* in M. Prestwich, ed. *International Calvinism 1541–1715* (Oxford, 1985); W. Monter, *Calvin's Geneva* (New York, 1967); C. Borgeaud, *Histoire de l'Université de Genève,* vol. 1: *L'Académie de Calvin, 1559–1798* (Geneva, 1900); F. Wendel, *Calvin: The Origins and Development of His Religious Thought* trans. by P. Mairet (London, 1965), pp. 15–110; J.W. Baker, "Calvin's Discipline and the Early Reformed Tradition: Bullinger and Calvin," in R. V. Schnucker, ed., *Calviniana: Ideas and Influence of Jean Calvin* vol. X, Sixteenth Century Essays and Studies (Kirksville, 1988); M. Mullett, *Calvin* (London, 1989); H. Höpel, *The Christian Polity of John Calvin* (Cambridge, 1982).

men. Indeed, the Reformed confessions acknowledged that only the Scriptures as found in the *original* languages, in which they had been given by inspiration, could be considered normative for all religious concerns (Westminster Confession of Faith 1:8).[14]

This was a return to what amounted to a unique Protestant blend of both ancient catholic traditions: the Greek New Testament text of the Eastern Church and the Hebrew Bible that Jerome had returned to in providing an official ecclesiastical recension for the Western Church. And, for a brief moment, a genuine rapprochement actually existed between some Protestants of Western Europe and the Eastern Church under the patriarchate of Cyril Lucaris (1572–1638), Patriarch of Constantinople from 1612 till his death.

Lucaris made contact with Protestants in his opposition to Rome and eventually became friends with the Archbishop of Canterbury, presenting Charles I with the precious Codex *Alexandrinus* as a gift. He sent his most promising priests to Oxford and to Geneva and came to accept the Protestant understanding of Predestination and election, justification by faith alone, two sacraments, and embodied these doctrines in a very

---

[14]Typical of this Protestant working out of the confession's requirements in Calvinistic lands is the model of the Scottish Reformation where it was established that "in the more notable towns, especially the old Cathedral cities . . . there should be a college in which at least logic, rhetoric, and the languages— i.e., Latin and Greek—should be taught by competent masters. . . . " D. H. Fleming, *The Scottish Reformation* (Edinburgh, 1800), p. 175. While translations were certainly encouraged for the use of laymen in all the Reformation traditions, only the original language texts were considered normative for theology. While the Anglicans and the Lutherans never made a credal statement on this it was a presupposition stated in nearly all the dogmatics written by them in the sixteenth and seventeenth centuries. On this see, T.P. Letis, "The Protestant Dogmaticians and the Late Princeton School on the Status of the Sacred Apographa," *The Scottish Bulletin of Evangelical Theology* Vol. 8, no. 1 (Spring, 1990): 16–42. This gave stress to the importance of the Bishop (pastor) within Protestantism and was another point at which the magisterial Reformation retained a direct link with ancient catholic tradition. On this point of continuity within the German Reformation cf., J. Pelikan's classic, *Obedient Rebels: Catholic Substance and Protestant Principle in Luther's Reformation* (New York, 1964).

Protestant *Confessio Fidei* published in Geneva in 1629.[15] The Protestants never received any such approbation from Rome, as the legacy of the Council of Trent makes clear.[16]

The Council of Trent

On the fifteenth of February 1546 Luther died. News of this soon reached the Council at Trent, then meeting to put back together everything this "wild boar" had destroyed. Father Paolo Sarpi records in his celebrated *History of the Council of Trent*, the reaction at the council to the news of Luther's death:

> The fifteenth of February Martin Luther died also. This news being sent to Trent and Rome, there was not so much grief . . . as joy. . . . The Fathers in Trent, and the Court of Rome conceived great hope, seeing that so potent an instrument, to contradict the doctrine and rites of the Church of Rome, was dead, who was the principle, and almost the total cause of the divisions and innovations introduced, and held it for a presage of the good success of the Council.[17]

Sarpi went on to explain why the council so completely rejected the Protestant's program of going back to the Greek and the Hebrew texts as the final authority for the Church:

> On the contrary, the major part of the Divines said, that it was necessary to account that translation, which formerly hath been read in the Churches [*Vulgata Latina*], and used in the schools, to be divine and authentical, otherwise they should yield the cause to the Lutherans, and open a gate to innumerable heresies hereafter, and continually trouble the peace of Christendom. . . . The Inquisitors will not be able to proceed against the Lutherans, in case they know not Hebrew and Greek, because

---

[15]A very readable and popular treatment of Lucaris is, G. A. Hadjiantoniou, *Protestant Patriarch: The Life of Cyril Lucaris (1572–1638) Patriarch of Constantinople* (Richmond, 1961).

[16]Unless, of course, one views Vatican II as a rather late concession to Protestant advances made during the sixteenth century Reformation.

[17][Paolo Sarpi] *The History of the Council of Trent* trans. by N. Brent 2nd ed. (London, 1629), pp. 148–149.

they will suddenly answer, "the text is not so," and "that translation is false": every novity [*sic*], or toy, that shall come into the head of any grammarian, either for malice, or want of knowledge in Divinity, so that he may but find some grammatical trick in those tongues to confirm it, will be sufficient to ground himself thereon, and he will never make an end.[18]

Here we see the same resistance to the Protestants that Jerome received from Augustine and other critics in the fourth and fifth centuries. Moreover, Sarpi tells us further that some at Trent put forth the same argument as Augustine, claiming that, "the same Holy Ghost, who did dictate the holy books, hath dictated also that translation which ought to be accepted by the Church of Rome."[19]

But by now Augustine's argument was no longer seen to be a compelling one—no doubt because of the influences of the humanists—and so others at Trent mentioned Augustine's contemporary and sometime sparring partner, Jerome, as saying that, "no interpreter hath spoken by the Holy Ghost," and that since the *Vulgata Latina* is for the most part Jerome's, "it would be strange to attribute the assistance of God to him that knoweth and affirmeth he hath it not."[20]

A popular belief prevailed in both cases, Augustine's and at Trent, that ascribed complete authority to an officially sanctioned *ecclesiastical* translation, believing that it alone was "*authentica*" and authoritative, over the original language texts. Moreover, as with Augustine, Sarpi tells us that the majority who voted for the Vulgate at Trent were those "ignorant in the tongues."[21] In both cases, the churchmen were wrong and the humanists and the humanist influenced Protestants were correct.

---

[18]Ibid, p. 156.

[19]Ibid.

[20]Ibid, p. 157. What the majority eventually agreed to was that while the translation was not dictated by the same degree of influence by the Spirit, it was influenced to a degree "very near" that which produced the original.

[21]Ibid, p. 155, i.e. the original Hebrew and Greek. Augustine knew no Hebrew and but a little Greek.

Schwärmerei
("Enthusiasm")

Not only did Luther and the other Reformers have to contend with the Council of Trent, on the right; they had also to deal with another force, on the left: the *Schwärmer*. Roughly translated "enthusiasts," this English equivalent no longer has the punch it once delivered. Today, "fanatics" would communicate more of the meaning of the German. They are sometimes referred to as those of the "Radical Reformation." I choose to refer to them here generally as Anabaptists.

While Anabaptists have come to be classed as specific religious groups from the sixteenth century, with contemporary remnant communities found all over the world and known today as Hutterites, Amish, Mennonites, etc., I have a more general meaning in mind when I use the term here. I have reference to a broad third category which has been around since the post-apostolic era. They have generally shared three traits: 1) they are ultra-separatists and generally recognise no visible institutional expression of catholic orthodoxy, whether Eastern, Western, or Protestant; 2) they all share a "restorationist" mentality. That is, they are not generally concerned with other historical or cultural expressions of Christianity because they are certain that they alone are a living expression of a primitive, or apostolic, or first-century, or original, *Biblical* Christianity; 3) they generally do not believe baptism is a sacrament intended for their infants.[22]

---

[22]Hence, when I make reference to groups that I believe broadly share these characteristics, while they may, or may not, actually be connected in any organic way with historic sixteenth century Anabaptist communities, I will, nevertheless, use the term "anabaptists," or "anabaptist culture," using a lower case letter. When referring specifically to sixteenth-century Anabaptists, or to their contemporary descendants, I shall use the upper case letter. May this treatise *not* be misunderstood as a polemic against all contemporary independent-separatist Baptists. Some of my dearest and closest friends are of this persuasion. Rather, I have in mind *exclusively* the radical fringe separatists, found almost entirely on American soil, and unresponsive to any other Christian tradition. I once had someone

The Medieval Manichee

During the middle-ages many of these separatists were known as the *Manichee*. The *Manichee* were a collection of sects (all of which seemed to share the same dualist heresy), known sometimes as *Paulicians*, sometimes as the *Bogomils*, sometimes as the *Patarenes*, sometimes as the *Cathars* and sometimes as the *Albigensians*.

They seem to have all shared some connection with earlier Gnostic tradition but because they were always found on the margins of Christian culture and society a clear picture is not always easy to come by.[23]

It is this kind of heretical sectarianism that disturbed not only those at Trent, who believed the Protestant Reformation would unleash hordes of such pestilent sects, but the magisterial Reformers were just as concerned not to give place to the advancement of such anarchistic political and religious tendencies.

Luther first encountered the *Schwärmer* while he was locked away in hiding in the Wartburg Castle. In his absence they in-

---

of my own tradition tell me that to pray with someone other than a Lutheran is to indulge in "promiscuous prayer," a more noxious phrase I would not want to consider. This sentiment reflects the extremism of the anabaptist *(Schwärmeri)* spirit I have in mind, though here it is actually found within a sub-set of the magisterial Reformation tradition.

[23]The best brief introduction to the phenomenon may still be S. Runciman, *The Medieval Manichee: A Study of the Christian Dualist Heresy* 2nd ed. (Cambridge, 1955, reprt. 1982). For a convenient and fair treatment of the historical circumstances of the crusade against the Cathars see, J. Madaule, *The Albigensian Crusade: An Historical Essay* trans. by B. Wall (London, 1967). These groups are not to be confused with the *Vaudois*, or the *Waldenses*. A wonderful study of them was produced by Euan Cameron, *The Reformation of the Heretics: The Waldenses of the Alps 1480–1580* (Oxford, 1984). The *Vaudois* were not particularly heretical, they were not separatists from the Western catholic tradition—they freely partook of the sacraments, in fact, "they would not go without them" (p. 85). Moreover, "there is no credible trial evidence from this period to prove that the Waldenses of the Western Alps entertained any heresy about Baptism whatsoever" [i.e. they fully partook of baptism for their infants within the Roman Catholic Church] (Ibid). Finally, "the reformers approached the Waldenses in order to educate them, and because they admired their tradition of dissent, not because they wished to assimilate Waldensian ideas or modify their own" (p. 199). In fact, most Waldenses became good Calvinists under the influence of Calvin and Beza.

vaded Wittenberg and began to systematically destroy all the religious art in the city. Once Luther heard of this he left his safe hiding place, took his life in his own hands, and against the instructions of his Elector, Frederick the Wise, he returned to Wittenberg to dispel the pretentious *Zwickau* prophets who took orders from no one because they were in direct communication with the Holy Ghost. Luther later said he did not care if they had swallowed the Holy Ghost, feathers and all, they were false prophets because they were not in submission to Scripture, but to their own stubborn will.

Luther had a clear sense of where this was all going: in the name of *his* reform, which was very conservative by nature, these radicals were out for insurrection and anarchy in the name of religious freedom. Hence, in 1521, he published his *Admonition Against Insurrection and Rebellion.*

Here he argued that those acting in *his* name, believing they had *his* approval, were actually moved by Satan, who "was trying to stir up rebellion through supporters of the Gospel in order to bring their teaching into disrepute."[24] The Harvard Church historian, Mark Edwards, continues on this theme:

> Luther's subsequent attack . . . suggests that he felt it necessary to make the issue of responsibility clear-cut. Believing that his own reputation and, more important, the reputation of the Reformation movement to be at stake, he went out of his way to disavow those allegedly responsible as unequivocally and convincingly as possible. . . . Drawing on Scriptural accounts and episodes in the long history of heresy, the Reformer thus warned that Satan had once again sent false prophets to confound the true Church. Although such prophets appeared to follow the Gospel, they were in fact "Judases"; and Luther laid all responsibility for their excesses on the satanic spirit which he claimed motivated each one of them.[25]

---

[24]M. U. Edwards, "*Suermerus*: Luther's Own Fanatics," in P.N. Brooks, ed., *Seven-Headed Luther: Essays in Commemoration of a Quincentenary 1483–1983* (Oxford, 1983), p. 128.

[25]Ibid, pp. 128–29. For other works treating Luther's stance on the Anabaptists see, J.S. Oyer, *Lutheran Reformers Against Anabaptists: Luther, Melanchthon*

Calvin and the *Schwärmerei*

Calvin was no less fearful of what would happen at the hands of the anabaptists, than was Luther. Willem Balke's marvellously comprehensive treatment of Calvin and the anabaptists ends in the following summary:

> Calvin accused them of an unspiritual, biblicistic use of Scripture. He charged that their doctrinal positions regarding government, the oath, discipline, and sanctification were exegetically untenable and based on incorrect interpretations of Scripture. . . . Calvin insisted that anyone who wanted to go back to the Bible while rejecting dogmatic theology should not be so naive as to ignore the record of history. Calvin therefore charged that the Anabaptists broke the *consensus interpretationis* with the Church Fathers. Their biblicism and lack of doctrinal concern was therefore the trapdoor that opened upon impurity of doctrine. In their radicalism, the kingdom-wide aspect of God's commandments and promises was curtailed by their *im-*

---

and Menius, and the Anabaptists of Central Germany* (the Hague, 1964); M.U. Edwards, *Luther and the False Brethren* (Stanford, 1975); J.S. Preus, *Carlstadt's Ordinaciones and Luther's Liberty: A Study of the Wittenberg Movement, 1521–1522* (Cambridge, 1974); E. W. Gritsch, "Thomas Müntzer and Luther: A Tragedy of Error," in H. J. Hillerbrand, ed., *Radical Tendencies in the Reformation: Divergent Perspectives*, Vol IX *Sixteenth Century Essays and Studies* (Kirksville, 1988) On the Anabaptists and the English Reformation, see, I.B. Horst, *The Radical Brethren: Anabaptism and the English Reformation to 1558* (Nieuwkoop, 1972); On the Anabaptist ecclesiology, see, F.H. Littell, "The Anabaptist Doctrine of the Restitution of the True Church," *Mennonite Quarterly Review* 24 (1950): 33–52; *The Anabaptist View of the Church: An Introduction to Sectarian Protestantism* (n.p., 1952); F. J. Wray, "The Anabaptist Doctrine of the Restitution of the Church," *Mennonite Quarterly Review* 28 (1954): 187–196; E. A. Payne, *The Anabaptists of the Sixteenth Century and Their Influence in the Modern World* (London, 1949). The best overall treatment of the Anabaptists in general is, G.H. Williams, *The Radical Reformation* 3rd ed. (Kirksville, 1992). A bibliography of early sources is H. J. Hillerbrand, *A Bibliography of Anabaptists 1520–1630* (Indiana, 1962). A helpful, brief, up-to-date bibliographical essay, introduction, biographical notes and a series of primary sources in translation can be found in M. G. Baylor, ed. *The Radical Reformation* (Cambridge, 1991). A useful collection of essays is also, H. J. Hillerbrand, ed., *Radical Tendencies in the Reformation*; G. H. Williams and A. M. Mergal, eds., *Spiritual and Anabaptist Writers* (Philadelphia, 1957).

periolum or their *ecclesiola*. This involved a serious curtailment of the riches of Holy Scripture.[26]

New Jerusalem

Luther and Calvin both saw their worst fears realised. During the years 1533–5 a community of anabaptists turned their backs on ancient Christendom, "separated themselves from the world" by gathering in the Westphalian city of Münster, and led by an arch-fanatic, John Matthys—who claimed to be Enoch— they persuaded the entire city that the end of the world was at hand and that Münster was now the New Jerusalem.

Cut off from both Catholic as well as Protestant Europe, without external restraints, the city soon became a grim den of all manner of excess: All goods were to be held in common, and polygamy was now sanctioned. Those who would not be re-baptised, were either forced to flee or else were slaughtered. [27]

Eventually, this infection was surgically removed once the civil authorities moved in, took over the city, and restored order. Here was perhaps the first manifestation, in the early modern age, of an unbounded religious community of those who would

---

[26]Willem Balke, *Calvin and the Anabaptist Radicals* trans. by W.J. Heynen (Grand Rapids, 1981), pp. 326–237. See also, J. Calvin, *Treatises Against the Anabaptists and Against the Libertines*, ed. and trans. by B. W. Farley (Grand Rapids, 1982); "Against Menno," in M. Beaty and B. W. Farley, *Calvin's Ecclesiastical Advice* (Edinburgh, 1991) On Zwingli's view see *Refutation of the Tricks of the Catabaptists* in *Ulrich Zwingli 1484–1531* (Philadelphia, 1972). The sentimentality expressed by the editor in a footnote on this treatise is less than satisfying. For a more rigourously historical interpretation, Ulrich Gäbler, perhaps the most important Zwingli scholar alive today, provides a better treatment on this point in his *Huldrych Zwingli: His Life and Work* (Philadelphia, 1986), pp. 125–131.

[27]For an ever so brief treatment of this see, Littell, *The Anabaptist View*, pp. 39–42. For more extensive treatments, see Williams, *The Radical*, pp. 362–381; L. von Ranke, *History of the Reformation in Germany* trans. by S. Austin (London, 1905), pp. 724–757; J. Horsch, "The Rise and Fall of the Anabaptists of Münster," *Mennonite Quarterly Review* 9 1935): 92 ff; 129 ff. For two recent close studies, see, G. Vogler, "The Anabaptist Kingdom of Münster in the Tension Between Anabaptism and Imperial Policy," in Hillerbrand, *Radical Tendencies*, pp. 99–116; J.M. Stayer, "Christianity in One City: Anabaptist Münster, 1534–35," in Hillerbrand, Ibid., 117–134. On Münzer himself see Abraham Friesen, *Thomas Muentzer, a Destroyer of the Godless* (University of California Press, 1990).

reconstruct *primitive* Christianity without reference to any other historic manifestation, or institutional precedent; an a-historical Christianity, leading to an unaccountable Christianity. Such is what the Reformers feared most; such is what the Roman Catholics predicted would be the fruit of Luther's "Reformation"; such was one result of putting vernacular translations of the Bible into the hands of the people.

All of Europe now knew one direction in which this "Reformation" of the Church might go. Christian Europe, both Roman Catholic and Protestant, consolidated in resisting this *restorationist Christianity*.[28]

The Protestants saw the wisdom of retaining an official Church/State connection to assure the preservation both of social order, but also for the preservation of the integrity of the now renewed Church and the promise of a *renewed* Christendom.

Those who would have nothing to do with the state-established forms of this renewed catholic orthodoxy (whether it be the Calvinism established in Switzerland, the Netherlands, and Scotland; or the now Reformed Anglicanism of England; or the Lutheranism of Germany and the Scandinavian countries), now fled to the haven of religious freedom in the New World—colonial America.

America: A Haven for the Scwärmerei

In time, this new republic broke free from all formal political connections with old Christendom. The Lockean social philosophy of the Enlightenment animated most of the American intellectual political thinkers who agitated for revolution. They determined that the Christian religion would be, for the first time in the history of the Christian West, disestablished and re-

---

[28]Both Roman Catholic and Protestant troops marched into Münster in order to restore order. If one can imagine the fear released during both the execution of the king of France with the subsequent reign of terror during the French Revolution, and the butchering of the Czar of Russia along with his family, and the revolution that followed there, one can begin to appreciate how menacing such *religious* revolutions appeared to both the average Protestant and Roman Catholic citizen in 16th century Europe.

garded as, at best, just an option within the boundaries of this now post-Enlightenment state. The result was the development of a truly anabaptistic religious culture. In Valerie Dodd's words, modern religious movements such as Unitarianism and Universalism had their roots "in the Anabaptist movement in sixteenth century Germany. From that movement derived groups which were often notable for their populist, democratic tendencies."[29]

Giving vent to such populist, democratic tendencies, America now became the breeding ground for every independent religious impulse conceivable to human consciousness. A cocktail of cults now bubbled up from the caldron of this state without a religion. Jon Butler has recently written of an America that became "awash in a sea of faith,"[30] while Nathan Hatch has discussed the "sea of sectarian rivalries"[31] that have washed over the landscape of American society.

W. A. Clebsch, in his *From Sacred to Profane America: The Role of Religion in American History*, has attempted to put this religious pluralism in the best possible light calling it, "a polypolitan culture," in contrast to the Puritan Cotton Mather who advocated in 1710 his hope for a *theopolis Americana*. Clebsch's analysis accurately captures the dynamic of American religious culture:

> In America pluralism has been resolved less and less by appeal to order that yields unity and more and more by tolerance that diminishes the ultimacy implicit in any cause's demand for loyalty. Save for nationalism in time of putative military danger, the religious city alone states its claims over modern Americans in ultimate terms of absolute allegiance. But these claims ring hollow; American religion increasingly finds ways to express in doctrine its new-world experience and therefore also its distance

---

[29]V. A. Dodd, "Strauss's English Propagandists and the Politics of Unitarianism, 1841–1845," *Church History* 50:3 (March 1981), p. 429.

[30]J. Butler, *Awash in a Sea of Faith: Christinizing the American People* (Cambridge, 1990).

[31]N. O. Hatch, *The Democratization of American Christianity* (New Haven, 1989), pp. 49–66.

from European Christendom. Although lacking explicit testimony to its own relativity as one cause among many, as one tolerant member of this plural culture, religion tacitly concedes by its internally pluralistic form that it is not the overarching cause which collects all other loyalties.[32]

Every ancient heresy was now given state sanction: one of the earliest major heresies with which the early Church was challenged, Arianism, was revived on American soil.[33] Polygamy now appeared again.[34] The ancient heresy of Sabellianism also saw its rebirth in America.[35] More than one Pentecostal cult announced the arrival of Elijah, or that New Jerusalem had yet again appeared in various cities in the U.S., each to fall yet again. The American dream became so entangled with religious aspiration that faith was turned into a means of health, wealth and power, and gain was equated with godliness.[36]

---

[32]W. A. Clebsch, *From Sacred to Profane America: The Role of Religion in American History* (Chico, 1968), p. 208. Nevertheless, the many religious cults that have found a home in America have not always played by the unwritten rules in Clebsch's conclusion that "the American aspiration for plural culture and plural religion has reached achievement" (p. 209). Many of these cults are still militant in promoting their brand of absolutism. See T. Robbins, W.C. Shepherd and J. McBride, eds., *Cults, Culture and the Law: Perspectives on New Religious Movements* (Chico, 1985).

[33]J. A. Beckford, *The Trumpet of Prophecy: A Sociological Study of Jehovah's Witnesses* (Oxford, 1975); M.J. Penton, *Apocalypse Delayed: the Story of the Jehovah's Witnesses* (Toronto, 1985).

[34]K. J. Hansen, *Mormonism and the American Experience* (Chicago, 1981); P. L. Barlow, *Mormons and the Bible: The Place of the Latter-Day Saints in American Religion* (Oxford, 1991).

[35]V. Synan, *The Holiness/Pentecostal Movement* (Grand Rapids, 1971), pp. 154–163; R. M. Anderson, *Vision of the Disinherited: the Making of Pentecostalism* (Oxford, 1979), pp. 176–194.

[36]D. E. Harrell, *All Things are Possible: the Healing and Charismatic Revivals in Modern America* (Bloomington, 1975). On the wealth and success ethos that has been part of the American religious experience, particularly among later generations of Charismatics see, D. Meyer, *The Positive Thinkers: A Study of the American Quest for Health, Wealth and Personal Power from Mary Baker Eddy to Norman Vincent Peale* (New York, 1965); D. Voskuil, *Mountains into Goldmines: Robert Schuller and the Gospel of Success* (Grand Rapids, 1983). Two perceptive treatments of the failure of this quest for success and the accompanying contemporary crisis within the most popular expressions of American Anabaptist religious

Predicting the second coming of Christ became a near national pastime as Darbyite dispensationalism (which never took hold in its native England where the established state church was still firmly in control, promoting ancient catholic orthodoxy), flourished in the now dominant anabaptist culture of 20th century America.[37]

Not only did the Reformation faiths never really flourish in the United States[38] (but perhaps for a brief moment in New England),[39] even the Roman Catholic Church in time eventu-

---

culture (which have used the media with the most force in America) are, M. D'Antonio, *Fall From Grace: the Failed Crusade of the Christian Right* (London, 1990); M. M. Poloma, *The Assemblies of God at the Crossroad: Charisma and Institutional Dilemmas* (Knoxville, 1989).

[37]T. P. Weber, *Living in the Shadow of the Second Coming: American Premillennialism 1875–1925* (Oxford, 1979); Edwin Gaustad, ed., *The Rise of Adventism: Religion and Society in Mid-Nineteenth-Century America* (New York, 1974) On the background of dispensationalism particularly see, C. R. Bass, *Backgrounds of Dispensationalism: Its Historical Genesis and Ecclesiastical Implications* (Grand Rapids, 1960); C. N. Kraus, *Dispensationalism in America: Its Rise and Development* (Richmond, 1958); C. I. Crenshaw and G. E. Gunn, III, *Dispensationalism Today, Yesterday and Tomorrow* (Memphis, 1985); J. M. Canfield, *The Incredible Scofield and His Book* (Vallecito, 1988); J. H. Gerstner *Wrongly Dividing the Word of Truth: a Critique of Dispensationalism* (Brentwood, 1991).

[38]M. E. Marty recorded in his *Righteous Empire: The Protestant Experience in America* (New York, 1970), a classic account of how the American cultural and social influences transformed nearly every European Protestant tradition that gained a foothold in America.

[39]On New England Puritanism, the following are good introductions, P. Miller, *Errand Into the Wilderness* (New York, 1956); *The New England Mind: From Colony to Province* (Cambridge, 1953); *The New England Mind: The Seventeenth-Century* (Boston, 1961); P. Miller and T. H. Johnson, *The Puritans* 2 Vols. 2nd ed. (New York, 1963). W. G. Wilcox, *New England Covenant Theology: Its English Precursors and Early American Exponents*, Unpublished Ph.D. Dissertation, Duke University, 1959. Another possible exception might be the German Lutherans, particularly those who came from Saxony and who retained their German identity until the post WW II era by retaining the German language in their theological training and in their liturgy. On them see, M. L. Rudnick, *Fundamentalism and the Missouri Synod: A Historical Study of Their Interaction and Mutual Influence* (St. Louis, 1966), pp.103–113. I differ with Rudnick, however, in his interpretation that the fundamentalist influence on the Missouri Synod has been slight if at all. The shift from defending the apographa to defending the autographa as the locus of final biblical authority was an external influence from American fundamentalism. Moreover, acceptance of the *New International Version* as the unofficially endorsed vernacular translation of the Missouri Synod, a

ally took on more of the appearance of a large democratic lodge rather than the most autocratic institution in the modern world.[40]

The New Schwärmerei: Fundamentalism

Cut off from the archetype of ancient catholic orthodoxy, America invented its own orthodoxy—Fundamentalism.[41] Fundamentalism was a synthesis: an Enlightenment reductionism

---

work produced by fundamentalist Reformed and Anabaptist communities, would surely lead Rudnick to change his mind were he writing his book today. Other exceptions might be Dutch Calvinism, J. D. Bratt, *Dutch Calvinism in Modern America: History of a Conservative Subculture* (Grand Rapids, 1984), and the Mercersburg theology of Schaff and Nevin, G. Shriver, *Philip Schaff: Christian Scholar and Ecumenical Prophet*, (Macon, 1987); J. L. Binkley, *The Mercersburg Theology* (Manheim, 1953). None of these traditions, however, have ever made any appreciable impact on the dominant contours of American religious culture (but for small ethnic communities). The United States has always been the domain of Anabaptist culture. Moreover, even the classic Anabaptists (e.g. Mennonites, etc.) as well as all other classic Protestant traditions, were modified by Pietism early on their arrival in America, see F. Ernest Stoeffler, ed., *Continental Pietism and Early American Christianity* (Grand Rapids, 1976).

[40]P. W. Carey, *People, Priests, and Prelates: Ecclesiastical Democracy and the Tensions of Trusteeism* (Notre Dame, 1987). As early as 1899 Pope Leo XIII had condemned "Americanism," noting that "there are some among you who conceive and desire a church in America different from that which is in the rest of the world." *Testem benevolentiae* as quoted in Clebsch, *op. cit.,* p. 216.

[41]The literature on American Fundamentalism is an ever growing mass of material. Standard introductions are, S. G. Cole, *The History of Fundamentalism* (New York, 1931); N. F. Furniss, *The Fundamentalist Controversy, 1918-1931* (New Haven, 1954); G. Hebert, *Fundamentalism and the Church* (Philadelphia, 1957); E. R. Sandeen, *The Roots of Fundamentalism, British and American Millenarianism* (Chicago, 1970); G. M. Marsden, *Fundamentalism and American Culture* (Oxford, 1980); *Reforming Fundamentalism: Fuller Seminary and the New Evangelicalism* (Grand Rapids, 1987); *Understanding Fundamentalism and Evangelicalism* (Grand Rapids, 1991); C. A. Russell, *Voices of American Fundamentalism* (Philadelphia, 1976); L. I. Sweet, ed., *The Evangelical Tradition in America* (Macon, 1984); J. A. Carpenter, *The Renewal of American Fundamentalism, 1930-1945*, forthcoming from Oxford University Press; M. E. Marty, *Modern American Religion: the Irony of it All, 1893-1919* (Chicago, 1986); D. Hunter, *American Evangelicalism: Conservative Religion and the Quandary of Modernity* (New Brunswick, 1983); *Evangelicalism: The Coming Generation* (Chicago, 1987); B. B. Lawrence, *Defenders of God: The Fundamentalist Revolt Against the Modern Age* (London, 1990); F.M. Szasz, *The Divided Mind of Protestant America, 1800-1930* (1982); A very useful bibliographical survey of the literature is found in V. L. Brereton, *Training God's Army: The American Bible School 1880-1940* (Bloomington, 1990),

to the *essence of Christianity* expressed in a handful of propositions regarding what must be believed to be a Christian, mar-
ried to elaborate theories regarding the second Advent of
Christ. Finally, this was all clothed in a Scottish Common-
Sense apologetic appeal to empiricism as an absolute guarantor
of external verification.[42]

Since there was no longer the possibility of appealing to the
catholic witness of the Church for certification of the Christian
religion, appeal was now made to science.[43]

Furthermore, now that everyone had their own designer religion, reflecting their own socio-economic and cultural concerns
and values, it was just a matter of time before free-market forces
provided each major group with their own designer Bibles to re-
inforce their given perspectives.[44]

And with the emergence of the twentieth-century chapter on
the controversy of Bible translation we finally return to the
theme of this essay. Market forces intruded into the equation in
direct proportion to the disintegration of ecclesiastical consensus and so the problem that emerged was inevitable: how was

---

pp. 197-208. A further helpful forty-five volume facsimile series reproducing primary documents from American fundamentalist authors is, J. A. Carpenter,
Fundamentalism in American Religion 1880–1950 (New York, 1988).

[42]C. D. Cashdollar, *The Transformation of Theology, 1830–1890: Positivism and
Protestant Thought in Britain and America* (Princeton, 1989). Cf. also, M.A. Noll,
Princeton, Scottish Enlightenment and the American College Ideal (New York,
1971); D. Bozeman, *Protestants in an Age of Science: the Baconian Ideal and Ante-
bellum American Religious Thought* (Chapel Hill, 1977).

[43]G. Marsden has written several insightful studies on this theme, *Fundamen-
talism*, pp. 55–62; 109–117; "The Collapse of American Evangelical Academia," in
A. Plantinga and N. Wolterstorff, eds., *Faith and Rationality* (South Bend, 1984);
Understanding Fundamentalism, pp. 122–181; "Evangelicals and the Scientific
Culture: An Overview," in *Religion and Twentieth-Century American Intellectual
Life*, ed. M.J. Lacy (Cambridge, 1989), pp. 23–48.

[44]For a good general survey with excellent bibliographies for each of the
major translations since the publishing of the seventeenth century Anglican
Church Bible, see, J.P. Lewis, *The English Bible From the KJV to the NIV: A History and Evaluation* 2nd ed. (Grand Rapids, 1991). It must be added, however,
that the author's treatment of the old English liturgical Bible tradition is
painfully one-sided and reflects more the values and ideology of the modern
Bible publishing industry, than a dispassionate professional assessment at the
hands of an expert in the field.

one to choose between so many commercial vernacular Bible options, proliferating at a dizzying rate, with no authoritative ecclesiastical guidance?

Burgon and Revision

Retreating for a moment to nineteenth-century Britain we discover the precursor to this problem in the controversy surrounding the first attempt to officially and publicly up-date the established liturgical Bible of the Anglican Church. Anyone with any exposure to the problems of the old *Authorized Version* knew by the middle of the nineteenth century that it was due to be corrected, just as Jerome had to correct the old *Itala*, or Old Latin (which had been translated from the LXX), and just as Erasmus, in turn, had to correct Jerome's Vulgate with his own fresh Latin translation from the Greek during the Renaissance.[45]

---

[45]Some of the wide ranging calls for revision of the A.V., extending as far back as the seventeenth century are, R. Gell, *An Essay Toward the Amendment of the Last English Translation of the Bible* (London, 1659); [H. Ross], *An Essay for a New Translation of the Bible* (London, 1702); *Reasons for Revising by Authority Our Present Version of the Bible* (Cambridge, 1788); J. Symonds, *Observations on the Expediency of Revising the Present English Version of the Four Gospels and the Acts of the Apostles* (Cambridge, 1789); *Observations . . . of the Epistles* (Cambridge, 1794); B. Burgess, *Reasons in Favour of a New Translation of the Holy Scripture* (London, 1819); H. Scrivener, *A Supplement to the Authorized English Version of the New Testament* (London, 1845); J. Scholefield, *Hints for an Improved Translation of the New Testament* (London, 1850); W. Harness, *The State of the English Bible* (London, 1856); E. Slater, *Biblical Revision: Considerations in Favour of a Revised Translation of Holy Scripture* (London, 1856); W. Selwyn, *Notes on the Proposed Amendment of the Authorized Version of the Holy Scriptures* (Cambridge, 1856); F. Iliff, *A Plea for the Revisal of the Translation of the Bible of 1611* (Sunderland, 1857); J. Beard, *A Revised English Bible, the Want of the Church, and the Demand of the Age* (London, 1857); G. E. Biber *A Plea for an Edition of the Authorized Version of the Holy Scripture with Explanatory and Emendatory Marginal Notes* (London, 1857); H. Burgess, *Revision of the Holy Scriptures: An Argument Against Objectors,* (London, 1857); R. Trench, *On the Authorized Version of the New Testament* (London, 1858); A. Dewes, *Plea for a New Translation of the Scriptures* (London, 1866); C. J. Ellicott, *Considerations on the Revision of the English Version* (London, 1870); J. B. Lightfoot, *On a Fresh Revision of the English New Testament* (London, 1871); T. K. Abbott, *The English Bible and Our Duty with Regard to It: A Plea for Revision* 2nd ed. Dublin, 1871; J. Eadie, *The English Bible: An External and Critical History of the Various English Translations of Scripture* 2 vols. (London, 1876), Vol. 2, pp. 242–484.

Even the most adamant defenders of the Anglican Bible were ready to concede the need for its adjustment at places. Rev. S. C. Malan in his *Vindication of the Authorized Version of the English Bible*, had confessed,

> At all events, all the necessary alterations in the text of the *Authorized Version* may be introduced into it by men of wisdom and judgement, without nine-tenths of the nation being aware of it. Would it not, therefore, be far better to do so, if it is to be done?[46]

One high church Anglican, John William Burgon, former Gresham Lecturer in Divinity, Oxford, a Fellow of Oriel College, Oxford, former Vicar of St. Mary's, Oxford (where Cardinal John Henry Newman had also been Vicar just a few years earlier) and finally, Dean of Chichester Cathedral, was more hesitant than most to see the old Bible altered in an official and public revision process.

While Burgon also readily conceded that a revision should take place he preferred that such a new critical edition be preserved for *private* use only, not to be employed in the public usage of the Church.[47] Here Burgon was echoing the advice Augustine had given to Jerome in a letter. Augustine had told Jerome he regarded the value of his new translation from the Hebrew, but desired that it not be given a place of authority in the public reading of the Church, "lest the faithful, accustomed as they were to the Septuagint, should be upset."[48]

The official English Bible of the Anglican Church at that time was known as the *Authorized Version* because it had been officially approved not only by all the Bishops of the Anglican

---

[46]S. C. Malan, *Vindication of the Authorized Version of the English Bible* (London, 1856), p. 346. This was, after all, the method used to revise the *Authorized Version* on at least four other occasions, not to mention those unauthorized alterations made unofficially by unknown persons, cf. F. H. A. Scrivener, *The Authorized Edition of the English Bible (1611): Its Subsequent Reprints and Modern Representatives* (Cambridge, 1910), pp. 3–39.

[47]J. W. Burgon, *The Revision Revised* (London, 1883), p. 113–114.

[48]Augustine's letter 82A, paraphrased in Kelly, *Jerome*, p. 271.

Church—it was, in fact, an official revision of the *Bishops Bible* (1572 edition)—but it was called "authorized" because James I, as Supereme Govenor of the Church, had given this translation his authority and sanction, as can be clearly seen on the title page of most editions to this day, where we read: "Appointed to be Read in Churches."[49]

Furthermore, this Bible had the *Cum Privilegio* ("with privilege") printed on it which meant that the Crown of England, as the Supreme Govenor of the state church, held the copyright to this Bible, giving permission for its printing only to those printers which the Crown had chosen. To this day this "copyright" is in place.[50]

Finally, only *Anglican* clergymen, or scholars, had ever been sanctioned to work on the English Bible within Britain since the Reformation.

Burgon had a particular apprehension, therefore, of the intrusion of an *anabaptist* (i.e. non-conformist) participation in such a project. When such a revision finally took place it was this that Burgon complained of most bitterly, believing it would lead to the dissolution of the orthodoxy and exclusive authority of the Church of England:

> I candidly avow that it was in my account a serious breach of Church order that, on engaging in so solemn an undertaking as the Revision of the *Authorized Version*, a body of Divines . . . should spontaneously associate with themselves Ministers of various denominations—Baptists, Congregationalists, Wesleyan Methodists, Independents, and the like: and especially that a successor of the Apostles should have presided over the deliberations of this *assemblage of Separatists*.[51]

---

[49]*Dictionary of English Church History*, s.v. "Bible." It has often been claimed that no official license or decree assured a place of authority for the A.V., but in that it was intended to be a revision of the Bishops Bible all of the original authority vested in this earlier edition would now naturally transfer to the A.V.

[50]This, contrary to the misinformation found in many anabaptist publications claiming the *Authorized Version* is the only Bible *not* copyrighted and so it can be freely printed by anyone at any time. All such illegal printing would be against the authority of the Crown of Great Britain.

[51]Ibid., pp. 504–505. Burgon was particularly offended at the presence of a

A more potent slur, intended to ruffle the feathers of high churchmen throughout the land, could not have been invoked by Burgon than to refer to the revision committee as an "assemblage of separatists."

Here we find yet another parallel with Jerome's controversy; and with that which Erasmus had with theologians in his day: the issue of *ecclesiology*. In Augustine's view, Jerome was pitting himself against the sanction of the *recognised usage of the early Church*. Erasmus was seen by his critics to be undermining the authority of the *Roman* Church and Jerome, whose Bible had by that time not only ecclesiastical sanction by means of continuous *church usage* throughout the middle ages, but initially he also had papal sanction from Pope Damasus.

Burgon felt that catholic orthodoxy was under threat by allowing the Anabaptists to have a free vote in determining the authentic text of Scripture. In his view, catholic divines within the Anglican communion, by means of usage, had already determined this standard by the seventeenth century:

> In my humble judgement, we shall in vain teach the sinfulness of Schism [i.e. separatism from the established state Church], if we show ourselves practically indifferent on the subject, and even set an example of irregularity to our flocks. My Divinity may appear unaccommodating and old-fashioned: but I am not prepared to unlearn the lessons long since got by heart in the school of Andrewes and Hooker, of Pearson and Bull, of Hammond and Sanderson, of Beveridge and Bramhall.[52]

All of those named by Burgon were high churchmen like himself, who would, indeed, have been scandalised to know that non-conformists were being called on to assist Anglican

---

Unitarian on the committee, but this was just the most extreme result of allowing "separatists" to take part. From his perspective, once separatists of any stripe were admitted how could one in principle stop at Unitarians? In the footnote, he links all separatists and Unitarians, "But it is quite a different thing when Revisionists . . . co-opt Separatists and even Unitarians into their body" (p. 504, n. 1). Elsewhere Burgon referred to all these separatists as "sects" (p.6).

[52]Ibid., p. 105.

theologians and scholars to revise the English Bible of the state church.[53]

Mind you, it was not the lack of conservatism in these non-conformists that troubled Burgon, this was quite irrelevant to his objection. Burgon was incensed because they were *schismatics*, outside the catholic tradition of the Church of England.

Burgon, nearly single-handedly, succeeded in preventing the *Revised Version* of 1885 from gaining popular acceptance within the Anglican Church.[54] But English society by this time was changing rapidly and it was just a matter of time before a *Revised Version* would find full acceptance within the English Church.[55]

Burgon is to be commended, whether one accepts all his arguments, or not, because he became a bona fide authority in the field before entering the controversy.[56] In replying to one of his critics, Bishop Ellicott, Chairman of the revision committee,

---

[53]Burgon wrote perhaps his most widely read and popular work, *Lives of Twelve Good Men* 2nd ed. (London, 1891), in celebration of twelve high church-men, many of whom had personally influenced his own theological development. Moreover, his biographer and very dear friend, Edward Meyrick Goulburn, Dean of Norwich, another high churchman, was the author of, *The Holy Catholic Church: Its Divine Ideal, Ministry, and Institutions—a Short Treatise with a Catechism on Each Chapter Forming a Course of Methodical Instruction on the Subject* (London, 1873). Finally, it was on this principle that Burgon's high churchmanship far outreached that of those who have been ignorantly accused of Anglo-Catholic leanings by an irresponsible anabaptist press in North America. The very fact that Westcott and Hort could join in a company of non-conformists in this revision project is evidence of their *low* church leanings and complete incompatibility with Anglo-Catholic sentiments.

[54]Geoffrey Hunt is less than sensitive to the actual historical events when he says, "In the long run, it did not gain widespread support. The reason, no doubt, was that it was a compromise." *About the New English Bible* (Oxford and Cambridge, 1970), p. 5. The primary reason was Burgon's devastating public critique.

[55]Hunt, *op. cit.; An Introduction to the Revised Standard Version of the New Testament*, by Members of the Revision Committee, n.p. 1946.

[56]F.F. Bruce, no friend of Burgon's, frankly acknowledged this: "Burgon was an able textual scholar in his own right, and was actually ahead of his time in his appreciation of the importance for textual criticism of biblical citations in the early Christian writers and of early Christian lectionaries. In both these areas of study he did much valuable pioneer work" *The English Bible* 2nd ed. (London, 1970), p. 148. Bruce neglected to add that Burgon provided much new data from his many Greek MS. collations.

Burgon reminded him that unlike the Bishop, Burgon had, as few men by that time had, gone directly to the sources:

> The task of laboriously collating the five "old uncials" through-out the Gospels, occupied me for five-and-a-half years, and taxed me severely. But I was rewarded. I rose from the investiga-tion profoundly convinced that, however important they may be as instruments of Criticism, codices Aleph B C D are among the most corrupt documents extant. It was a conviction derived from exact *Knowledge* and based on solid grounds of *Reason*. You, my lord Bishop, who have never gone deeply into the sub-ject, repose simply on *Prejudice*. Never having at any time col-lated codices Aleph A B C D for yourself, you are unable to gainsay a single statement of mine by a counter-appeal to *facts*. Your textual learning proves to have been all obtained at second-hand,—taken on trust. And so, instead of marshalling against me a corresponding array of ANCIENT AUTHORITIES,— you invariably attempt to put me down by an appeal to Modern Opinion.[57]

And here, it must be said, Burgon had the best of his Bishop. Like the humanists and the Reformers of the sixteenth century, Burgon had indeed, whether you accepted his judgements or not, gone to the sources.

Fundamentalism and Education

By the middle of the this century, nearly everyone was now prepared to put down the old English Bible and take up one of the many modern options available—but for the fundamental-ists, nearly all of whom normally held emotionally, rather than in an informed way, to the old Bible of the Anglican Church:

> Whatever the variations among fundamentalists speakers, few were unaffected by the Bible, particularly the King James Ver-sion. Fundamentalists have constantly quoted, echoed, and al-luded to Scripture. They have employed biblical constructions ("builded," "used of God," "cometh," "unto," "thy") and archaic

---

[57]Burgon, *Revision Revised*, p. 376.

or old fashioned words that retained a "biblical" ring. . . .
The seventeenth century prose of the earlier Bible still exerts
considerable linguistic power.[58]

This surely is an inexplicable irony because no Anabaptist
ever worked on the committee that produced the A.V. while
they did, however, work on its rival, the R.V. Furthermore, one
would have expected them to rally around the Baptist Bible
produced last century. John Eadie, an Anglican who worked on
the R.V., described this nineteenth-century, revised, Baptist
Bible in the following terms:

> The Baptist translation of the American Bible Union merits
> commendation in many respects, though it is more than faithful
> to antipædobaptist opinions. It professedly makes the Bible the
> book of a sect. And we have such renderings as these: Matt. iii.
> 1, "John the immerser; xxi. 25, "John's immersion, whence was
> it? from heaven or from men?". . . .[59]

One reason the Anglican Bible became the Bible of the fundamentalists is because most had no intimate knowledge of the
actual history of the English Bible which would have made clear
this was the official Bible of the Anglican Church, which
Church had historically been consistently intolerant toward the
Anabaptist communities. Marsden has highlighted the significance of fundamentalist education which casts some light on
this problem:

> Fundamentalism did not develop in seminaries, but in Bible
> conferences, Bible schools, and, perhaps most importantly, on
> the personal level of small Bible-study groups where the
> prophetic truths could be made plain.[60]

Brereton's important study of the role American Bible
schools, as opposed to university or seminary training, played in

[58]Brereton, *op. cit.,* p. 24.
[59]J. Eadie, *The English Bible* , vol 2, p. 360.
[60]Marsden, *Fundamentalism,* p. 61–62.

insulating fundamentalists from a broad liberal arts education, is an insightful study of the dynamic at work here:

> Despite the considerable differences among these [fundamentalist] groups, they found commonality in their dissent from the intellectual currents represented by the universities and university-influenced seminaries. . . . Most of the early Bible school work was well below college level, and high school graduation was seldom a requirement for entrance. The early faculty, rarely professional educators, were often part-time employees or volunteers, and seldom boasted advanced (or even college) degrees. . . . To be sure, literature at Gordon [College] (and at other Bible schools) was more likely to be "edifying" than thought-provoking; the frame of reference supplied by history and philosophy was to teach an appreciation and defense of Christianity—and "Christian civilization"—rather than a critical stance toward it.[61]

In short, if the humanities were taught at all, it was through a rather dense filter.

Hence, without reference to a sophisticated understanding of *why* the *Authorized Version* was the dominant Bible in English speaking societies, it simply became the "Word of God" to the fundamentalist. The *Authorized Version* of the Anglican Church became for the American fundamentalist a dislocated entity; the unmediated *ipsissima verba*, without pedigree, without genealogy, without historical associations or context.[62] James Barr puts it like this:

---

[61]Brereton, *Training God's Army*, pp. 33; 35; 105. This, of course, is no longer the case among the mainline separatist Baptist institutions. Shining examples, such as Pensacola Christian College, with its phenomenal growth patterns coupled with high academic standards, reveals that a further stage of maturation has dawned in some leading light institutions, without their compromising their independence to the increasingly secular state, or to the modernism of mainline denominational religious institutions.

[62]There was one pseudo-historical account of the details surrounding the transmission of the *Authorized Version* produced by a fundamentalist, but the author was a Seventh-Day Adventist scholar who employed a rather conspiratorial approach to his subject (this conspiratorial dimension has subsequently always been found to be part of the Anabaptist treatment). According to this account,

In much popular fundamentalism there was practically no awareness of an original text at all, much less of any variations within that original: what functioned as the inspired text was the English of the *Authorized Version*. Officially, no doubt, there was some awareness that the translation was not the original, but in practice this made little or no difference, since for all practical (i.e. all religious) purposes the English translation was a precise transcript of the will of God.[63]

Hills and Revision

In 1956, however, after the fundamentalist/modernist controversy had spent its fury, a scholarly monograph emerged building on the foundation of many of Burgon's original arguments and data.[64]

Edward F. Hills, a conservative Presbyterian, trained in the classics at Yale and with a doctorate in N.T. text criticism from Harvard, set forth the first technical plea for retaining the old Anglican Bible since Burgon's attempt in the late nineteenth century.

Not being an Anglican himself, Hills's approach put less emphasis on an ecclesiological argument and more on a purely technical one, informed, nevertheless, by his own theological tradition.

As a Presbyterian he believed the Westminster Confession's affirmation that the Bible would be preserved in its integrity within the Christian Church (Westminster Confession of Faith 1:8) meant that those original language texts which had been uniformly used with the greatest degree of historic continuity,

---

the *Authorized Version* was produced from texts of the Bible preserved and transmitted by medieval separatists (mentioned earlier in this essay), who, the author implies, were Seventh-Day Adventists, B. G. Wilkinson, *Our Authorized Bible Vindicated* (Washington, 1930). For a contemporary work in a similar vein, please see Appendix B.

[63]J. Barr, *Fundamentalism* (Philadelphia, 1978), p. 280.

[64]Edward F. Hills, *The King James Version Defended: A Christian View of the New Testament Manuscripts* (Des Moines, 1956). In manuscript form this was to have been titled: *Text and Time: Textual Criticism from the Reformed Point of View*, actually a more descriptive indication of the actual content of the book.

qualified as the providentially preserved editions. This was, in fact, the position of most of the Protestant dogmaticians, Lutheran and Reformed, since the seventeenth century.[65]

Hills came to many of the same conclusions as Burgon, but in the place of the high church argument of apostolic succession as a guarantee (perhaps more implicit than explicit in Burgon), he appealed directly to the affirmation of the Presbyterian West-minster Confession of Faith.

Hence, Hills was much more content to abide by the form of the Greek N.T. which actually underlay the *Authorized Version*, with all of its historic accidents, because it was this recension that had been sanctioned by the Westminster Confession.

Burgon, on the other hand, wanted to revise this Greek tradi-tion in a number of cases where he felt it had been corrupted. Being a well trained classicist, however, as well as a theologian, Hills laboured under no perfectionist view of the *Textus Recep-tus,* frankly admitting, "Some of the non-Byzantine readings which Erasmus introduced into his New Testament text are un-questionably erroneous."[66]

Nevertheless, Hills agreed with Burgon that the only stabilis-ing force that would keep the sceptical tendencies found within the discipline of text criticism from affecting the public good of the Presbyterian Church, as well as among the confessional churches at large, was to keep in place the old Anglican Bible which still retained substantial wider cultural significance by mid-century. Earlier, Burgon had said:

> Whatever may be urged in favour of Biblical revision, it is at least undeniable that the undertaking involves a tremendous risk. Our A.V. is the one religious link which at present binds together ninety millions of English-speaking men scattered over the earth's surface. Is it reasonable that so unutterably precious, so sa-cred a bond should be endangered, for the sake of representing

---

[65]For a brief introduction to this see, Letis, "The Protestant Dogmaticians.".

[66]Hills, *The King James Version Defended*, 1st ed., p. 122. Although, it must be said that in later editions he modified this language. For a study of Hills's life and thought, see, T. P. Letis, *Edward Freer Hills's Contribution to the Revival of the Ec-clesiastical Text,* M.T.S. Thesis, Emory University, Atlanta, 1987.

certain words more accurately—here and there translating a tense with greater precision—getting rid of a few archaisms? It may be confidently assumed that no revision of our A.V., however judiciously executed, will ever occupy the place in publick [sic] esteem which is actually enjoyed by the work of the Translators of 1611—the noblest literary work in the Anglo-Saxon language. We shall in fact never have another "*Authorized Version.*"[67]

Hills echoed this sentiment with a little more desperation seventy-three years later:

Thus naturalistic New Testament textual criticism is inclining more and more toward a free handling of the text. The final authority is not the testimony of the extant manuscripts, even in places in which they all agree, but the subjective insight and judgement of the critics. Thus the future of the New Testament text is unpredictable, since it depends on these intangible factors. The way is open for a multiplicity of texts—as many as there are critics. Who knows what forms the New Testament may assume fifty years hence? At present the one great stabilizing factor (in English speaking countries) is the persistent devotion of the Bible reading public to the King James Version. But if this loyalty should fade, what would prevent the full effects of naturalistic textual criticism from being felt in the field of New Testament translations also?[68]

The Legacy of Burgon and Hills

Both Burgon and Hills have always received approbation from the more learned conservative classes of modern Christians who find enrichment, not an insurmountable challenge, in the literary qualities of the old English Bible.[69] Contemporary literary critics still hail the A.V. as an enduring masterpiece.

---

[67]Burgon, *Revision Revised*, p. 113.

[68]Hills, *The King James Version* 1st ed., p. 14.

[69]Here in Great Britain during the Easter season this year (1992) a most remarkable dramatic presentation of the Gospel accounts of the life of Jesus, by a small group of British actors, titled simply, *The Gospels,* was serialized in evening television broadcasts on the BBC. It was the *Authorized Version* they chose to recite, verbatim, to an astounding effect.

One of the most important modern, one volume, literary analysis of the entire Bible is the Harvard University publication, edited by Robert Alter and Frank Kermode, titled, *The Literary Guide to the Bible* (1987). Here the editors chose not the more popular *Revised Standard Version*, nor the *New English Bible*. Instead, they used the *Authorized Version*, giving the following criteria for their choice, qualities both Burgon and Hills were attempting to preserve:

> We have as a rule used the King James Version in Translations, and our reasons for doing so must be obvious: it is the version most English readers associate with the literary qualities of the Bible, and it is still arguably the version that best preserves the literary effects of the original languages.[70]

Stephen Prickett, a highly acclaimed literary critic, and Robert Barnes, a lecturer in religious studies, have recently amplified this theme while discussing the translation philosophy behind the old Anglican Bible:

> Explicit commitment [by the translators] both to tradition and consensus left its mark on the text in two very important ways. Firstly, it meant that the language of the translation was *deliberately archaic* [emphasis mine]. In a period when the English language was changing more rapidly than ever before or since, the Bible was set in words that were designed to stress the essential continuity of the Anglican settlement with the past by recalling the phraseology, not merely of the familiar Geneva Bible, but of Coverdale and Tyndale—and beyond that even of the Vulgate itself. At a time of threatened disorder—that within a generation was to culminate in Civil War—the new Bible was a statement of stability, order, and above all continuity with the past. It was, in the fullest sense of the word, a political document. Secondly, there was no room for individual interpretation. Not merely was it politically inexpedient; it was also theologically inappropriate and even, in extreme cases, blasphemous. If the

---

[70]R. Alter and F. Kermode, *The Literary Guide to the Bible* (Cambridge, 1987), p. 7.

Bible was inspired by the Holy Spirit and was the source of its own authority, then it was doubly dangerous for man to seek to amend it in any way. . . . Thus John Boyes (or Bois), a fellow of St. John's College, Cambridge, who was . . . a translator of a section of the New Testament for the AV . . . recorded in his notes that he and his committee had been careful to preserve ambiguities in the original text. . . . Seventeenth-century translators, whether Protestant or Catholic, were under no doubt that, whatever the difficulties or peculiarities of the Hebrew or Greek, they were there for a divinely ordained purpose, and were therefore not to be corrected by human agency.[71]

Finally, Prickett concludes regarding the legacy of modern translations in general. What disturbs him, was also a nuisance to Burgon and Hills:

Not the modern language, but the assumption, so clearly expressed in the preface to the GNB [Good News Bible], that the Bible (and by inference, religious experience) can be reduced to things that are "natural, clear, simple and unambiguous"—a conclusion that would have greatly puzzled the sixteenth and seventeenth-century translators, not to mention a long procession of saints, mystics, and poets over the last 2000 years.[72]

In short, there have always been and always will be those to whom the past is a living, and vital reality, and in religious cultural terms, this always entails a literary appreciation for the matchless qualities of the A.V. found impressed upon every dimension of English language tradition.

And then there are those souls dislocated from the past, self absorbed in the immediacy of contemporary living, to whom

---

[71]S. Prickett and R. Barnes, *The Bible* (Cambridge, 1991), pp. 120–121. Here Prickett relates a wonderful story illustrative of the impact of the *Authorized Version* on the English language: "There is a story (possibly apocryphal) that when the translators of the NEB came to the parable of the Prodigal Son they decided to find out the *modern* English equivalent of the 'fatted calf.' Accordingly, they consulted a butcher at Smithfield market in London as to what one called a calf that had been specially fattened up for a particular occasion. He explained that the technical phrase was 'fatted calf'—and that it came from the Bible!" (p. 130)

[72]Ibid., p. 132.

the past is an unnerving and troubling unknown quantity to be avoided at all costs. Modern translations provide them with just the barrier needed to keep them blissful.

One last testimony to the enduring significance of the platform for which both Burgon and Hills toiled.

Robin Lane Fox, a Fellow of New College, Oxford and University Reader in Ancient History, has recently written a most provocative book, titled: *The UnAuthorized Version: Truth and Fiction in the Bible.* There are a number of wonderfully refreshing perspectives offered in this entertaining and thought-provoking study, but none more relevant to our topic than the following:

In the Old Testament, especially, historians have helped us to realize that we cannot hope to recover the first, the 'original' text: it is in others, especially non-historians, that the urge to reconstruct it is still extremely strong. . . . As for the New Testament. . . . the very aim, a standard version [i.e. Nestle/ Aland Novum Testamentum 26th ed.], is misleading and unrealistic. From the variety which we have, any standard involves loss: it does not, and cannot, give us exactly what Paul or the Evangelists originally wrote. Historians, therefore, are not straining for the flawless original. . . . It is one thing to change the Lutheran Bible's German or the English of the King James version because we are now certain that a Hebrew or Greek word had a different meaning. It is quite another to change it with the aim of drawing closer to the original scripture. For the original text of the Old Testament is lost to us, and the Greek texts of the New Testament do not take us beyond small variants and alternatives a hundred years or more after the Gospels' likely date of composition. 'Literary authenticity' is a misplaced ideal for Old Testament translations, and in my view, it is misplaced for the New Testament too. . . . There are scriptures but no exact scripture within the range of our surviving knowledge: each group of readers, then, should be free to use the particular form of scripture which is historically rooted in its own traditions of liturgy, prayer, hymns and surrounding language. In English, the *Authorized Version* has a special place which ought, even now, to be unshakeable. . . . We cannot work back to the original: one consequence is that the best-loved translations have more authority than some of their modern critics realize.[73]

This eloquent and informed opinion cuts through much emotionalism and clears away so many of the sacred cows which both in Burgon's day as well as in Hills's, prevented the semi-learned from grasping their arguments: the untutored common folk within the Anglican Church knew intuitively that the old English Bible provided them with a profound continuity with the past; and the historians and textual critics—those free from the modern dogma of belief in "inerrant autographs"—knew well enough that the ecclesiastically sanctioned editions might be the best we could ever hope for.

It is that massive consumer-class in the middle, whom the Bible publishers and armchair anthropologists so easily dazzle with their promise of keeping the Bible relevant, who could not, and cannot, understand the speech of Burgon or Hills.[74]

Burgon and Hills were, in the best sense of the word, conservative by temperament, which meant they were also responsible scholars. They attempted to state their case as compellingly as possible and with as much learning as their subject actually demanded. They were both experts in their field—no one has ever doubted this—whether one accepted their judgements, or not.

In the later half of this century, however, particularly in the United States among the anabaptist communities, what has emerged is a vulgar profanation of their effort.

---

[73]R. L. Fox, *The UnAuthorized Version: Truth and Fiction in the Bible* (London, 1991), pp. 156–157.

[74]Evidence of this can be found in typical publications, well-packaged for mass consumption, such as, P. W. Comfort, *Early Manuscripts and Modern Translations of the New Testament* (Wheaton, 1990); P. W. Comfort, ed. *The Origin of the Bible* (Wheaton, 1992); P.W. Comfort, *The Complete Guide to Bible Versions* 2nd ed. (Wheaton, 1996). These books are all authored by the senior editor of the Bible Department of Tyndale House Publishers, publishers of the *Living Bible* and the *New Living Translation*. It is a tacit witness to the gullibility of the Christian purchasing public that such an odd arrangement could be put into place. That this is the most blatant example of the fox guarding the chicken house, no doubt, goes altogether unnoticed!

A Society for Burgon?

A group of twice separated, fundamentalist Baptists, formed a society some years back calling it the "Dean Burgon Society." This was not a society in the usual sense of the word, "a voluntary association of individuals for common ends; *esp.*: an organised group working together or periodically meeting because of common interests, beliefs, or profession."[75]

The name would seem to imply that the common interest that brought together the members of this society would be an interest in Burgon and his views, in the same way that those who are members of the Audubon Society share a common interest in bird watching. If, however, in order to become a member of the Audubon Society one had also to agree to be a faithful member of and supporter of the Republican Party in the United States, or of the Tory Party in Great Britain, they would cease to be *just* a society interested in bird watching. They would now be a much narrower group, which would be better termed, "The Republicans, or Tories, for Bird Watching Society."

This Burgon society is so organised that not only could Dean Burgon *not* be a committee member, he could not even be a member in any way of this society that, nevertheless, sees fit to *use* his name! It is organised more like a local, independent, Baptist Church, to which Burgon would never have been associated.

The irony is a profound one. A group that Burgon publicly called a "sect," organised to use his name in a society to which he could not be a member.[76] This is confounding in its own right, but it is the public platform of this organisation, claiming that it represents Burgon's own views, which constitutes the real scandal.

---

[75] *Webster's New Collegiate Dictionary*, s.v. "society."

[76] I once pointed out this irony to a member of this group and was promptly told that were Burgon alive today he would not be a member of the Anglican Church, but he would, instead, be a Baptist.

Burgon Against the Burgon Society

Within the pages of one recent collection of talks given by members of this organisation, it was claimed, contrary to Burgon's own opinion, that,

> The King James Bible does not "lag behind" any of the "recent translations because of its inferior textual basis." It has a *superior textual base!* We do not concur . . . that the King James Bible is *inferior* in any way.

Burgon certainly did. This statement does not reflect the position of John William Burgon. He spent a great deal of time deflecting attempts by his critics to paint him as someone who was advocating the perfection of the textus receptus. Again in reply to Bishop Ellicott, Burgon complained of unfair treatment in the following reply:

> I should enter at once on an examination of your Reply, but I am constrained at the outset to remonstrate with you on the exceeding unfairness of your entire method of procedure. . . . you labour to enlist vulgar prejudice against me:—partly, by insisting that I am for determining disputed Readings by an appeal to the "Textus Receptus,"—which (according to you) I look upon as *faultless*:—partly, by exhibiting me in disagreement with Lachmann, Tischendorf and Tregelles. The irrelevancy of this later contention,—*the groundlessness of the former,*—may not be passed over. . . . (italics mine)[77]

Elsewhere he had made his position quite explicit:

> Once for all, we request it may be clearly understood that we do not, by any means, claim *perfection* for the Received Text. We entertain no extravagant notions on this subject. Again and again we shall have occasion to point out (e.g. at page 107) that the *Textus Receptus* needs correction.[78]

---

[77]Burgon *Revision Revised*, p. 372–373. Cf. also, pp. 17; 107–108.

[78]Ibid. p. 21, n. 2. Elsewhere he affirmed unequivocally, "In not a few particulars, the "Textus Receptus" *does* call for Revision, certainly. . . ."(p. 107); He told Ellicott that while he found it a useful standard for collation purposes, he

In fact, Burgon cited one correction to the textus receptus he was ready to make immediately, and he chided the *Revised Version* committee for retaining this T.R. reading in the *Revised Version*!:

> For, in not a few particulars, the "Textus Receptus" *does* call for Revision, certainly. . . . To mention a single instance:— When our Lord first sent forth His Twelve Apostles, it was certainly no part of His ministerial commission to them to *"raise the dead"* (νεκροὺς ἐγείρετε Matthew x. 8). This is easily demonstrable. Yet is the spurious clause retained by our Revisionists.[79]

Miller and Scrivener Against the Burgon Society

Moreover, Burgon's coadjutor, Edward Miller, in his little handbook, made this same point clear. Referring to the school that he and Burgon belonged to as the "Sound School" of textual criticism, Miller remarked that,

> it is unjust to insinuate that they [the "Sound School"] are set against all revision of the Greek Text. They would not be Textualists at all if they were not ready to adopt what are really the verdicts upon all the evidence. "Again and again," says Dean Burgon, "we shall have to point out that the Textus Receptus needs correction." No one can read Dr. Scrivener's "Plain Introduction," a work which every clergyman should possess and study, without observing that so stiff an adhesion to the Text re-

---

was "far . . . from pinning my faith to it, . . . I *eagerly* (emphasis mine) make my appeal *from* (emphasis his) it [the textus receptus] to the threefold witness of Copies, Versions, Fathers, whenever I find its testimony challenged" (p. 392).

[79]Ibid., p. 107–108. This has further serious implications for this "Burgon Society." They have published reams of very irresponsible publications criticising another group of fundamentalist restorationists, "the Majority Text Society," who, in a much more responsible manner, are, ironically, actually attempting to implement Burgon's theories. The "Burgon Society" claims *they* are advocating Burgon's true position and not this "Majority Text Society," members of which have produced a revised edition of the Received Text according to the methods Burgon advocated. Like Burgon, this *Majority Text* rejects the above passage, Z. C. Hodges and A. L. Farstad, *The Greek New Testament According to the Majority Text* (Nashville, 1982), p. 29. The facts obviously speak for themselves as to who is actually carrying out Burgon's blueprint.

ceived from the last three centuries has no place in his thoughts. Quotation or proof of so notorious a circumstance are absolutely unnecessary.[80]

Here we find that this Burgon society misrepresents Burgon's actual views and the views of those considered his allies, on a rather remarkable point.

Another interesting irony is that this organisation has as one of its "Articles of Faith," that it will republish Burgon's works, and some of these have appeared, in a rather inferior fashion (merely photo-copied and bound at the spine), but to date, perhaps his most important work of all has yet to see the light of day. His *A Textual Commentary Upon the Holy Gospels, Largely from the Use of Materials, and Mainly on the Text, Left by the Late John William Burgon* Part I, St. Matthew, Division I. I–XIV. This was Burgon's actual revision of the Textus Receptus.

The reason this has not appeared is because here would be tangible proof of the many corrections which Burgon had actually made to the T.R. before his death.[81] He expressed in his *Revision Revised* that he wanted to be free from controversy around this subject so that he could arrive at his ultimate desire, the work of interpretation. This textual commentary, therefore, was the first step in that direction because it provided Burgon with what he judged to be the bed-rock of textual certainty. That it differed from the T.R., in scores of places, is important in understanding his over-all position and goal.

In the *Introduction* of this work Miller frankly admits that for the fourteen chapters of Matthew here treated, "on a small proportion of passages where we do not follow the Textus Recep-

---

[80]E. Miller, *A Guide to the Textual Criticism of the New Testament* (London, 1886), p. 60–61.

[81]I am informed that, surprisingly, this has now appeared. Ironically, this is further evidence that Burgon's would-be-advocates simply do not actually *read* what he wrote, but rather they tend to read secondary sources that have so distorted Burgon's views that he is completely unrecognizable in his own terms.

tus, Burgon and myself present results which are printed in spaced type, and are accounted for in the notes."[82]

I have collated this revised edition of the T.R. produced by Burgon and Miller with another revision that appeared back in 1982, *The Majority Text*, which was an attempt to further the work that Burgon had begun. I also collated these two with the old T.R., discovering that Burgon and Miller differed from the T.R. sixty-one times in the space of just fourteen chapters. The M.T. differs from the T.R. fifty-four times in the same part of this Gospel. Burgon and Miller agree with the M.T. fifty-six times, but interestingly, Burgon disagreed with the M.T. nine times when it agreed with the T.R..

So not only does the "Burgon Society" deliberately misrepresent Burgon, they have reprehensibly misstated the case when they say the *Majority Text* does not represent the kind of revision Burgon himself was pursuing and wished to see brought to fruition.

Another talk found in the collection already referred to earlier celebrates the technique that gives oxygen to this group— the use of *ad hominem*. The platform of this organisation is that anyone who differs from them religiously, qualifies for criticism on that basis if they also choose not to hold to the old Anglican Bible as perfect. Greek scholars are particularly held up for scorn. A few specimens will suffice:

> Last year I spoke about the unorthodox theological and political views of Hort and Westcott. Since that time I have seen the DBS scolded by critics for engaging in ad hominem, or personal, arguments. . . . Ad hominem arguments are often helpful and many times can shed light on why people, scholars included, behave as they do. Their exclusion [i.e. ad hominem arguments] is simply another way of limiting debate to Greek scholars, and harks back to the medieval idea that only the church hierarchy can interpret Scripture.

Here we have someone who blatantly traffics in using an opponent's political or theological beliefs as a means of undermin-

---

[82]E. Miller, *A Textual Commentary Upon the Holy Gospels* (London, 1899), p. vii.

ing the authority of their theory of textual criticism, and then celebrates the act as a virtue.[83]

The *Encyclopaedia of Philosophy* has this to say about the use of *ad hominem* :

> fallacy. An argument which seems to be valid but really is not. There are many possible types of fallacy; traditional logicians have discussed the following ones:. . . . (6) *argumentum ad hominem*, an argument that attempts to disprove the truth of what is asserted by attacking the asserter or attempts to prove the truth of what is asserted by appealing to the opponent's special circumstances.[84]

The author in question is neither a text critic, nor an academically trained historian, nor a theologian; he is a medical doctor. And here we find another common practice among fundamentalists who enter this field. They want to repudiate bona fide scholarship as the domain of unbelief, but they want to assume the stature of a scholar when making proclamation in favour of their own cause. In this author's case, we have another fallacy in operation—"(8) *argumentum ad verecundiam*, an argument in which an authority is appealed to on matters outside his field of authority."

Several serious errors of historical fact are found in this talk. A. Alexander is said not to have believed in *verbal* inspiration. He certainly did believe in verbal inspiration.

After this author admitted he had not consulted a particular translation, he then stated that "it is likely to omit I John 5:7 and to read 'He who was manifest in the flesh' in I Timothy 3:16."

This technique of guilty-before-tried is pursued throughout. The venerable Charles Hodge is guilty because in a review of

---

[83]Here again it is perfectly evident that those in this group have never actually read the man whose name they use and abuse. I have never found a personal attack by Burgon on the theology or political views of any of his opponents. It was always the technical points of either theory or fact that he made the occasion of his rhetoric. Since none of the members of this organization have the training for such a task, *ad hominem* serves their purpose.

[84]*The Encyclopedia of Philosophy*, s.v. "Logical Terms, Glossary of."

Lachmann's Greek text, he expressed no alarm at certain omissions. Furthermore, Hodge, "noted without disapproval that Griesbach divided manuscripts . . . into classes." This is the use of another fallacy, "(7) *argumentum ad ignorantiam*, an argument that a proposition is true because it has not been shown to be false, or vice versa."

Perhaps the most telling insight on this author's confused judgement, is his disapproval of Hodge's criticism of the very obscurantism which Burgon also opposed. While admitting that Hodge opposed the idea of revising the A.V., our author is dismayed that Hodge said further that, nevertheless,

> those who wish to retain the A.V. must "repudiate themselves, and discountenance in others, the habit of regarding the Authorized or any other version as precisely equal in authority to the ipsissima verba of the sacred oracles and still more the illiterate and indolent treatment of its very inaccuracies and deficiencies as part and parcel of the Christian revelation." We must instead continually compare "this exclusive version and acknowledged standard with the immediately inspired originals."

The author here is offended at Hodge's remarks because they are, in fact, directed at his own irresponsible position of wanting to hold that the KJV is perfect. He is doubly confused, however, because he then claims that Hodge's views just stated are "not consistent with the claim of the Westminster Confession," when in fact it is on the basis of the WCF that Hodge is making such a statement.

Another member of this society attempted to enlist Edward Hills as an advocate of this society's extreme views, in a separate talk printed and distributed by the former Trinitarian Bible Society in Canada.[85]

This work, titled, *Dr. Edward Freer Hills' Position on the KJV,*

---

[85]This organisation should not be confused with the current Trinitarian Bible Society in England, or that which is now in Canada. The Canadian organisation was, for a time, taken captive by a crew of extremist mutineers under the influence of the "Dean Burgon Society," but by legal means has been brought back under the umbrella of the responsible London headquarters.

is in fact, a serious misrepresentation of Hills's views. A series of secondary errors are found here: Griesbach is consistently spelled "Griesback"; John Owen is consistently called, "Owens"; Owen who died in 1683 is said to have dealt with "Griesback's [sic] claimed 30,000 variants," but Griesbach was not born until 1745. He claims that Theodore Beza did not want the A.V. revised, but Beza died in 1605, six years before the A.V. was even produced.

Finally, his most serious error is his attempt to claim Hills, like himself, believed the A.V. was superior to the original language texts:

> The above statement of facts by Dr. Hills could explain how it could be possible when defending our English canon of Holy Scripture to have places called into question where our English will be held by faith to be superior to any Greek or Hebrew text.

This is a blatant falsehood, for which there is no justification. No text in any of Hills's works could be so misconstrued as to support this assertion. The Westminster Confession of Faith, the basis of all of Hills's arguments, maintains that always and only the original language texts—the Greek and the Hebrew—are normative for the Christian religion.

Hills was alive to this element attempting to use his published works to defend the indefensible and published a disclaimer putting distance between himself and his would be advocates:

> Do we . . . "worship" the King James Version? Do we regard it as inspired, just as the ancient Jewish philosopher Philo (d. 42 A.D.) and many early Christians regarded the Septuagint as inspired? Or do we claim the same supremacy for the King James Version that Roman Catholics claim for the Latin Vulgate? Do we magnify its authority above that of the Hebrew and Greek Old and New Testament Scriptures? We have often been accused of such excessive veneration for the King James Version, but these accusations are false. . . . Admittedly this version [A.V.] is not absolutely perfect, but it is trustworthy.[86]

---

[86]Hills, *King James Version Defended*, 4th ed, pp. 229–230.

Furthermore, this is all the more insidious because the party subject to this abuse is no longer alive to defend himself.

Burgon in the Hands of the Anabaptists

One of the saddest developments among the anabaptists on this subject has been the use of Burgon's works to justify *their* cause.

On the cover of a reprint of Burgon's *Inspiration and Interpretation*, a reference is made in bold letters to "Burgon's Militant Fundamentalism," and on the inside it is said, "Burgon shows himself as a Militant Fundamentalist." This phrase, "militant fundamentalist" is code language within the circle of the most extreme wing of fundamentalism and is worn as a badge of honour by those in this group.

Here, an attempt is made to claim that Burgon is of the same pedigree as these American fundamentalists. That this high churchman and Dean of one of Britain's oldest cathedrals, should be so classed is a further indication of American fundamentalism's ethnocentrism.

Worst yet has been the compilation of many of Burgon's works in a heavily edited, one volume work (published by another organisation), titled, *Unholy Hands on the Bible*. A wonderful review of this appeared shortly after its publication which revealed it to be an unconscionable mutilation of Burgon.[87] The following are the conclusions found in this review:

---

[87]M. A. Robinson, *Whose Unholy Hands on What?: A Review Article*. Dr. Robinson, a well trained textual critic who produced a major contribution on the scribal habits of the Byzantine scribes, "Scribal Habits among Manuscripts of the Apocalypse," Ph.D. Dissertation, Southwestern Baptist Theological Seminary, Forth Worth, TX, 1982, is Professor of New Testament at Southeastern Baptist Seminary. He is to be commended for taking the time to go over this material in detail. Professor Robinson has also co-edited a critical edition of Burgon's *Traditional Text*, M. A. Robinson and W. G. Pierpont, *The New Testament in the Original Greek According to the Byzantine/Majority Textform* (Atlanta, 1991). Unlike the *Majority Text*, however, this work can boast having had as its editor a seasoned text critic in Professor Robinson. The Introduction, the work of Professor Robinson, is the most compelling theoretical work treating the Byzantine text type I have read on the subject since the days of Burgon and Hoskier. It can be obtained from: The Original Word, P.O. Box 799, Roswell, GA 30077.

There are three main factors which force this reviewer not to recommend the present book under any circumstances. . . . the volume fails utterly because of its multifarious typesetting errors, its thoroughgoing revision by the present editor, and in that editor's introductory invective. . . . Most editorial revisions...alter Burgon's original words, and cumulatively transform Burgon's unique contribution to New Testament textual criticism significantly. Burgon is clearly remoulded by the hand of the editor, even to the order of his words. . . . Edward F. Hills fares no better in his own "Introduction,". . . . Hills is reworked even more than Burgon; in many places to Hills's detriment. The same disregard for the original integrity of authors is clearly seen there as well.[88]

The saddest feature in all of this is that earnest students of this subject who might actually want to know the views of either Burgon or Hills, will rightly be so offended by these works that they would not consider the arguments of these genuine scholars for fear of the company they might have to keep.[89]

The A.V. Superior to the Greek and Hebrew Texts: Trent Revisited

Another group of anabaptists in California calling themselves the "Tychonian Society," advocates geocentricity and, "that the KJV 1611 IS the inspired Bible, correcting any Greek or Hebrew text or manuscript."[90]

---

[88]Robinson, *Whose Unholy Hands on What?*, pp. 2; 5; 6.

[89]Responsible works have appeared in print by careful laymen, but they tend to be produced on this side of the Atlantic [U.K.]. For a delightful model of such work see the prize winning brief, accurate and well documented layman's introduction to the life and thought of Burgon, Douglas W. Taylor, "The Words of Inspiration: John William Burgon and the Traditional Text of the New Testament," in *The Evangelical Library Bulletin* 88 (Spring 1992):8–17.

[90]*Bulletin of the Tychonian Society* 53 (Spring 1990):27. Another anabaptist has argued in this same vein in the conspiratorial sounding, "Modern Bibles—the Dark Secret," *Foundation* (September–October 1992): 41–48. The author claims that he has not discovered a "proven error" in the KJV, which he believes to be inerrant; but it is obvious he lacks the basic equipment to demonstrate such an indefensible position.

Furthermore, the president of this organisation, who boasts a Ph.D., tells us that in reality Erasmus was,

> actually born and raised a Bogomile [a medieval separatist group] (in modern terms, a Baptist,) and there is no record of his having converted to Catholicism. On the contrary, his powerful arguments against Catholicism are entirely consistent with his Bogomile upbringing. . . . The Reformers had little love for millennial "Anabaptists" as Erasmus's group came to be known.[91]

Here Erasmus is transformed into a millenarian separatist. There is no clearer evidence than that for Erasmus's inextricable attachment to the Roman Catholic Church. He was ordained a priest in this Church 1492 and died within her bosom in 1536. The Roman Church was not in the habit of offering Cardinal's hats to medieval heretics, such as the Bogomils.

A Profile of Fundamentalism

The question naturally emerges, how can so much misinformation, on such commonly established points of fact, be held and publicly advocated in print by fundamentalists?

Again, James Barr's assessment seems on target. He characterises much of fundamentalism as "a pathological condition of Christianity."[92] He further explains what this means:

> In this respect, though we have not tried to *explain* fundamentalism from psychological causes, we cannot but observe that it may in certain situations have psychological *results*. Where the band of doctrinal purity is drawn tight enough, freedom and

---

[91]*Bulletin of the Tychonian Society* 54 (Summer 1990):40. A Baptist missionary to Nepal once sent me a pamphlet he had written for publication where he argued that Erasmus was a "Protestant," and not a Roman Catholic. When I told him he was in error and that the pamphlet should not be published because of this and several other problems I was called, "a Protestant Pope," and in so many words told to mind my own business. Why Erasmus is subject to so much abuse I can little understand. Anyone interested in finding the actual details of Erasmus's life need only consult the sources in footnote 9.

[92]Barr, *Fundamentalism,* p. 318. He qualifies this, however, by saying he does not mean it is "psychologically pathological."

spontaneity can easily and quickly be lost. Lack of contact with non-conservative Christians produces a marked in-group mentality. Suspicion of unorthodox and non-evangelical tendencies becomes marked. Free exchange of ideas with those outside the group comes to be lost, because all ideas are immediately measured according to whether they appear to favour the group's ideology or not. . . . It is, in fact, not surprising if an ideology so powerful and so exclusive as the fundamentalist one should have its effects on the personality. I do not suggest that this necessarily happens; but surely few with experience will doubt that it does sometimes happen.[93]

Barr observed on another occasion that,

because of the peculiar character of fundamentalism, it is unlikely that any more than a tiny minority of fundamentalists will ever be able to hear a contrary voice at all, since the nature of the movement and its organisations is to prevent them from doing so.[94]

What this means, therefore, is that if the leaders of this movement assert something as a fact, and an authority in the field, who may not be a fundamentalist, says the contrary, the fundamentalist leader will be believed, and the authority rejected.

The Lessons of Münster Considered

And this is how such gross misinformation gets perpetuated without correction, sometimes for years and among numerous pockets of insulated groups. How else could Jan Matthys have convinced an entire city of anabaptists that he was now Enoch and that Münster was now *New Jerusalem*?

It is, therefore, the anabaptist leaders who knowingly mislead their followers, who will bear the greater responsibility. As a reminder to all who continued to live in Münster after it was liberated and for the benefit of those who would come to visit the troubled city in the future, Jan van Leyden, self-proclaimed King of this New Jerusalem, had his corpse kept in a cage which

---

[93]Ibid., p. 319.
[94]J. Barr, *The Scope and Authority of the Bible* (Philadelphia, 1980), p. ix.

was hung from the tower of St. Lambert's Church for some time as a reminder to all of the end results of such political, religious and intellectual anarchy.[95]

Moreover, as a result of the anabaptist affair, Münster, which was for a season a Lutheran city as a result of the Reformation, now became once again a Roman Catholic city as a direct result of the Münster travesty. In fact, some,

> appeared to want, to complete their satisfaction, that Lutherans should be disposed of in the same manner. The Lutherans did not disguise from themselves that, for the present, there remained no hope for the progress of their doctrines in Münster.[96]

Von Ranke concludes his mournful account of the Münster affair in the following terms, and with this we close:

> The colonies of North America now lay open to them. Those things for which there was no room in a constituted society, where such experiments could produce nothing but disorder and destruction, were practicable in a world where everything had to be created.[97]

---

[95]This cage along with the others used to display other Anabaptist leaders from the Münster affair remained hanging from the tower until into the modern era. Van Ranke reminds us that van Leyden was, in the final analysis, an opportunist. After his capture "he now confessed that the resistance he had offered to the authorities was unlawful, polygamy rash and untimely, and he even acknowledged the obligation of infant baptism. He promised, if he were pardoned...to try to bring all Anabaptists to silence and submission. . . . " But his last minute strategy failed him: "They were all condemned to be put to death with red-hot pincers in the marketplace of Münster" p. 755.

[96]von Ranke, *History of the Reformation*, p. 756.

[97]Ibid., pp. 756–757. Since the first edition of this work appeared one of the most striking contemporary examples of a manifestation of the spirit of the *Schwärmer* in the United States has been forever burnt into the consciousness of its citizens. The Branch Davidian cult in Waco, Texas shared many explicit and chilling parallels with the sixteenth-century Münsterites: 1) they were completely "separated from the world" in a fortified compound; 2) they were led by someone who had delusions of being a Biblical character, namely, Jesus Christ; 3) they were Millenarians waiting for the end of the world; 4) they practiced polygamy; 5) they took up arms against the State; 6) they were eradicated by the military force of the State. *Afflavit Deus et dissipantur* ("God sent forth His breath and they are scattered")

Book Reviews

Accuracy of Translation and the New International Version: The Primary Criterion in Evaluating Bible Versions. By Robert P. Martin. Edinburgh: The Banner of Truth Trust, 1989. Pp. 89. £2.95.

It has been a long time coming, but finally a major publisher has offered a sensible and substantive evaluation of the *NIV*. This criticism is all the more timely because of late, Zondervan has been boasting that finally the *NIV* has replaced the *Authorized Version* as the best selling English Bible in the world. Not much credence should be credited to this triumphalism, though. Thomas Nelson has its own poll which says that not only is the old *AV* still number one, but they claim the *New King James Version* is number two, the *NIV* not even appearing in the running. So much for polls released by the public relations offices of large publishers.

This book is all the more important because of the publisher. The Banner of Truth has consistently produced the very cream of the crop of Reformation, Calvinistic, and Puritan history, Bible commentaries and theology, in the English speaking world.

The publishers took on this subject some years ago in their journal, *The Banner*, (October, 1976), and presented a commendable, even-handed, pro and con debate regarding the *NIV*. Nevertheless, the issue was left quite open-ended, suggesting, perhaps, that nothing of any consequence was at stake. In this present publication, the publishers have endorsed a critique that claims the *NIV* undermines the very foundation of historic Protestantism: the verbal view of inspiration.

In centring the argument here, Robert Martin has indeed cut through all the advertising verbiage and glowing endorsements of the *NIV*. In eighty-two, easy to read pages, he makes really only one decisive point: one cannot claim to hold to a verbal view of inspiration and still use the *NIV*.

This is more than just an abstract doctrinal issue. Martin has shown the practical results, once the actual constraining influence of the Hebrew and Greek texts is abandoned in favour of an overly interpretive model (not, what does the text *say*, but what does it *mean*). His personal worry is the influence of Darbyite, dispensationalism in the *NIV*; but those from a sacramental and liturgical tradition have also seen further betrayals of the original texts (cf. David P. Scaer, "The International Version—Nothing New," *Concordia Theological Quarterly* 43 [June 1979]: 242–43).

Yet, those who should know better have officially endorsed and flocked to the *NIV* (many confessional Reformed and Lutheran bodies). What a puzzle. But is it really? The *NIV* is a marketing wonder; a merchandising feat. It stands as a tribute to the possibilities existing in a consumer crazed and sensitized culture, currently experiencing "the closing of the American mind" (the *NIV* is hardly international—it is as American as Coca-Cola and MacDonalds). With enough money and time behind a project and the involvement of enough church leaders (strategic seminary faculty), no mountain is too big—even *verbal inspiration.*

Martin has six chapters, each nicely leading the reader along in his argument. Stating first the philosophy behind the translation technique used in producing the *NIV* (chapters 2–3), he next documents, with the hard data of examples, the results of this philosophy and its implications for verbal inspiration (chapters 4–6). In appendix A he notes the many changes in the revisions of the *NIV* since it first appeared. In appendix B he tackles the issue of archaic language and modern translations. Finally, in appendix C he makes clear that he has no interest in defending the Protestant *Textus Receptus* and offers some sound criticism of certain extreme elements, particularly in the United States, who argue for this textual standard more from an emotional, rather than from a well thought-out *apologia.* It would be difficult to fault him here. There are both author and Scripture indices.

Regarding Martin's appendix C treating the issue of text criticism, only a word need be added. Martin earned his doctorate from the Southern Baptist school, Southwestern Baptist Theological Seminary (the largest seminary in America), where a flood of dissertations on N.T. text criticism have flowed forth in recent years, Martin's among them. He reflects in his assessment of the discipline the typical confidence that conservative theologians in America have carefully projected since the days of B.B. Warfield, the first conservative churchman in America to gain proficiency in the discipline. In truth, prior to the nineteenth century, the discipline of text criticism was seen by confessional Protestants, as well as Roman Catholics, as the single greatest threat to *verbal inspiration.* This is because the variety of textual variants seemed to invite an infinite number of possibilities. This did not seem to fit the paradigm of *verbal* certainty.

Furthermore, Martin neglects to note that christological issues were fought, from Servetus onward, with Socinians, Arians and Deists, just around certain key textual variants. This provides the neglected context for explaining the quotations Martin employs from Bengel, Kenyon and others, who were pressed to calm the waters (p 76, n. 1). These authors stressed the innocuous nature of textual criticism just because it was around this issue that the antitrinitarians of the seventeenth and eighteenth centuries offered the greatest challenge to traditional orthodoxy and to the Reformation editions of the original language texts.

Furthermore, textual criticism still provides plenty of theological controversy. Martin lulls us all to sleep when he assures us,

> far from being an enemy of truth, where its task is pursued using sound principles, textual criticism is the friend of truth and a valuable aid to the church in drawing the precise boundaries of 'biblical' faith and practice. (p. 76).

But nowhere does he mention what these "sound principles" are. For the last thirty years, there have been at least three major schools of textual criticism, each of which, like the three popes of Avignon, have anathematised the others. 1) the rational, or reasoned eclectics; 2) the rigourous eclectics; 3) and the Majority text school. In turn, each group has its own minor sub-groups. Each school has produced its own edition of the *original* Greek N.T.; each differs from the others, sometimes on important points, because each is operating from a different set of "sound principles". Perhaps we are to discover which school Martin belongs to by means of the open United Bible Societies third edition of the Greek New Testament which appears on the cover of Martin's book. Or perhaps this is the preferred edition of the publishers. Whatever the case, appendix C is the weakest link in Martin's otherwise excellent essay.

This is an easy to read, brief treatment of a very important analysis of the *NIV.* It is not the best work on the subject, Jakob van Bruggen's *The Future of the Bible* (Nashville: Thomas Nelson, 1978), still holds that position. It is, however, the very best in print at the moment.

The Byzantine Text-Type and New Testament Textual Criticism, Harry A. Sturz. Nashville: Thomas Nelson, 1984, 305 pp., hardback, $18.95.

Sturz's study is one of a flood of recent works (which began as a trickle in 1956 with the publishing of E.F. Hills's *The King James Version Defended*: *A Christian View of the New Testament Manuscripts*) calling for either a favorable reevaluation of the Byzantine text or else a full-scale return to it as the "proper" textual base for the N.T.

Sturz, professor emeritus and former Chairman of the Greek Department (contra the dust jacket of his book) at Biola University, wrote this originally as his doctoral dissertation at Grace Theological Seminary, 1967. While it has been slightly revised it is essentially this MS which was circulated for many years by Biola as a syllabus, and then was picked up by Thomas Nelson in 1984.

Within the discipline of N.T. text criticism Sturz's proposal is a modest one. In fact, it practically echos the position of Herman von Soden (1852–1913). Although, in an earlier review of Sturz, Professor M. Silva expressed an opinion that Sturz position was that of F.H.A. Scrivener (1813–1891), the coadjutor of Burgon. However, Scrivener's own assessment was that "I stand midway between the two schools, inclining much more to Burgon than Hort" (*Life of Burgon* vol. 1, p.229). Furthermore, a glimpse at Scrivener's Introduction reveals that he nearly always defended as authentic the Byzantine reading, thus giving priority to this text-type.

Regarding von Soden, Metzger notes,

> Von Soden tends to give preference to readings supported by two of the three main texts, by this procedure the Koine type [Byzantine] of text is elevated to a rank co-ordinate in importance with the other two texts. (*The Text of the New Testament*, p.142.)

The unique contribution that Sturz brings to von Soden's approach is his detailed presentation of the data represented by early papyri, which did not exist in von Soden's day. In so doing Sturz destroyed forever Hort's theory that the Byzantine text was constructed in the fourth century by combining earlier text-types. Hort believed "distinctively" Byzantine readings could not be found before the recension that produced the Byzantine text in the fourth century. Since Sturz has provided an array of papyri readings from the second and third centuries, containing *distinctively* Byzantine readings (readings not shared by other text-types), he insists the Byzantine text, as von Soden argued, should be given equal authority with the other text-types when making a textual judgement.

But even here Sturz is not saying anything new. In 1940, C.C. Tarelli, investigated the papyri and revealed the Byzantine text merited greater consideration:

> The readings of the Byzantine text which the papyrus [p.45] supports, moreover, include at least as many with a pure "Syrian" attestation as those which it opposes, which cannot but weaken the presumption against readings so attested . . . the occurrence of such readings . . . in this early manuscript suggests that it is at least unsafe to assume a late date for a reading which might be explained as an "improvement". (*The Journal of Theological Studies* vol xli. p 258.)

However, while nearly everyone now admits that on the basis of external evidence, the Byzantine text cannot merely be dismissed when determining a reading, few accept the proposal that because some Byzantine readings are found in the papyri we can now assume that the Byzantine text is as old as the Egyptian or Western texts—old "readings" do not an old "text" make. Hence, when Zuntz made his confession that the Byzantine text must now be given greater respect because of the evidence from the papyri, he noted that "A number of Byzantine readings, most of them genuine, which previously were discarded as 'late', are anticipated by P46," for him this did not mean we were "to resume the hopeless fight of Dean Burgon." (*The Text of the Epistles: A Disquisition Upon the Corpus Paulinum*, 1953, P. 55.)

The invoking of Burgon's name has great significance: the papyri do lend support to Burgon's thesis that the Byzantine text can be demonstrated not just to be equal in significance to the other text types, but rather the trunk from which the others diverged in a secondary fashion. This, as anyone who has studied the history of the discipline knows, is the decisive debate. Sturz's modest proposal has not been accepted just because it tends in the direction of Burgon. Hence, as modest as it may be, Sturz's position has not found acceptance among American N.T. text critics, because as Metzger says, "so far from regarding the Koine as an independent entity...most scholars today follow the view of Griesbach, Hort, and others, that this text is largely secondary and derivative from the others." (Ibid.)

Furthermore, Sturz makes it clear that he, too, has no intention of "resuming the hopeless fight of Dean Burgon." He spends all of chapter four debunking Burgon and Hills for using a theological framework for interpreting the data of N.T. text criticism.

For the record, let it be known that Hills was the first text critic to make use of the papyri to vindicate Burgon's argument that the Byzantine text reaches back well before the fourth century. In fact, in 1942, while a doctoral student under E.C. Cowell, Hills proposed a dissertation topic that would prove "the K MSS [Byzantine] that had attestation among the oldest witnesses [papyri] would be older than those that had many variants without such attestation." (Theodore P. Letis, "Edward Freer Hills's Contribution to the Revival of the Ecclesiastical Text," Unpublished M.T.S. Thesis, Emory University, 1987. p. 141.) If his proposal had been accepted he would have accomplished what Sturz set out to do, and more, twenty-five years in advance of Sturz. The proposal was refused. So Hills wrote his dissertation on another topic, (the so-called "Caesarean text), under a different Director (H. Cadbury), at a different institution (Harvard).

However, in 1956, still eleven years in advance of Sturz, Hills argued,

> When the Chester Beatty Papyri were discovered, still other Byzantine readings which previously had been regarded as late were found to be early . . . [this] has given material aid to the cause for which Burgon stood. (*The King James Version Defendfed* P. 74.)

Furthermore, in his Introduction (1959) to the reprint of Burgon's monograph defending the last verses of Mark's Gospel, Hills listed a table of seventeen distinctively Byzantine readings discovered by him in P66, the famous Papyrus Bodmer II, published just two years earlier. Sturz is silent about all of this, focusing rather on Hills's theology of the text, something of which he seems not to have had a firm grasp (on this, see my contributions to, *The Majority Text: Essays and Reviews in the Continuing Debate*, The Institute for Biblical Textual Studies, 1987).

Sturz did, nevertheless, provide an important contribution in continuing to keep the data before those who want to dismiss the Ecclesiastical Text as though it was without substance or support in the early Church.

Theory and Practice in Renaissance Textual Criticism: Beatus Rhenanus Between Conjecture and History. By John F. D'Amico. Berkeley: University of California Press, 1988. Pp. 310. $38.00

John F. D'Amico, who died in 1987, was Associate Professor of History at George Mason University in Fairfax, Virginia. He won great acclaim as well as the Howard R. Marraro Prize for Best Book in Italian History in 1984 with the publishing of his earlier work, *Renaissance Humanism in Papal Rome: Humanists and Churchmen on the Eve of the Reformation* (Baltimore: The Johns Hopkins University Press, 1983).

This present study treats probably the most neglected humanist and historian of the Northern Renaissance. Till now, Beatus Rhenanus, was better known as the first biographer of Erasmus, published in 1540 (see the Latin text in Allen, I, 56–71 and an English translation in John C. Olin, ed., *Christian Humanism and the Reformation* 1965, pp. 31–54), in connection with the first authorised *Opera Omnia* of Erasmus. As of this stimulating and well researched study, Beatus will now be better known for having far surpassed his Dutch mentor as both an historian and as a text critic.

Beatus Rhenanus (1485–1547), the son of a German butcher, studied at the University of Paris (1503–7) at the same time as Lefèvre d'Étaples was lecturing there on Aristotelian philosophy and for a time Beatus fell under his spell. Beatus arrived in Basel in 1511, in order to further his study of Greek (he studied with the Dominican Hellenist and patrologist, Johannes Cuno), and was to remain there working with Johannes Froben at his press until 1526. During this time he published through Froben's press, among other things, a minor historical work on the popular lay preacher, Geiler von Kaiserberg (1510); Seneca's *Ludus de morte Claudii* or *Apocolocyntosis* (1515); *Opera Tertulliani* (1521); and after he left Basel, an important history of Germany, *Rerum Germanicarum libri tres* (1531).

For a time Beatus was attracted to the German Reformers, seeing Luther as the possible fulfilment of Erasmus's blueprint for change. The violence precipitated by Luther's extreme measures, however, particularly the peasants revolt, eventually caused Beatus to turn away from the German Reformation. In the end it was patristic studies that animated Beatus, not the innovative theology of Luther. Here we see that Erasmus's influence was decisive. Beatus remained in every sense a humanist (see his long letter to Lefèvre prefacing Beatus's edition of Nemesius of Emesa's *De natura hominis*, 1512).

Once Erasmus arrived in Basel (1514), Beatus became much devoted to the Prince of Humanists (who could have resisted?), though this cooled considerably in later life. D'Amico tells us it was Erasmus who moved Beatus away from the mystical philosophy of Lefèvre, toward the art of text criticism. While seeing his own and other's works through Froben's press, Beatus's attention was drawn to the problem of textual errors in MSS. By observing Erasmus's practice of editing, Beatus was soon to surpass his teacher, refining and mastering the art of *conjectural emendation* (the practice of restoring a text on the assumption that all extant copies are corrupt at a given point).

D'Amico judged that while "Erasmus' genius lay in his ability to conjecture brilliantly," (p. 52) it would be his student, Beatus, who would use the technique with the most force in reconstructing historical texts. In contrast with Beatus, "the text—even Sacred Scripture—had for Erasmus a certain autonomy distinct from its historical context" (p. 38). Beatus, on the other hand, was much more concerned "to establish the past in its integrity" (ibid). It was this that led to his mastery, both as an historian and a text critic.

It is interesting to note, nevertheless, that even Beatus exercised reserve in his practice of conjecture when editing his edition of Tertullian's works. He passed by opportunities to practice his art on occasions, even when he was confident he had come upon a corruption, "wishing not to tamper with a religious work" (p. 63).

Moreover, in wanting to make a contrast between Beatus and Erasmus, D'Amico may have neglected to take note of an all too obvious point: it was Erasmus's own historical concern that pushed him to restore what he considered to be the more primitive Greek edition of the New Testament, in order to correct the *Vulgata Latina*. This showed his concern, if less thoroughgoing, to also reconstruct the past as fully as possible. Furthermore, it should not be forgotten that Erasmus's first two editions of his Greek N.T. (1516, 1519), omitted for the first time in over six hundred years within the Western Church, the famous proof-text for the Trinity, the *comma Johanneum*. He did so from the conviction that he was recapturing a form of the text that had not been influenced by later doctrinal development (this, in contrast to his Spanish colleagues in Alcalá, working on the *Complutensian Polyglot,* N.T. printed in 1514, published in 1520).

Nevertheless, it is true that Erasmus was more concerned to restore the *Greek* text over the *Latin* (his contribution to the historical method) than to spend great effort in restoring a *critical* edition of the Greek text. It would be the textual approach of his student, Beatus, who "was neither Catholic nor Protestant, rather he was first an Erasmian and then his own man," (p. 68) and what D'Amico called his "New Textual Critical Method," (chapter three) that would play a major role in New Testament text criticism in the eighteenth century. Other Erasmians, such as Wetstein (cf. Joannis Jacobi Wetstenii, *Novum Testamentum Graecum* 2 Vols. Amsterdam, 1751–52, vol I, *Prolegomena);* and William Bowyer *(Critical Conjectures and Observations on the New Testament*, London, 1772 [4th ed. 1812]) would apply Beatus's method of conjecture, in a comprehensive way, to the text of the Greek N.T.

In this respect, I think D'Amico's close study of Beatus provides further evidence to substantiate Jerry Bentley's argument that Erasmus (if not always in his own pioneering work, nevertheless, in the influence he exerted on others), was the father who inspired what would become the historical critical method of Bible study (cf. Bentley's *Humanists and Holy Writ*, 1983).

The scope of literature treated in this work is rich indeed and the analysis of Beatus as a major contributor to the emergence of a genuine historical approach to texts is a convincing one. As the final work of a careful scholar one could not have asked for more.

Tyndale's New Testament Translated from the Greek by William Tyndale in 1534. Edited by David Daniel. New Haven and London: Yale University Press, 1989. Pp. 429. $29.95.

When Tyndale arrived at Cambridge, Desiderius Erasmus (c.1456–1536), who lectured on Greek while there,[1] was already gone—but his influence remained.[2] Breathing the Erasmian atmosphere, Tyndale determined to learn Greek while also reading the works of Erasmus and eventually those of Luther.[3] As a result, he came to embody a wonderful blend from both men. He owned Erasmus's philological care and sense of respect for the integrity of ancient texts—both sacred and secular[4]—and Luther's theology.[5]

Probably the most celebrated aspect of Erasmian influence on Tyndale has been his reply to one of his opponents that, God granting him the grace (and here we have Luther's notion of *sola gratia*), he would make "the boy that driveth the plough" to know more Scripture than the typical English prelate.[6]

---

[1]On Erasmus at Cambridge see *Erasmus in Cambridge: the Cambridge Letters of Erasmus*, trans. by D.F.S. Thompson, introduction and commentary by H.C. Porter (Toronto: University of Toronto Press, 1963); and E.E. Reynolds, *Thomas More and Erasmus* (London: Burns and Oats, 1965). Erasmus taught Greek during this stay at Cambridge which lasted from August 1511 to February 1514. It was also during this time that he began his work of editing the Greek New Testament.

[2]On Erasmus's influence at Cambridge and how he himself was influenced see F. Seebolam, *The Oxford Reformers: John Colet, Erasmus and Thomas More* (London, 1896); on Erasmus's influence on Tyndale see W.E. Campbell, *Erasmus, Tyndale and More* (London: Eyre and Spottiswoode, 1949).

[3]It is believed Tyndale was the first to translate Erasmus's *Enchiridon Militis Christiani* (first printed in 1504 bound with a series of other works and then published by itself in 1518), translated as *The Manual of the Christian Knight* (1533).

[4]On Erasmus as translator see E. Rummel, *Erasmus as a Translator of the Classics* (Toronto: University of Toronto Press, 1985). On Erasmus's view of language and rhetoric see M. O'Rouke Boyle, *Erasmus on Language and Method in Theology* (Toronto: The University of Toronto Press, 1977); *Rhetoric and Reform: Erasmus' Civil Dispute with Luther* (Cambridge: Harvard University Press, 1983).

[5]On Luther's influence on Tyndale see J.E. MacGoldrick, *Luther's English Connection: The Reformation Thought of Robert Barnes and William Tyndale* (Milwaukee, 1979).

[6]This sentiment was probably taken directly from Erasmus's preface to the first edition of his Greek New Testament, which he called the *Paraclesis* (the word is Greek and means an exhortation) where Erasmus spoke of the hope that "the countryman might sing them [the Scripture] at his plough, the weaver chant them at his loom, the traveller beguile with them the weariness of his jour-

This wonderful blend of the best of the Northern Renaissance and the German Reformation resulted in the character of Tyndale's Biblical translations. In recent days, no one has assessed this better than Gerald Hammond, Professor of English Language and Literature, the University of Manchester:

> While the Renaissance Bible translator [Tyndale] saw half of his task as reshaping English so that it could adapt itself to Hebraic idiom the modern translator wants to make no demands on the language he translates into.... The basic distinction between the Renaissance and the modern translators is one of fidelity to their original. Partly the loss of faith in the Hebrew and Greek as the definitive word of God has led to the translators' loss of contact with it, but more responsibility lies in the belief that a modern Bible should aim not to tax its reader's linguistic or interpretive abilities one bit. If this aim is to be achieved then it seems clear that a new Bible will have to be produced for every generation—each one probably moving us further away from the original text, now that the initial break has been made.[7]

Moreover, Hammond has noted regretfully,

> It is partly a matter of the creative inferiority of the modern translators: normally they are scholars and exegetes whose instincts are to replace the dangerous ambiguities of poetry with the safer specificities of prose. They do not see that the life of anything written lies in its words and syntax.[8]

Professor Jakob van Bruggen of the Reformed Theological College,

---

ney." For a translation of this complete work see J.C. Olin, ed. *Christian Humanism and the Reformation* (New York: Harper and Row, 1965):92–106.

[7]G. Hammond, *The Making of the English Bible* (New York: Philosophical Library, 1983):2;12–13. For further analysis of Tyndale's approach to translation see T.P. Letis, ed. *The Majority Text: Essays and Reviews in the Continuing Debate* (Grand Rapids: The Institute For Biblical Textual Studies, 1987):69–112.

[8]Hammond, Ibid., p. 2. For a study that pursues further this theme of preserving the ambiguity of original language texts in translation as a criteria of accuracy see S. Prickett, *Words and the Word: Language, Poetics and Biblical Interpretation* (Cambridge: Cambridge University Press, 1986) and W. Allen, "The Translation of ἀπο τῆς εὐλα βείας at Hebrews 5.7," *The Bulletin of the Institute for Reformation Biblical Studies,* 1:1 (Fall, 1989):9–10. [P.O. Box 5114, Ft. Wayne, Indiana, 46895, U.S.A.]

Kampen, has reminded us that unlike many modern exegetical pedants, Tyndale "was a reformer and theologian and he evaluated the English usage by Scripture rather than accommodating Scripture to English usage."[9]

Tyndale and his translation legacy are lost on most twentieth-century readers of the English Bible. Worse yet, there seems to be few left to even mourn the fact. The modern reader, no longer really interested in what the original text said, prefers to get at Biblical mysteries by way of a new priesthood. These are the new translation technicians who promise to provide the nectar of divine truth—as distiled and mediated through them—by making ancient Near-Eastern texts speak with all the vapidity and sterility of modern, twentieth century *conversational* English.[10]

The supreme example of their work is the translation that did not blush to make bold in its earliest advertising claims to be the beginning of a *New Tradition* in the history of the Englished Bible. This was a deliberate disowning of the Renaissance Bible tradition to make way for the corporate boardroom Bible. Though it was given life by the Zondervan Corporation, the *New International Version* than fell into the hands of the Harper and Row Publishers as a result of a corporate take-over.[11] This company, in turn, was also taken over by Rupert Murdock, the publisher of among other things the British daily paper *the Sun,* notorious for its nude pin-ups. Such is the modern world of the designer Bible.[12]

---

[9]J.van Bruggen, *The Future of the Bible* (Nashville: Thomas Nelson, 1978):48–49.

[10]The Renaissance Bible translation tradition never attempted to put the Bible into conversational English. To these editors fidelity to the original language texts prevailed thus a deliberate archaism was perpetuated from the sixteenth century until the twentieth century when secular communications theory took captive the English Bible. Thus, Archbishop Trench could say in the nineteenth century, "It is good that the phraseology of Scripture should not be exactly that of our common life; that it should be removed from the vulgarities, and even the familiarities of this; just as there is a sense of fitness which dictates that the architecture of a church should be different from that of a house."

[11]They are the publishers of such notable contributions to the history of Christian thought as Jane Schaberg's *The Illegitimacy of Jesus: A Feminist Theological Interpretation of the Infancy Narratives* (San Fransisco: Harper and Row, 1987).

[12]We mention this not to indulge in *ad hominem,* but rather to drive home the fact that modern Bible publishers—not to be confused with Bible societies—are not religious organizations or missionary societies, deserving our unexamined trust. They operate in the cold world of profit, like any other business organization. It is not the edification of men's souls they are after, it is their purchasing power.

Moreover, those clergy who have obediently fallen in line with the *New Tradition* have sent a clear signal to their parishioners and colleagues that, unlike William Tyndale, they no longer find the verbal view of inspiration compelling.[13]

Nevertheless, while the *New Tradition* takes captive much of the modern church (would we be cruel to suggest that perhaps they deserve one another?) we can be thankful that the literary community still holds as a most important ideal the integrity of original language texts. Thus we find the Tindalian tradition, as embodied in nine-tenths of the Authorized Version,[14] given a high seat of honour in the very important Harvard University Press publication, *The Literary Guide to the Bible* (1987). When choosing an English translation of Scripture for the literary analyses of each of the books of the Bible the editors of this formidable work did not find the advertising slogans of the *New Tradition* convincing. Instead, they confess,

> We have as a rule used the King James Version in translations, and our reasons for doing so must be obvious: it is the version most English readers associate with the literary qualities of the Bible, and it is still arguably the version that best preserves the literary effects of the original languages.[15]

The editors have Tyndale to thank for this.

Furthermore, modern readers have David Daniell and Yale University Press to thank for allowing us to once again make friends with this masterpiece of Renaissance Bible translation.[16] It is attractively

---

[13]This point has again been made in a grand fashion by Robert Martin, *Accuracy of Translation and the New International Version: The Primary Criterion in Evaluating Bible Versions* (Edinburgh: The Banner of Truth Trust, 1989). Professor van Bruggen's *the Future of the Bible* (1978) was the first monograph offering such a critique of the NIV and is still the most important work on this subject.

[14]Unfortunately, Tyndale was never able to complete a translation of the entire Old Testament, but the percentage holds true for all those books he completed.

[15]R. Alter and F. Kermode, *The Literary Guide to the Bible* (Cambridge: Harvard University Press, 1987):7.

[16]There was a time when Bible-belt Christianity scorned the New England academies for contributing to the loss of the Bible's authority in America. Ironic it is that the presses of these New England institutions are producing these quality productions, while the fundamentalist communities contribute most to the sales of translations no longer interested in reproducing faithfully the original language texts.

bound in quality clothe (though there is no mention of the use of acid-free paper, probably because this has become unnecessary to mention, most university presses having now seen the prudence of this). Daniell has provided a suitable introduction, addressing, among other things, the mad philosophy behind the *Good News Bible:*

> Tyndale's opening of John 14, "let not your hearts be troubled", renders the Greek exactly. The popular Good News Bible has "Do not be worried and upset", wrong both in sense and tone (viii).

Daniell then puts his finger on the problem,

> In their new allegiance to "relevance", publishers and the public have been allowed to forget the man who laid the foundation of the bible in English, who so astonishingly gave the bible to the people (ibid.).

Such is the crisis to which, hopefully, this edition can speak.

Other features in this edition include a wonderful detailed facsimile, courtesy of the British Library, of a page from Tyndale's 1534; a very helpful glossary; Tyndale's preface, as well as all of his prologues to each book. Finally, Daniell has not failed to include all the interesting end material found in the back of Tyndale's edition. In possessing this edition one truly has, in modern spelling, Tyndale's entire 1534 (aside from a few minor adjustments Daniell has made and noted in his introduction).

I recall as a student at Westminster Seminary coming to register for the fall classes and finding in the registration room a mountain of boxes containing newly published editions of the NIV Reference Bible. Zondervan had presented the seminary with an offer they could not refuse: each student was allowed to have one of these very costly volumes for $2.00 as I recall. Quite a strategy. Would it not be wonderful if such an arrangement could be made with Yale to provide those at seminary who consider themselves the heirs of the Protestant Reformers, and others as well, with this splendid volume? I fear it will never happen. Nevertheless, I do challenge the clergy to buy this and prepare their sermons from it for one year, in order to rediscover the original genius of Tyndale. Also, Bible study groups should consider a study from at least one book (Romans?) from this edition. What fun it might bring; and what good it might do!

Appendices

Appendix A

The Following are private reviews replying to circulated off-prints of the essays "B.B. Warfield, Common-Sense Philosophy and Biblical Criticism" as it appeared in the *Journal of the Presbyterian Historical Society (American Presbyterians)* and "Brevard Childs and the Protestant Dogmaticians: A Window to a New Paradigm of Biblical Interpretation," as it appeared in *Churchman.*

Dear Mr. Letis, Thank you for your recent letter and the off-print "B.B. Warfield...Biblical Criticism." I have read the essay with much interest and profit. . . . Very few of those interested in Warfield have picked up on his radical reinterpretation of N.T. text criticism. I continue to be amazed that he had such success, at least for a while, in convincing rather traditional Reformed groups of his position and even in making an explicit adjustment in the credal formulation. . . . It is great that you are breaking fresh ground in this area.
> —**Professor Brevard Childs, Yale Divinity School**

Dear Mr. Letis, Thank you kindly for your letter of December 17 and the enclosed copy of your article on Warfield. I am delighted you zeroed in on this critical turn in B.B.W[arfield]. The use of "autographs" in his view and those who came after him, esp. at WTS, has always been baffling to me. It shows what compromise with Enlightenment (in terms of science and scientific criticism) may compel one to resort to in order to find an island of so-called safety/security. Your article is clear, convincing, and disturbing (for those who advocate the view).
> —**Professor John Vander Stelt, author of *Philosophy and Scripture:**
> *A Study of Old Princeton Westminster Theology*, **Dordt College**

Dear Mr. Letis, I wish to thank you for the off-print of your article on "B.B. Warfield, Common-Sense Philosophy and Biblical Criticism." I have learned much from it, particularly the crucial nature of textual crit-

icism as a theological watershed for conservatives in the periods you dis-cuss—something of which I was quite unaware. You help me also to un-derstand why textual criticism was considered a "safe" discipline for con-temporary evangelicals—something which always puzzled me.

—Eldon Jay Epp, **Harness Professor of Biblical Literature,**
Case Western Reserve University and former chair of the
New Testament Text Criticism Section,
the *Society of Biblical Literature*

Dear Mr. Letis, Thank you for sending me a copy of your lecture, which I found very interesting. I was particularly instructed by the contrast you draw between Warfield and Hodge. I have not previously seen it worked out so clearly . . . best wishes for your future work.

—Professor Brian A. Gerrish, *John Nuveen Professor,*
The University of Chicago Divinity School

Dear Ted, Many thanks for an off-print of your lecture on "B.B. Warfield, Common-sense Philosophy and Biblical Criticism," which I have just read with great interest. I had no idea textual criticism was so important for Warfield. You have shown how crucial his theological move to make autographs inerrant was in the history of Princeton. Congratulations.

—Professor John C. O'Neill, Chair, Department of
New Testament Language, Literature and Theology,
the University of Edinburgh and author of *The Bible's Authority:
A Portrait Gallery of Thinkers from Lessing to Bultmann.*

Dear Mr. Letis, I am glad finally to get a chance to read your piece. Though I can not sort out all the nuances, . . . it does seem to me to shed some interesting new light on the Princetonians. . . . You are right that Warfield's acceptance of lower criticism is one instance of illustrating my point. It seems to me that his position made sense (it was an ingenious resolution of the problem) so far as it went; but it was difficult to explain why they should not go along with Briggs and further. So thank you for your insight.

—Professor George Marsden, Professor of Church History,
Duke University, President of the American Society of Church
History and author of *Fundamentalism and American Culture*

Dear Ted, I shared your essay with a Warfield fan in Florida at a conference, after having read it and profited from it. . . . The critique of "autographism" is to the point. . . . You make modest claims, and that helps. At the same time . . . this shakes the foundations of one kind of propositional fundamentalism or evangelicalism. I'll be eager to see more of your work.

—Professor Martin E. Marty, Professor of Church History,
The University of Chicago Divinity School and editor of
Church History and the **Christian Century.**

Dear Mr. Letis, I found your Warfield essay highly illuminating. Rousing my interest in the Hodges and Warfield is something of a feat, I'm afraid. . . . So I was delighted to see what you were able to do with, and for, Warfield. I've never doubted his importance, but in showing his divergence from the Hodges you have identified a dimension that the historians—and, I take it, the N.T. scholars—have not appreciated. I have no particular suggestions, probably because I have no expertise in biblical studies. I do think we've now reached a stage at which we need to present and understand these rather forbidding figures as the teachers, counselors, and very human persons they were. Perhaps you'll do this in a Warfield biography.

—Professor William R. Hutchison, Professor of Church History,
Harvard University Divinity School, and author of
The Modernist Impulse in American Protestantism.

Dear Mr. Letis, Thank you for your letter and article. I had already read it in American Presbyterians *and was even more appreciative when I read it a second time. Since all my research has been in the earlier Princeton Theologians (I wrote a dissertation at the University of Michigan entitled, "The Tethered Theology: Biblical Criticism, Common Sense Realism and the Princeton Theologians, 1812–1860" and a revised manuscript is currently in the offices of two publishers), I really know very little about Warfield. Thus I found your careful article all the more provocative. You sense, I gather, what many others are pointing to: the Princeton Theologians as a lot are undergoing major reappraisal by historians of American culture. Nichol's polemical analysis . . . will not last much longer.*

—Professor John W. Stewart,
Lecturer in American Church History,
Yale Divinity School

218

Dear Mr. Letis, Thank you for your . . . offprint which I enjoyed reading greatly. Increasingly, I find that it is the nineteenth century that needs and deserves scholarly attention, rather than the eighteenth or, certainly, the seventeenth, where we have an over-abundance of historical studies, especially on things Puritan. . . . Your fine article was a joy to read, and I appreciate having it very much.

—Dr. Jon Butler, Professor of American Studies, History, and Religious Studies at Yale University and author of *The Huguenots in America* and *Awash in a Sea of Faith: Christianizing the American People.*

Dear Ted, Thank you very much for your gracious letter and for your two articles. I especially appreciated the one on B.B. Warfield which provided some new insights concerning his contribution to fundamentalism. At least, these were new to me. I am presently working to complete a volume on Scriptural authority and intend to include a reference to your article. You impress me as a person of scholarly promise, and it is my hope that you will find a position when you return to this country.

—Dr. Donald G. Bloesch, Professor of Theology, University of Dubuque Theological Seminary

Dear Mr. Letis, I have been able to read your articles with real attention, and found them most illuminating. . . . Having stayed some years ago (1979) at the Schaeffer community—L'abri in Switzerland—I was dimly aware of the Princeton controversies . . . [while at Princeton Semianry] I, too, came to think that text criticism was the only domain left to 'evangelical' biblical study, so it was very interesting to find your argument about text criticism being the thin edge of the modern wedge.

—Dr. Mark G. Brett, Lecturer in Old Testament, Lincoln Theological College, England, and author of, *Biblical Criticism in Crisis? The Impact of the Canonical Approach on Old Testament Studies.*

Dear Mr. Letis, Thanks for your letter and offprints. I am interested in the distinctions that you draw between Charles Hodge and Warfield—particularly because I am convinced that a clear distinction must already be drawn between Hodge and Turretin on such issues as theology as a science, theological certainty, and theological method. . . . You are entirely correct to see a difference in the use of the concept autographa *be-*

tween the Princetonians and the Protestant scholastics—the latter were interested in the authority of the apographa, *given their relationship* quoad verba *with the* autographa. *I am somewhat surprised to find that Warfield invented the emphasis on the* autographa—*although I realized that it was not found in Charles Hodge, and I have tended to regard its use in A. Hodge and Warfield's* Inspiration, *as apologetic. . . . Best wishes on the progress of your work.*

—Dr. Richard A. Muller, Professor of Historical Theology,
Fuller Theological Seminary and author of
*Dictionary of Latin and Greek Theological Terms
Drawn Principally from Protestant Scholastic Theology*
and the three volume work,
Post-Reformation Reformed Dogmatics.

Dear Mr. Letis, Thank you for the reprint of your article on Warfield. It is a fine piece, and it has caused me to think in new ways about the coming of biblical criticism to America. It has also helped me to understand better why American Reformed theologians were so attracted to Westcott and reprinted even some of his articles on Compte. I continue to find it intriguing to observe how thinkers like Warfield can borrow from those who might be considered their foes and turn the ideas to their own creative purposes. This, of course, is what Westcott was doing with Compte. It illustrates again, I think, how ideas spread in unpredictable, nonlinear ways.

—Dr. Charles D. Cashdollar, Director of Liberal Studies
and Professor of History, Indiana University of Pennsylvania
and author of *The Transformation of Theology 1830–1890:
Positivism and Protestant Thought in Britain and America.*

II. "Brevard Childs and the Protestant Dogmaticians: A Window to a New Paradigm of Biblical Interpretation":

Dear Mr. Letis, I was fascinated by your article in "Churchman" on Brevard Childs and the attempt to discover a new evangelical paradigm. . . . I thought this was an admirably and refreshingly searching and self-critical article to appear in what might be felt to be a rather strongly conservative evangelical setting and that it raised questions which have to be faced by evangelicals, but not only by evangelicals. Having grown-up the-

ologically as a Barthian, I was particularly fascinated by your defense of the whole "pre-critical" doctrine of inspiration and your exploration of a way in which it might be able to be re-appropriated "in a post-critical, post-modern way." . . . *I am so grateful* . . . *for a liberating article.*

—The Very Reverend Simon Barrington-Ward
The Bishop of Coventry, Great Britain

Dear Mr. Letis, Thank you very much for the off-print of your essay in the Churchman. *I read it with great interest and profit. Actually I found it quite remarkable that you had anticipated a move which I make now really for the first time explicitly in my forthcoming book,* Biblical Theology of the Old and New Testament: Theological Reflection on the Christian Bible. *I have just sent off a rather large manuscript—1200 typed pages—to SCM and Fortress. In this volume I recognize the difficulty of adequately consulting both testaments, but then argue that the greater challenge is to gain entry into dogmatic/systematic theology.* . . . *Thank you again for your essay.* . . .

—Professor Brevard Childs, Yale Divinity School

Appendix B

Reviews of James R. White's *The King James Only Controversy: Can You Trust the Modern Versions?* (1995) and Gail Riplinger's *New Age Versions* (1993)

AN ASSESSMENT OF JAMES R. WHITE'S THE KING JAMES ONLY CONTROVERSY: CAN YOU TRUST THE MODERN TRANSLATIONS? (1995)

James White and Gail Riplinger are both cut from the same bolt of cloth. Hence, the old saying holds true: "it takes one to know one." They are, in fact, "kissing cousins," in terms of religious genus. The very fact that White felt that Riplinger's book, *New Age Bible Versions* (which will be addressed below), merited an entire book length reply indicates that he must have felt that her propositions were compelling enough to deserve such treatment.[1] In other words, her superficial treatment of the subject was, nevertheless, disturbing enough for him to treat it seriously. This speaks as much about his grasp of the subject—or lack of—as it does about Riplinger's effort.

I dealt with her work in three or four double spaced pages and said all that could responsibly be said without granting her more validation than her book demands. Some arguments having no merit can be enlivened and given artificial significance simply by treating them as though they did. I suspect that were it not for Riplinger offering White a soft target he would still be labouring away in near obscurity. Her book, in effect, made his high-profile publishing career possible.

---

[1] He does, of course, treat other authors as well as the movement itself, though he provides no historical analysis or even a sociological analysis of the roots of this movement and its advocates. I believe this is because it is all rather close to his own religious point of reference.

White's Qualifications to Address Text Critical Theory, Praxis, and its History, and His Qualifications to Address the Topics of Translation Philosophy and Philology

White has a B.A. from Grand Canyon University and an M.A. from Fuller Seminary. He admits to taking several years of N.T. Greek but I read nowhere that he has any training in the classics, a near necessary foundation for doing text critical studies. Nor do I note that he has done any work under a trained and recognized text critic. Nor does he have a Ph.D. in this, or even a related field. In short, he has little more than a ministerial level of education.

Granted, some have gone on to do substantial text critical work with such a background by pure industry and ability. But this always manifests itself in the literature where peer assessment in the discipline ratifies one's work in the field. I see no such body of published literature from the pen of James White, either in the area of text criticism, translation philosophy, or philology. In short, he has no qualifications for writing on these subjects other than the basic ability to read secondary sources and so critique a woman even less qualified than himself. Prior to the publishing of this book he was a self-styled crusader against the cults. Little more than a generalist at best.

White's Distortions
1) White's Lack of Connection With Current Literature

Because of these rather substantial short-comings in his background preparation his treatment of the subject shows some glaring and substantive problems. I say these things not to be mean-spirited but to make a very valid point. When one is not at the core of one's discipline, mistakes, over simplifications, and misjudgments of arguments and data are bound to take place. And we are not disappointed by White on this occasion.

On pp. 27–28 White wants to make the claim that text criticism never affects doctrine and that only the higher criticism does so. He is, of course, quite wrong about this, as nearly all text critics would agree, but on page 40 he makes this claim very explicit:

The simple fact of the matter is that no textual variants in either the Old or New Testaments in any way, shape, or form materially disrupt or destroy any essential doctrine of the Christian faith. This is a fact that any semi-impartial review will substantiate (p. 40).

Because White does not know the literature on this subject he has no knowledge of my essay: "B.B. Warfield, Common-Sense Philosophy and Biblical Criticism," which appeared in the *Journal of the Presbyterian Historical Society* a few years back (1991), where I show that not only did text criticism—formerly known as "lower" criticism—open the way for the higher criticism, but that Warfield's introduction of this discipline to Princeton Seminary led in a significant way to its eventually adopting higher criticism. Warfield himself, therefore, I argued, contributed in a substantive way to the eventual reorganization of Princeton to allow for the modern critical approach to studying the Bible, currently practiced in most mainline seminaries and religious studies departments in universities throughout the world. He did this by teaching his colleagues and students the art of lower criticism.[2]

Nor does White know of my Ph.D. dissertation research which established that his assertion, that doctrine is never affected by text criticism, is a rather old one and not without a pedigree: it was an ideological stratagem created as early as the 18th century during debates by the orthodox with the challenges of the English Deists.[3]

But the most damning indictment of White's book is the fact that because he is not, properly speaking, part of the text critical guild, he shows no knowledge whatsoever of the most important book written in text critical studies in the past fifty years, that is, Professor Bart Ehrman's *The Orthodox Corruption of Scripture: The Effect of Early Christological Controversies on the Text of the New Testament* (Oxford University Press, 1993). This, it should be added, was published the same year as Riplinger's. Riplinger's he knows, this book he does not know.

This, the most important book ever written on the very subject of the doctrinal influence of text critical practice—which White raises with such certainty—by the world's leading authority on the subject,

---

[2]Theodore P. Letis, "B.B. Warfield, Common-Sense Philosophy and Biblical Criticism," *Journal of the Presbyterian Historical Society (American Presbyterians)* 69:3 (1991): 175–190.

[3]Theodore P. Letis, "From Sacred Text to Religious: An Intellectual History of the Impact of Erasmian Lower Criticism on Dogma As a Contribution to the English Enlightenment and the Victorian Crisis of Faith," unpublished Ph.D. dissertation, the University of Edinburgh, 1995. This is soon to appear as a monograph.

comes to just the opposite conclusion to which White himself arrives! Professor Ehrman would remind White that,

> *The textual problems we have examined affect the interpretation of many of the familiar and historically significant passages of the New Testament: the birth naratives of Matthew and Luke, the prologue of the Fourth Gospel, the baptismal accounts of the Synoptics, the passion narratives, and other familiar passages in Acts, Paul, Hebrews, and the Catholic epistles. In some instances, the interpretations of these passages <u>were</u> understood by scribes who "read" their interpretations not only out of the text but actually into it, as they modified the words in accordance with what they were taken to mean. . . . Naturally, the same data relate to the basic doctrinal concerns of early Christians—theologians and, presumably, laypersons alike: Was Jesus the Messiah, predicted in the Old Testament? Was Joseph his father? Was Jesus born as a human? Was he tempted? Was he able to sin? Was he adopted to be the Son of God at his baptism? At his resurrection? Or was he himself God? Was Jesus one person or two persons? Did he have a physical body after his resurrection? And many others. The ways scribes answered these questions affected the way they transcribed their texts. And the way they transcribed their texts has affected, to some degree, the way modern exegetes and theologians have answered these questions (pp. 276; 281–82, n. 11).*

This puts White's confident assertion that no doctrine is ever affected by text criticism in a very dim light indeed.

Furthermore, White seems not to be aware of other essays of mine that demonstrate the connection between the lower criticism—which White wants to sanitize—and the higher criticism, as found in a book I had published in 1987 titled: *The Majority Text: Essays and Reviews in the Continuing Debate.* Because of this gap in his reading he misses entirely the point of the Jesus Seminar and its debt to the lower criticism (*cf.* p. 28).

2) White's Distortion of the Position and Contribution of Edward F. Hills

White addresses Edward Hills more favorably than anyone in his book, e.g. pp. 83, n.18; 85; 92; But then lumps him with the likes of

Riplinger, Gipp, Grady and Ruckman (p.93). This is known as the fallacy of "guilt by association" and he plays this hand with deft skill. Hills is given a backhanded compliment only to be brought needlessly in connection with those with whom he shared neither a theological method, nor manner of presentation:

> *Dr. Edward F. Hills represents the best of the KJV Only position* [this, in fact, was *never* Hills's position, as will be demonstrated below] *in the sense that he does not engage in the kind of insulting rhetoric that is characteristic of the presentations made by other individuals (p. 92).*

Why not just add that and "at least he was not a child molester ;" or "at least he did not beat his wife" or "cheat on his income taxes." Only in *this* sense was his position superior to the rabble-rousers? This is crucifixion by faint praise.

By never providing his readers with Hills's qualifications White succeeds in leaving the impression that Hills is a bit of a misguided populist, not unlike the other irresponsible authors White wishes to deservedly castigate. A "polite" representative, but nevertheless, of the same class.

In reality, Hills was a Yale University classics graduate with a Th.D. from Harvard University in New Testament text criticism. His doctoral dissertation addressed the harmonizations of Caesarean text-type, and was a rather significant contribution to the discipline in its day, as can be seen by the fact that it is still referred to in the literature.[4] Three essays followed in the *Journal of Biblical Literature.*[5] The omission of this material in White's analysis of Hills's position is a grossly unfair distortion that others who differed from Hills from within the discipline would not have dreamed of doing to a colleague. Moreover, White does his readers no service at all in offering them something qualitatively short of a true measure of who Hills was.

---

[4] See Larry W. Hurtado's important, *Text-Critical Methodology and the Pre-Caesarean Text:: Codex W in the Gospel of Mark* in the *Studies and Documents* series (Grand Rapids: Wm. B. Eerdmans, 1981), pp. 4; 8; 9; 15; 18; 33; 66; 97;100.

[5] For details on the history and analysis of Hills's life and work see my master's thesis, "Edward Freer Hills's Contribution to the Revival of the Ecclesiastical Text," unpublished M.T.S. thesis, Emory University, 1987.

To return to the theme that it "takes one to know one," ironically, one of the severest charges White lodges against the hapless Riplinger is the following:

> *Belief in grand conspiratorial schemes often leads one to sacrifice commitment to fairness when it comes to representing "THEM," whoever <u>they</u> might be. . . . Sadly, modern Christianity provides us with all too many examples of less-than-exemplary reporting in the cause of "good." It seems we are often guilty of focusing upon the extreme, the exciting, the sensational, all at the cost of being honest, forthright, and accurate in our speech and writing. . . . Christians are to be lovers of truth, and as such, should hold to the highest standards thereof. Misrepresenting others—even those we <u>strongly</u> feel are in error—is not an option for one who follows Jesus (p. 95).*

Eloquently put! Now let's see if what is good for the goose is also equally good for the gander.

Like Riplinger, his antagonist, White, too, has fallen prey to his own snare. He says of Hills that,

> *[t]he desire for <u>absolute</u> certainty in all matters plainly lies behind [Hills's] statements . . . [emphasis mine] (p. 93).*

Hence, on this basis he lumps the Harvard Ph.D. with the lady home economics teacher. In my preface to the fourth edition of Hills work, *The King James Version Defended*, (1984), I make it perfectly clear that this certainly *was not* Hills position:

> *Finally, it must be stated that Hills did not hold to an uncritical, perfectionist view of the TR as some have assumed. . . . What he did argue for, however, was a "canonical" view of the text (KJV Defended p. 106), because, in his experience, this was the only way to be assured of "<u>maximum</u> certainty" (KJV Defended pp. 224–225) versus the results of a purely naturalistic approach to the text of the New Testament [emphasis mine] (p. viii).*

"Maximum" is not "absolute."

In Hills own words on this matter of certainty, he put his argument deliberately in the following terms so as *not* to be classed with White's antagonists:

In other words, God does not reveal every truth with equal clarity. In biblical textual criticism, as in every other department of knowledge, there are some details in regard to which we must be content to remain uncertain. But the special providence of God has kept these uncertainties down to a <u>minimum</u>. Hence, if we believe in the special providential preservation of the Scriptures and make this the leading principle of our biblical textual criticism, we obtain <u>maximum certainty</u>, all the certainty that any mere man can obtain, all the certainty that we need (p. 224).

Here we see an example of a classically trained text critic, well familiar with the rules of semantics, of logic and, of rhetoric, offering a finely tuned and nuanced argument in one direction, while Mr. White publicly misrepresents him, steering him down a path Dr. Hills was consciously repudiating, and advocating that others avoid. The irony of Mr. White's earlier homily on honesty is palpable.

3) White's double standard

White next admonishes his readers that,

Protestants . . . should be <u>quick</u> to question any such notion of absolute religious certainty. The concept of the individual's responsibility before God is deeply ingrained in Protestant theology. We cannot hand off our responsibility in religious matters to someone else (p. 94).

Well put again. And yet White advocates that Christians surrender to the small committees who worked on the UBS[4], the Nestle/Aland[27], and the consensus represented by the committee who gave the world *The New International Version*, which would be better termed the *The Rupert Murdoch New International Diversified Media Conglomerate Corporate Boardroom Bible for Maximum Profits.*

4) White's Text Critical Case Studies

These amount to childish displays of pedantry with little critical value whatsoever. His evaluations appear as just so many borrowings from the UBS *Textual Commentary.* He treats each variant in a deplorably superficial way, devoting a paragraph or two to variants that could well require an entire Ph.D. dissertation to crack, or at least a full journal essay, but he is content to come off as an authority to an audience that cannot discriminate.[6]

In summary, White would have done well to remain in his own terrain treating cults, or at best he should have followed his own good advice while addressing a subject beyond his reach.

An Assessment of Gail Riplinger's book
New Age Bible Versions
(1993)

The author seems sincere but her comments on p. 420 sum up her audience as well as her method:
"Conspiracy buffs will prick up their ears to hear . . ."
Most of the time her logic works like this:

1. Westcott knew Blavatsky, therefore
2. Westcott *read* Blavatsky, therefore,
3. "It appears then that Westcott was a theosophist, of sorts . . ." (p. 415).

How can one be a theosophist "of sorts." Either you are, or you aren't. Where are the quotes from Blavatsky in Westcott's works? Yes, she shows that Blavastsky read Westcott, but he was a *very popular* author (I have nearly everything he wrote). If I had to bear the burden of guilt by association from everyone who has quoted from *my* works, I would be in real trouble.

Elsewhere J.B. Phillips drank sherry; Westcott and Hort drank Ale; and so this proves their translation work was influenced by "evil spirits," so she argues. But what are we then to do about the fact that Burgon drank as well: this *must* have influenced his famous book, *Revision Revised*. And nearly all the A.V. translators drank—some *very* heavily, indeed—and so this also *must* mean that it was the work of evil spirits as well. And Luther's imbibing is notorious, so we should conclude that the doctrines of grace, which he re-established, are inspired by the Devil. You see how silly all this is.

---

[6]For an example of how demanding each textual variant can be see my "John 1:18, the Egyptian Manuscripts, and Gnostic Influences: A Case Study in the Canonical Approach."

Yes, they (Westcott and Hort) were both part of this guild—intended to collect data on the paranormal, what in their day they called the "metaphysical"—but there was a craze in British society around such matters during this time and it appeared to me long ago when I looked into all of this (about ten years ago) that they wanted to objectify the study of this in a somewhat scientific manner. That is, they busied themselves with collecting supposed accounts of paranormal activity. Nowhere in any of the accounts I read in the life and letters of either Hort or Westcott does it *ever* say *they practiced spiritualism* or *advocated this* as a religion, and yet, from Riplinger's account one would think that this was the case. She has *completely* misrepresented the sources in a very prejudicial manner. This does not justify what they were doing, mind you, but I do not read that they were holding hands around a table.

The same type of Greek text like the W&H edition had already been produced in Germany by Griesbach, which differs very little from W&H's Greek text and shall we also look for the spiritualist connection here as well? (perhaps this will be her sequel).

This kind of book is one long sermon to the already converted (and a very bad sermon at that). Only those who already hold to the A.V. would take the time to read this nonsense. Others will find it as ludicrous as I do. The modern translations tend to be a problem not because all the translators are part of a New Age conspiracy—how surprised most of them would be to learn this—but because they are 1) based on questionable translation philosophy; 2) and are founded on highly confusing and dubious textual theories. If we are ever to make a dent on the academic world—it can be done if we do our home work and really make valid arguments, such as Burgon did in his day and Hills did in our own—we simply must give-up the amateur mystery novel approach so loved by the marginalized conspiracy obsessed.

Both Burgon and Hills were learned men who knew about W&H's silly association with this guild, but neither of these good scholars ever used this fallacious *ad hominem* approach to the subject because they knew it always backfires, i.e. it can always be turned against *you* and *your* allies as well, without ever really getting at the merit of the arguments at hand. But then, perhaps Burgon and Hills are part of the "conspiracy" as well because neither of them attacked W&H for being in the ghostly guild? You see how this begins to work?

One could go further in using this technique by asking: what does the author's training as a home economics teacher have to do with attempting to interpret demanding historical, theological and biographical sources treating text criticism and religious traditions?

As for W&H, they were against the Oxford Movement and so whatever they said about Mary worship they were speaking as historians *not* as advocates of Mary worship. On this Hort's extensive letter to a women contemplating joining the Roman Catholic Church, is very interesting, indeed. Here Hort says:

> *I cannot see that the doctrine of the Roman supremacy has a shred of support from the Bible, or from the history of the early Church. . . . [I]ts influence on society has been almost wholly mischievous (**Life and Letters** vol.I, p. 464).*

As for their comments on the word "Evangelical," it had a different connotation in Victorian England from what it has in 20th century American society. Evangelicals were then looked upon as Jehovah's Witnesses are today which explains Hort's comments. Evangelicals tended to be non-conformist dissenters from the Church of England which meant there were all kinds of political implications to being an "Evangelical," outside the established state Church, to which Church W&H *and* Scrivener *and* Burgon *and* Miller all belonged. The latter three would have shared very similar sentiments to those of Westcott and Hort regarding 19th century English "Evangelicals."

By the standards of *their* day both W&H were considered orthodox. They held to the orthodoxy of the Church of England and never advocated theosophy, or spiritualism, or German rationalism as alternative religions. The following is a typical example of Riplinger's complete mishandling of the evidence which she has twisted and distorted beyond all recognition on p. 407 of her "book" (and sadly this *is* typical of the *entire* book):

> *What happened to this guild in the end I have not discovered. My father [Westcott] ceased to interest himself in these matters, not altogether, I believe, from want of faith in [i.e. belief in, that is, that such phenomena really exist], what for lack of a better name, one must call Spiritualism, but because he was seriously convinced that such investigations led to no good (**Life and Letters** vol. 1, p. 119).*

Westcott's son says nothing here of Westcott's "life long" faith in spiritualism. In fact, he is making the opposite claim, namely, that Westcott gave up all such investigations! Here she just misled her readers on a very serious point—there is no other way of putting the matter—about what was actually in her source. This was in the 1850's, at least twenty years before the R.V. committee ever met.

W&H's ready acceptance of Darwin was wrong—but then there was no creation science in those days, Darwin was the only *scientific* theory.

Such irresponsible "conspiracy theory" in the long run keeps real criticisms of the corporate boardroom bibles from being taken seriously.